New Jersey's
Special Places

Other Books by Arline Zatz
New Jersey's Great Gardens (Backcountry Guides)
30 Bicycle Tours in New Jersey (Backcountry Guides)
Best Hikes with Children in New Jersey (The Mountaineers)
100 Years of Volunteer Wildlife Law Enforcement (New Jersey Division of Fish, Game, and Wildlife)

NEW JERSEY'S SPECIAL PLACES

Scenic, Historic, and Cultural Treasures
in the Garden State

Arline Zatz

Photographs by the author

Second Edition

The Countryman Press · Woodstock, Vermont

Published by The Countryman Press, PO Box 748, Woodstock, Vermont
05091
Distributed by W.W. Norton & Company, Inc., 500 Fifth Avenue, New York,
New York 10110
©1990, 1994 by Arline Zatz

Second edition 1994

Printed in the United States of America

Library of Congress Cataloging-in-Publication Data

Zatz, Arline, 1937–
    New Jersey's special places : scenic, historic, and cultural treasures in
the Garden State / Arline Zatz : photographs by the author. — 2nd ed.
        p.   cm.
Includes bibliographical references and index.
ISBN 0-88150-290-1
    1. New Jersey—Guidebooks.   I. Title.
F132.3.Z38   1994
917.4904'43—dc20   94-10153
                                               CIP

Cover design by Petey Becker

Text design and page composition by Julie Gray

Interior photographs by Arline Zatz

Cover photographs, by Joel Zatz, taken at Skylands Botanical Garden (upper
left), Liberty Science Center (lower left), Allaire Church (upper right), and
Mount Tammany (lower right)

Map on page 6 by Alex Wallach

10 9 8 7 6

"There is only one happiness in life,
to love and be loved."

—George Sand

This book is dedicated to a truly special person—
my husband

Joel Zatz

—for all the fun, happiness, and love
he has brought into my life.

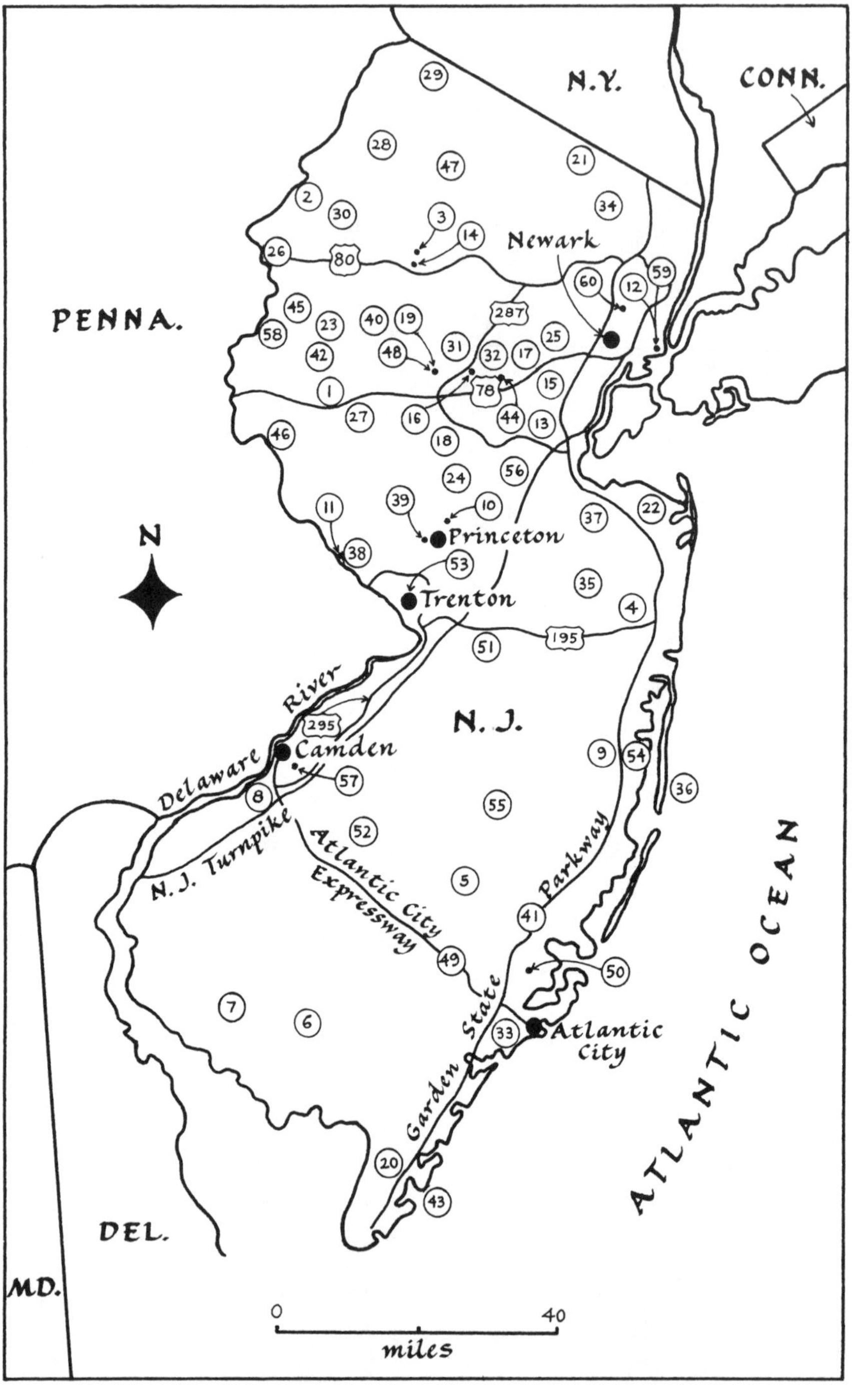
N.Y.
CONN.
PENNA.
Newark
Princeton
Trenton
Camden
N. J.
Delaware River
N. J. Turnpike
Atlantic City Expressway
Garden State Parkway
Atlantic City
ATLANTIC OCEAN
DEL.
MD.
N
80
287
78
195
295
0
40
miles
29
28
47
21
2
30
3
14
34
26
60
12
59
45
23
40
19
58
42
48
31
32
17
25
1
15
27
16
44
13
46
18
24
56
11
39
10
37
22
38
53
35
4
51
9
54
36
57
8
55
52
5
41
50
49
7
6
33
20
43

Contents

SPECIAL INTERESTS

Acknowledgments

Foremost thanks to Carl Taylor, Editor in Chief at The Countryman Press, for offering me the opportunity to revise *New Jersey's Special Places*. His faith, optimism, and encouragement are sincerely appreciated. Working with the staff at Countryman has been a delight. I thank those who have contributed their time and effort to this project, including Bob Mastejulia, Sales Manager, for his cheerful, positive attitude and his willingness to explore my ideas; Helen Whybrow, Managing Editor, for fine-tuning my words; Michael Gray, Production Manager, for his efforts in producing a super cover; and Chelsea Dippel, Production Editor, for her infinite patience and understanding.

An author writes the words, but many people play key roles in the completion of a book. Sincere thanks to those who helped with the first edition of *New Jersey's Special Places* and to the many people who spent time checking on the accuracy of the chapters appearing in the revised edition. They include, in alphabetical order: Mike Anderson, Naturalist, Scherman-Hoffman Sanctuary; Jack Aprill, Leaming's Run Gardens; Karen Bednarski, Golf House; Ed Bird, Assistant Director, Duke Gardens; Cathy Bodson, Curator, Red Bank Battlefield; Peter Both, Manager, James A. McFaul Environmental Center; David Breslauer, Director, Clinton Village; Charles Brown, Volendam Windmill; Jane Bullis, Naturalist, Merrill Creek Reservoir; George Campbell, Curator, Edison Tower and Museum; Colin Conway, Waterloo Village; Cathy Dobson, Historian, Redbank Battlefield; Cindy Gibson, Renault Winery; Peg Hartnett, Waterloo Village; Carol D'Alessandro, HMDC Trash Museum; Ellen Hodges, Princeton Chamber of Commerce; Holly Hoffman, Director, Trailside Nature & Science Center; Carol Hunfinger, Franklin Mineral Museum; Alisa Jones, Naturalist, Lord Stirling Environmental Education Center; Kathleen Kripin, Curator, Allaire Village; Nancy Marley, Reference Librarian, Woodbridge Public Library.

Also, Betty McAndrews, Director, and Ellen Myers, Reeves-Reed Arboretum; Ellyn Meyers, Horticulture Department Head, Leonard J. Buck Garden; Lucinda O'Connor, Executive Director, The Wetlands Institute; Margaret O'Reilly, New Jersey State Museum; Ken Oravsky, Naturalist, Swartswood State Park; Bonnie L. Pover, Assistant Director, Noyes Museum; Elbertus Prol, Curator, Ringwood Manor; Linda Riley, New Jersey State Aquarium; Joe Schmeltz, Naturalist, Herrontown Woods; Robert F. Sommers, Naturalist, Cheesequake State Park; Mary Stabile, Wild West City; Paul Tarlowe, Senior Biologist, Pequest Natural Resource Education Center; Ilmar Vanderer, Public Affairs Assistant, Liberty Science Center; Jeff Van Pelt, Garden Supervisor, Colonial Park; Beverly A. Weaver, Historic Preservation Specialist, Wharton State Forest; and Elaine Clements Zopes, Director, Museum of Early Trades and Crafts.

Friends have also played an important role in this book, by offering sweet words of encouragement on days when my mind was blocked or by enhancing my scouting expeditions by simply being there. Big hugs to Jean Bayrock, Joyce Becker, Rose Buono, Veronika Diener, Mary Elwood, Lila Garfield, Marcia Greenwald, Laura Mausner, Janet Savin, Mary Ann Simon, and Virginia Stoudt.

Huge thanks—and lots of love—to my husband, Joel, for accompanying me on many scouting expeditions and offering excellent suggestions in the original and revised editions; and to my son, David, for checking the manuscript and adding useful tips.

Introduction

Everyone needs a place to "get away from it all," somewhere to relieve stress, refresh the spirit, and have fun. Over the past years, while researching travel features for newspapers and magazines, I have discovered a multitude of "special" places that exist in New Jersey. Webster's dictionary defines "special" as "unique, highly regarded, or distinctive." This book is a collection of places I never tire of visiting and which I'd recommend to friends without hesitation.

When *New Jersey's Special Places* was originally published in 1990, it received state and national first-place awards, having been judged "best non-fiction book in the general travel category." In compiling material for the revised edition, I expected to find the usual changes that occur regarding hours, addresses, and phone numbers. However, what I wasn't prepared for were changes in historical facts. I quickly discovered that as historians probe deeper into our past, new facts emerge. These facts have been incorporated.

Also, new chapters have been added to reflect newly opened outstanding attractions and others I've recently discovered and feel are special. These include the Liberty Science Center, the New Jersey State Aquarium, the Museum of Early Trades and Crafts, Four Sisters Winery, Merrill Creek Reservoir, The Wetlands Institute, Great Swamp Outdoor Education Center, and, believe it or not, the Trash Museum. Additional "not-to-be-missed" places appear at the end of the book.

Atlantic City, a very popular tourist destination in the United States, wasn't mentioned in the first edition of *New Jersey's Special Places*, nor is it mentioned in this revised edition. The boardwalk—the first one in the nation—is still there; so is the beautiful sand beach and fresh salt air spray. But, if you like to gamble or watch top-name entertainment, you've probably already been there.

Instead, this book contains many lesser known places that are truly special—places where, for example, you can visit a working Dutch windmill; watch artisans scoop up molten glass and shape the oozing, fiery balls into magnificent colored shapes; or hunt for buried treasure at a former zinc mine and view a stunning display of fluorescent minerals.

History buffs can explore a battlefield along the Delaware River, where a brave lady refused to leave her spinning loom even after a cannonball nearly landed in her lap! Edison fans can visit the inventor's first laboratory in Menlo Park to see his inventions and a light in the tower that has burned continuously since 1929. If you prefer, paddle down a meandering stream in the heart of the Pine Barrens; relax beneath towering hemlocks while listening to the music of a flowing stream; help a sheriff capture "bad guys"

A short distance from Kingston is the Princeton campus—a marvelous place to stroll, enjoy campus plantings, see the modern art museum, and shop at elegant Palmer Square.

in a wild western town; or hike to the highest point in the state.

In the pages ahead, you'll find detailed information on dozens of special places to visit year round, including location, the best season to visit, highlights, admission, hours, and facilities. Since hours and admissions are subject to change, it's always best to call before going. While some places have exhibits and facilities especially for children, most of the adult attractions will also entice them—even the Renault Winery, where they can view old oak casks and are served grape juice instead of wine. The notes at the end of chapters offer hints on where to eat, nearby attractions, and other pertinent information. In addition, there is a listing of "too-good-to-be-missed" places.

The special places in this book—written for all ages and for all seasons—are found in a state that is truly exceptional. New Jersey, only 166 miles long and 32 miles wide at the center, boasts 127 miles of shoreline, 1,400 miles of trout streams, over 800 lakes and ponds, 40 state parks, 11 state forests, 5 recreation areas, 38 natural areas, and 24 historic sites. It's no wonder that over seven million people choose to live in the nation's most densely populated state.

New Jersey is headquarters not only to AT&T, Prudential, and more than 100 international corporations but also to over 30,000 artists. Besides producing famous personalities, including John Travolta, Lou Costello, Count Basie, Jerry Lewis, Bruce Springsteen, Dionne Warwick, Valerie Harper, and Flip Wilson, it is a state that has celebrated many "firsts."

In 1820 Judge Robert Gibbon consumed one "love apple" after another while standing on the steps of the Salem County Courthouse as people watched in horror. At the time, it was believed that one bite of this fruit would prove fatal. In eliminating this superstition, Gibbon convinced the nation to accept the tomato as part of their diet, and today, the "redder than red" Jersey tomato is the state's largest farm cash crop. Often the target of humor because of the industrial strip along a small portion of the New Jersey Turnpike, New Jersey is, indeed, still the "Garden State." Its farms rank highest for the average value of land per acre, and they are among the most productive per acre in the United States.

Other "firsts" in the Garden State include the inventing of celluloid, the carbon telephone transmitter, the phonograph, the submarine, the steamboat, streptomycin, synthetic vitamin B-1, the electronic tube, the motion picture, the incandescent lamp, transistors, the first brewery in America, the first china for restaurant use, the first hot-blast furnace, the first ball bearings for electric motors, the first condensed soup in the country, saltwater taffy, smokeless gunpowder, the first adhesive and medicated plaster with a rubber base, the first organized baseball game, the first intercollegiate football game, the first Miss America contest, the first wagon road, and the first copper mine in America.

The list goes on and on, proving New Jersey to be a "first" in diversity. Perhaps nowhere else can you hunt for "diamonds" on a beach, follow General George Washington's road to victory, explore as many historic towns and unusual places, or travel over terrain from the rocky Palisades along the Hudson River to the flat, sandy Pinelands in the southern part of the state.

There's absolutely nothing wrong with curling up with a good book or watching television, but be forewarned: Sampling the places I've written about can become habit-forming! I hope that they will and that as you visit these special places again and again, you'll discover many new ones on your own. Please write and tell me about your favorites.

Enjoy!

New Jersey Tidbits

Size: Fourth smallest state in the nation
State motto: Liberty and Prosperity
State flower: Purple violet
State bird: Eastern goldfinch
State animal: Horse
State insect: Honeybee
State tree: Red oak
State dinosaur: Hadrosaurus Foulkii
State fish: Brook trout
State nickname: Garden State
State seal: The Great Seal of New Jersey features the figures of Liberty and Ceres, mythical goddess of prosperity. The plows represent the state's agriculture; the helmet, sovereignty; and the horse, strength in war and commerce.

HISTORY LIVES

1. Hunterdon Historical Museum

LOCATION Hunterdon County
56 Main Street (off Route 78), Clinton 08809
(908) 735-4101

SEASON Spring, summer, fall

HIGHLIGHTS Historic mill; 19th-century domestic, agricultural, and commercial artifacts; quarry; stone crusher and screening house; blacksmith shop; turn-of-the-century general store and post office; 1860 schoolhouse; picturesque setting on the South Branch of the Raritan River

ADMISSION Fee

HOURS April 1–October 31, Tuesday–Sunday 10 A.M.–4 P.M.

FACILITIES Rest room, gift shop

EVENTS Concerts held throughout the summer; write for a free schedule

THE MILL RALPH HUNT BUILT IN 1810, KNOWN AS "THE OLD RED MILL," STILL stands. Thanks to the efforts of the "Red Mill Five," namely, James R. Marsh, Monroe DeMott, Cyrus Fox, Robert Lechner, and Ralph Howard, it was saved from destruction and opened to the public in 1963. Today, along with the other buildings and exhibits depicting family life, work, and customs in rural western New Jersey over 200 years ago, it brings history alive as part of Hunterdon Historical Museum.

After having taken over his father's earlier mill operation, Ralph built the Old Red Mill for carding, spinning, and weaving wool and wool products, and the new town that sprung up was named Hunt's Mills. Later, in honor of Governor Dewitt Clinton of New York, the name was changed to Clinton. Over the following years, the mill changed hands many times and was used for manufacturing grist, talc, and graphite. Today the Old Red Mill is notable to historians as the only known example of a 19th-century talc mill surviving in the United States.

Everything changed when the Mulligans came on the scene in 1837. Quarrying the surrounding cliffs and installing kilns, a stone crusher, and a screen house, the Mulligans began manufacturing limestone, which local

The Old Red Mill built by Ralph Hunt in 1810 still stands today. It brings history alive as part of Hunterdon Historical Museum.

farmers used for fertilizer. This wasn't an easy task. Blast holes had to be dug by hand, and even the most experienced worker couldn't dig more than five feet over a 10-hour shift. For this, the salary was two cents per inch!

Since most holes had to be "shot twice," black powder was used for blasting until the 1930s because it was less expensive than dynamite. The first charge usually cracked the quarry face. Powder was then placed in these cracks, and the second shot broke the stone further. Using 16-pound hammers, workers would then break these stones into smaller sizes. Once this chore was finished, the chunks were loaded by hand onto wagons and carted to the kiln by mule. The laborers earned about 13 cents for an average 10- to 12-hour workday.

On the self-guiding tour through the village you'll pass many structures. The metal part in front of the Screen House is what remains of the crusher. Wagons dumped the stones here. From this spot, the stones were carried up to the top of the grader, where they passed through revolving sieves to be sorted according to size. Once sorted, they tumbled into wagons below and were delivered for road work or for ballast used by local railroads in the early 1900s.

Approximately 125 tons of coal were needed to produce 4 tons of lime at the kiln site; it took two men from two to three days to charge the kiln. To prepare the charge, coal and alternating layers of large and small limestone were added, with clay added to the final batch. The kiln was ignited by starting a fire in the fire box, which was kept active by tending it through a small opening known as the "keyhole."

A "burn," lasting from two to three weeks, chemically changed the limestone from calcium carbonate to calcium oxide. Adding water created calcium hydroxide, the main agricultural liming material and outhouse sanitation agent. Whitewash, a preservative and sanitation material applied to barn exteriors, was made by adding more water to this solution. One average kiln charging created enough lime to cover approximately nine acres of land.

Supermarkets didn't exist in these days, but the General Store did. Plastic bags weren't invented yet, so most items were carted home in cloth bags or baskets brought in by the customer. And, if customers didn't have enough money, the storekeeper was happy to extend credit or barter goods for live chickens, eggs, or fresh-churned butter. Transactions were recorded in his thick ledger. The General Store was a place for men to congregate, exchange gossip, smoke, or play checkers by the pot-bellied stove while their wives shopped for food, clothing, and the latest fabrics.

Clinton's General Store was originally a tenant house for two of Mulligan's workers; it now displays many fascinating items including an old-time wringer, used to squeeze water from clothing; sleigh bells; bustles worn under dresses; scales used for weighing live chickens; and a variety of unique implements.

The Bunker Hill Schoolhouse, built in 1860, was moved in 1974 from its original site in Alexandria Township. Pupils had to use an outhouse and, in lieu of toilet tissue, used pages torn from old Sears, Roebuck catalogs. When they ran out of pages, corn husks were used! Grades kindergarten through eight were taught in the one-room schoolhouse, with the younger children sitting closest to the teacher. The maps on the walls, dating from the 1880s, are original, as are the children's desks and the stove. The children brought wood from home and were responsible for cleaning out the ashes. No one ever forgot to do this more than once, because if somebody did, that person was seated as far away from the warmth of the fire as possible.

The log cabin, a replica of General Daniel Morgan's childhood home, was originally located a few miles north of Clinton. It's believed that Morgan's sister, Sarah, married Squire Boone, moved to Kentucky, and named her son after her brother. Supposedly the son was Daniel Boone, the famous pioneer. Morgan, reputed to be an excellent marksman, was in command of 500 Continental Rangers, known as Morgan's Raiders, who suppressed the Whiskey Rebellion in Pennsylvania in 1794. Morgan served as a congressman for several years before retiring.

Log cabins were constructed by the settlers as temporary homes while they searched for farmland or gathered the materials to build a larger house. Mud and straw were placed between the logs by the children, while the wooden chimney was fireproofed on the inside by using a thick layer of clay that hardened from the fire. The doors, made of double planking, were secured with nails clinched for strength. These were referred to as "dead" nails because they couldn't be reused—thus the term "dead as a door nail." During winter months, all cooking took place inside. A fire was kept burning round the clock, not only for cooking and heat but also as a source of light. When summer came, cooking was done outside because the cabin's interior was too hot.

The bed springs were made of rope, which, each night, had to be tightened with a special wrench. This not only kept the mattress from sagging but allowed the occupants to "sleep tight!"

Life was never dull. There were always apples to cook for apple butter, maple trees waiting to be tapped, onions to be hung and stored from the cabin rafters, and a multitude of other chores to be done.

An herb garden, located in back of the cabin, is typical of those grown in colonial times. Earlier settlers were fortunate to receive many seeds from the Lenape Indians, who grew maize, beans, squash, pumpkins, and sunflowers. The Indians also shared their knowledge with the new arrivals, showing them how planting beans around the cornstalks provided a support for the bean vines. Wisely, the colonists brought flax seeds from Europe to this country, as well as some of their favorite flower seeds. Colonial vegetable gardens yielded beans, cabbage, carrots, turnips, brussels sprouts, and beets, but tomatoes were noticeably absent. The Europeans called them "love apples" and never ate them. Although Thomas Jefferson grew them, he made the mistake of saying they were members of the nightshade family. People were afraid to eat them, thinking they were poisonous, until 1820, when Judge Robert Gibbon promised to eat a basketful on the steps of the Salem courthouse. When he didn't get sick or die, others also took a chance.

Clinton was once a world without radio, movies, or chain stores. When the auto emerged in 1900, it was called a "devil-wagon" or horseless carriage. Today, a visit to Clinton—despite its modern rest rooms and electricity—is taking a step back in time. The mill, in days long gone, stood next to lovely, wide waterfalls. It still does today, and on hot summer afternoons it isn't unusual to see children and adults splashing in the shallow water or fishing for dinner.

Life might have been hard in earlier days, but strolling through the village is an enjoyable experience today.

NOTES: Bring a picnic lunch, or, if you prefer, restaurants are within a five-minute walk. Plan on stopping in at the Hunterdon Art Center next door. Gallery hours are Wednesday–Sunday, 11 A.M.–5 P.M., closed major holidays. Exhibits, which include paintings and pottery, change frequently, and special events are scheduled regularly. Contact the Hunterdon Art Center, 7 Center Street, Clinton 08809, (908) 735-8415, for a schedule. A walk through Clinton reveals many architectural gems; the downtown area has preserved its beauty and has Victorian, Greek Revival, and public buildings that look much the same as they did over 100 years ago. Round Valley Recreation Area (see chapter 27) is located a few miles away.

2. Millbrook Village

LOCATION Warren County
Old Mine Road (north of the Delaware Water Gap),
Millbrook 07832
(908) 841-9520

SEASON Late June–Labor Day

HIGHLIGHTS Restored village; craftspersons in period dress
demonstrating crafts such as spinning, weaving,
and blacksmithing

ADMISSION Free

HOURS Grounds open 9 A.M.–5 P.M. daily; building and
guided tour hours subject to change; call before
going

FACILITIES Rest room, picnic tables, trail

EVENTS First weekend in October, Millbrook Days,
featuring country crafts, home cooking, and
entertainment

WITH SWEAT POURING FROM HIS BROW, SEEMINGLY OBLIVIOUS TO THE INTENSE HEAT within the darkened area, he continued hammering a red-hot metal rod into shape. As I stood there, watching him turn bars of iron into tools, my mind wandered. What, I wondered, had life been like a century ago, here in Millbrook Village? The blacksmith standing before me was a reminder of another era when a great many people lived and worked in tiny, self-sufficient, rural communities just like this one.

At Millbrook Village, where National Park Service employees dress in period costumes and demonstrate handcrafts such as spinning, weaving, and blacksmithing, visitors have an opportunity to examine a way of life common in the Delaware River Valley not so long ago. The Lenape Indians discovered this beautiful valley thousands of years ago, making it their home and hunting grounds. Europeans, equally impressed, followed. By the late 19th century the area had become known as the "in" place to vacation. Hikers, hunters, bird watchers, fishermen, and canoeists still flock to what is now the Delaware Water Gap National Recreational Area, encompassing 70,000 acres along both the Pennsylvania and New Jersey banks of the Delaware River.

Most are familiar with the beauty of the Delaware River Water Gap. This

Guides in period dress meet visitors at Millbrook Village, where you can take a self-guided walk through time. This reconstructed church dates back to one that stood here in 1860.

distant mile-wide notch through the Kittatinny Ridge was cut by the Delaware River and by underground pressure folding the earth's crust. Rock layers are still visible in the gap, and at several places the folding of the rocks can be easily seen.

Visitors can journey back in time by visiting Millbrook Village, now a restored crossroads hamlet on the Old Mine Road, only minutes away from the scenic Water Gap. The village of Millbrook was put on the map in 1832, after Abraham Garris built a dam on Van Campen's Brook to power the wheel of his gristmill. It didn't take too long for others to realize that they could also make a living here by providing services to the surrounding agricultural community.

As you take a self-guiding tour through the village, walk into the General Store. Once vital to the community's economic life, it was here that farmers bartered for the necessities and luxuries of life, picking from shelves that held over 400 items, including hardware, groceries, dry goods, and medicines.

On the other side of the street stands the reconstructed Blacksmith Shop, which provided services for farmers bringing grain to the mill. During hot summer days you'll appreciate how hard the blacksmith labored over an open fire for hours at a time, while working the metal with heavy tools. As you watch, the blacksmith will demonstrate how iron is held in the flaming forge and then hammered into shape on the anvil. The blacksmith was among the first craftsmen to set up shop in the village; his responsibilities included repairing tools, sharpening blades, and creating hinges, horseshoes, and other useful farm and household items.

The Millbrook Hotel, now a private residence, was popular over 100 years ago with farm laborers who boarded here, as well as with travelers who stayed overnight and locals who hoisted a few drinks in the taproom. Before the village was well established, Methodist ministers also stopped here. Later, services were held in a private home. When the community grew, a church was erected, but after burning down, it was replaced in 1860 with a structure identical to the reconstruction you now see.

Opposite the church stands Hill House, named for Sylvester Hill, a carpenter who also ran a combination tavern and store. A friendly group, the Hill family often combined work with social affairs, arranging for quilting, sewing, and corn-husking get-togethers in exchange for the local gossip.

Take a peek at the Van Campen Farmhouse, an 18th-century farmhouse originally located two miles south of Millbrook but brought here in 1978. Abraham Van Campen, an early settler, arrived in the village around 1732; Millbrook is named for the water-powered mill he built along the stream. After accumulating 10,000 acres, he and his descendants became leading citizens in the vicinity.

Nearby is the DePue House, now furnished as a shoemaker's house. Philip Garris began his trade as a shoemaker but later operated a general store. Garris was a common name in Millbrook; you'll find many references to this family, such as the E. Garris House and the Garris Barn and Pond. At the Garris House you'll hear how difficult life was for the village women, who had to wash clothing with scrub boards, iron with heavy flat irons, churn butter by hand, and keep vegetable and herb gardens.

One of the major tasks assigned to the women was making clothes. Usually single women were given the job of spinning wool and flax into fabric; they became known as "spinsters." Since the married women were busy taking care of their families and doing other chores, they purchased cloth at the local store, handing down a homemade item to the youngsters until it couldn't be worn any longer. At that time the material would be torn into strips and braided into rugs.

The gristmill, built by Abraham Garris in 1832, allowed valley farmers to have their grain ground into flour without having to journey over the mountains. Millbrook, with a population of 75, reached its peak between 1870 and 1885, but when a railroad line was built along the opposite side of Kittatinny Ridge after the Civil War, modern mills sprung up, the miller lost business, and the village quickly declined.

NOTES: Since hours are subject to change, it's best to call the Kittatinny Visitor Center, (908) 496-4458, first. There are two visitor centers within the park. Dingmans Visitor Center at Dingmans Falls, one mile from Route 209, (717) 828-7802, features a half-mile-long nature trail that meanders through masses of rhododendron and hemlock to two waterfalls. The Kittatinny Visitor Center, located on Interstate 80 at the Water Gap on the New Jersey side of the river, offers hikes to Mount Tammany (see chapter 26) and Sunfish Pond, plus a scenic view of the Delaware River and excellent information on the area.

3. Waterloo Village

LOCATION Sussex County
Waterloo Village (off Route 80, Exit 25),
Stanhope 07874
(973) 347-0900

SEASON Spring, summer, fall

HIGHLIGHTS Restored 18th–19th-century village, re-created
Lenape Indian village, costumed guides, artisans,
scenic Morris Canal and Musconetcong River,
period furniture, beautiful landscaping and gardens

ADMISSION Fee

HOURS Tuesday–Sunday 10 A.M.–6 P.M. April 15–September
30; 10 A.M.–5 P.M. October 1–December 31; closed
January 1–April 14, Thanksgiving, Christmas, Easter,
and Tuesdays following Monday holidays

FACILITIES Rest room, drinking water, restaurant, snack bar,
picnicking on the lawn, gift shops, concert tent,
concert field

EVENTS Annual arts festival and craft shows held
May–September; Festival of Music including
classical and popular series; School of Music; write
or call for a free schedule of events: Waterloo
Foundation for the Arts, Inc., Stanhope 07874,
(973) 347-0900

IN THIS TINY HAMLET ALONG THE MUSCONETCONG RIVER, SITUATED IN A VALLEY between the Allamunchy and Schooley mountain ranges, visitors are invited to walk where time has stood still and glimpse a village that has been preserved as it was in colonial days when it was in its prime.

The village, designed to preserve the artifacts of our colonial roots, was once an ancient Indian meeting place and burial ground. As early as the mid-1740s, settlers recognized that this area, rich in forested hillsides and fertile meadows, would provide excellent homesteading land. After huge deposits of iron were discovered nearby, the Philadelphia firm of Allen and Turner purchased the land. By 1763 the partners had constructed a four-fire, two-hammer forge, a gristmill, a sawmill, and huge mansions for the iron master and forgeman. A settlement, named Andover, quickly rose around

A potter—one of many artists in Waterloo Village—demonstrates the art as it was done in the 1700s.

the forge; its name was taken from Turner's birthplace in Andover, England. Later the town became known as Andover Forge.

By 1780, because the surrounding hillsides had been stripped almost bare of the timber needed to fuel the forge, the operation had to be abandoned. Eventually the deforested land was leased to farmers by heirs of the original proprietors. Later, realizing that the land still had value, Brigadier General John Smith purchased the 282-acre forge farm.

While fishing at Lake Hopatcong, Morristown financier George P. McCullock noticed that the lake drained in two directions—west into the Delaware River and east to the Passaic River drainage area. He realized that this would be an ideal water supply for a trans–New Jersey canal. When it was completed in 1833, the Morris Canal was hailed as one of the greatest engineering accomplishments, because the 102-mile canal ran from Phillipsburg on the Delaware River to Jersey City on the Hudson. This was not an easy route, however, for the canal climbed and descended nearly 1,700 feet along its course.

Boats were lifted and lowered through the canal by a system of locks and 23 inclined planes designed by Robert Fulton, inventor of the first practical steamboat. Boats would ascend or descend grades on a short railroad setup, with the boat resting in a cradle on wheels so that it could be raised or lowered on an inclined track and pass over natural barriers up to 100 feet high. The canal boats were capable of carrying up to 75 tons, with cargo consisting of coal, iron ore, grain, wood, potables, bricks, and lumber.

Andover Forge quickly gained importance as a major stop between Phillipsburg and Jersey City. In 1840 the village was renamed again, this time Waterloo, in celebration of Wellington's victory over Napoleon at Waterloo, Belgium. The village thrived as an inland port. At this time it consisted of a forge, a gristmill, a sawmill, a tavern, a store, and 15 dwellings. As Smith's sons took over the business, each one constructed a mansion of his own on the property.

A railroad bypass, built around the village in 1901, proved to be a much faster and less expensive way to transport goods than the Morris Canal. Trade in the village slowly came to a standstill, and in the 1920s, when the canal was drained and closed by the state, the village became another sleepy hamlet.

For a short while, when Waterloo began shipping ice via railroad to the meat-packing industry in Newark, it seemed as though the village would again prosper, but this venture failed along with a later proposal to establish an exclusive lakeside community on the grounds. The stock market crash of 1929 was the final blow, leaving Waterloo Village a ghost town until Percival Leach and Louis Gualandi restored and opened it to the public in 1964.

Plan on spending an entire day walking through America's past, among authentically costumed guides and artisans, and restored period homes and structures—as well as a recreated Lenape Indian village—all now part of a living museum steeped in over 100 years of tradition. The Methodist Church, constructed in 1859, has been in continuous use since Peter Smith led the list of contributors with his donation of land and $500 to help defray the original cost of the $2,300 needed to build it.

Stroll down the curved path leading to "The Homestead," originally a stone horse barn, which was converted by Smith into living quarters. After making a fortune selling merchandise in his General Store and Towpath Tavern, situated along the busy canal, Smith enlarged the house. In addition to the original kitchen, the house has a fine collection of Royal Crown china; an unusual tricornered chair, said to be preferred by gentlemen wearing swords because they could sit comfortably; magnificent wallpaper depicting scenes of Niagara Falls and the Hudson River, among other places; a portable organ; a harp; and a Steinway grand piano, circa 1853.

The Apothecary and Herb-drying Room is fascinating. Herbs, much in demand, were used not only in making wreaths and other decorations but as cures for colds, sore throats, and minor afflictions. A beautiful array of green, yellow, and red bowls line the windows, which, according to the guide, were backlighted at night so that in case of an emergency people could locate the apothecary shop, awaken the pharmacist, and have medication prepared.

"When I was growing up," explained the guide as she pointed to a leech jar, "any young man who had a black eye would buy a leech for twenty-five cents. He'd put the leech over his eye, and if he had a date that night, by the time he went out the black and blue marks would be gone." The apothecary collection dates back to the 1740s, although the village was too tiny to have its own apothecary at the time. Almost as old was a poem the guide recited, handed down by a Quaker doctor, from an unknown source:

> When patients comes to I
> I physics, bleeds, and sweats 'em.
> Then if they should choose to die,
> Well, what's that to I?
> I lets 'em.

From here, you can walk to the Weaving Room, now occupied by textile artisans. The Pottery Shed, formerly a wood and ice storage shed, now houses a potter who demonstrates the art as it was done in the 1700s. In the Canal Museum you can learn how the Morris Canal was constructed. The Broom and Cabinet Shop was the former carriage house of the Homestead and is currently used as a woodworking shop. In the Meeting House you can view a 15-minute slide show reflecting on the history of the village.

Peek in at the Gristmill. In 1760 this structure served as a charcoal house for Allen & Turner. When the canal opened, it was converted into a gristmill. The water-powered sawmill located behind the gristmill is typical of mills operated in colonial New Jersey.

Scattered throughout the village are 23 authentically restored homes and buildings, each featuring period furniture, rare antiques, and objects of art.

Notes: Plan to picnic along the scenic Musconetcong River, or have lunch in a delightful atmosphere at the Towpath Tavern. Dogs are not allowed in the village.

LOCATION   Monmouth County
In Allaire State Park, Route 524 (Exit 98 off the Garden State Parkway), Farmingdale 07727
Village (732) 938-2253; Park (732) 938-2371

SEASON   Year round

HIGHLIGHTS   Restored 19th-century village; guides and craftspersons in period dress demonstrating blacksmithing, carpentry, spinning, weaving, and open-hearth cooking. Park offers camping, picnicking, fishing, hiking, bridle paths, nature center, antique steam train rides, and the New Jersey Museum of Transportation

ADMISSION   Village: free; fee for school and organized group tours
Park: free except Memorial Day–Labor Day (no charge Tuesdays); fee for camping

HOURS   Village: grounds open for walking during park hours; buildings open May–October 10 A.M.– 4 P.M. and for special events
Park: last week in October–last week in March 8 A.M.–4:30 P.M.; first week in April–Memorial Day weekend 8 A.M.–6 P.M.; Memorial Day–Labor Day 8 A.M.–8 P.M.; Labor Day–last week in October 8 A.M.–6 P.M.

FACILITIES   Village: visitor center, snack bar, gift shop, bakery, rest room
Park: rest room, modern bathhouse and dump station in campground, picnic tables, children's playground, nature center

EVENTS   Living history celebrations, contests, lawn games, concerts, storytelling; craft, antique, and flea markets; call for schedule of events

THOUGH THE ROAR OF THE BLAST FURNACE CAN NO LONGER BE HEARD, ALLAIRE Village stands as a reminder of one of the most successful bog iron operations in this area over 140 years ago.

Records in the late 1700s indicate that the site, originally called Williamsburg Forge, was renamed Howell Furnace in 1821 when the land, 15 or 16 houses, a furnace, a sawmill, and outhouses were leased to Benjamin Howell. That same year, James P. Allaire, a brass founder from New York, purchased the property for $19,000 and renamed it the Howell Works.

Having little more than a grade-school education, Allaire served as a druggist's clerk at age 15 and as an apprentice to a brassmaker at age 16. Allaire inherited the business when his employer died, and when he was 19 he fashioned the brass air chamber for Robert Fulton's steamship, the *Clermont*. Later he created the cylinder for the *Savannah*, the first American steamship to cross the Atlantic. His company, the James P. Allaire Works, quickly became one of the largest marine engine shops in the United States.

Allaire had purchased the land for its abundant quantities of bog iron, which he needed to operate his engine works in New York. Under Allaire's expertise the business flourished. Over 500 workers—carpenters, pattern makers, wheelwrights, millers, teamsters, stage drivers, grooms, and harness makers—and their families lived in Allaire's village, each dependent upon the furnace and beehive-shaped stack constructed in 1830 to extract the iron. Stoves, screws, pipes, hand irons, pots, and kettles were all manufactured here.

Over time Allaire rebuilt the village, replacing older wooden structures with brick buildings and adding quarters for the workmen, a gristmill, various shops, a company store, and an Episcopal church. Although he ruled with an iron hand and paid his workers in Howell Works script (good only at his company store), he was considered a generous and fair man. While learning the classics from a private tutor, he established a school for his employees' children. Tired of commuting between New York and the Howell Works, Allaire finally decided to remodel a large house in the village and spent his remaining years in what became commonly known as "Allaire Village."

Visitors are welcome to explore the village, which is managed by Allaire Village, Inc., a nonprofit educational organization. Stop in at the visitor center first; it occupies two of the original row houses, while the adjoining row houses have a false facade complete with 11 chimneys, 11 front doors, 22 first-floor windows, and 22 dormers. At the center you'll get an overview of the bog iron industry, the charcoal-making process, the use of water power, and the fabrication of cast-iron objects in addition to a slide presentation about Allaire, his village, and the ongoing preservation program at this site. This original end row house contains period furnishings, including a mid-19th-century shoemaker's bench, rush-bottom chairs, rugs, quilts, and children's toys.

Plan on spending several hours exploring the village and the pleasant

James P. Allaire built this Episcopal church for the workers of his village; services and weddings still take place here. Look closely at the unusual steeple; it's situated over the pulpit because the front of the building wasn't strong enough to support it.

trails within the park. The millpond, fed by a stream, originally was set up to hold water to act as a power source for the mill while the old wooden farmhouse, dating to the 1700s, was used by the ironwork's manager. The Episcopal church Allaire built for his community has an unusual steeple; it's situated over the pulpit because the front of the building wasn't strong enough to support it. Also unusual is the fact that Allaire did not require worshipers to pay pew rents. Today the church is used for wedding ceremonies; if you're here on Sunday, you may see an old-fashioned wedding taking place, with coach, horses, and driver waiting to whisk the bride and groom away.

One of the most interesting sites in the village is the remains of the casting house, where iron from the bog ore was extracted from the furnace and shaped into long bars known as "pigs." Legend tells of an early iron master who compared his furnace hearth and its products to a sow and her pigs, and since that time, the name "pig iron" has survived.

Manufacturing pig iron wasn't an easy task. The workers had to tend the furnace 24 hours a day when it was "in blast," until the winter freeze. In order to get pig iron from the furnace, layers of ore and charcoal were dumped into the top of the furnace stack. The intense fire in the furnace chamber was enough to turn these ingredients into a molten mass, resulting in a chemical action that caused the iron to separate and fall to the bottom. The remaining "slag" would float to the top and be drawn off. Finally, the molten iron would pour out through another opening, where it was then guided into long channels in sand, forming pigs, or made into molds. It became solid iron once the fluid metal cooled and hardened.

In 1846, when hardrock iron ore and anthracite were discovered in

Pennsylvania, the bog iron industry came to a halt. Workers left, and although Allaire's son, Hal, stayed on for four decades until his death in 1901, the village slowly decayed. Arthur Brisbane, one of William Randolph Hearst's top editors, bought the land a few years later. Many repairs were undertaken by the Boy Scouts after he leased out land to them in 1927, and when he died in 1941, his widow donated the village and surrounding acreage to the state.

After you've seen the beehive-shaped blast furnace and watched the demonstrations at the blacksmith shop, stretch your legs on one of the short trails within the park. The yellow-blazed trail follows along the Manasquan River—a good place to catch trout and look for violets and trout lilies blooming along the banks during the spring. Over 94 varieties of wildflowers can be found here.

It takes about 20 minutes to reach the campground from the village along the green-blazed trail. On this delightful walk you'll see pine, sweet gum, oak, and maple trees, while the only sounds are usually made by a squirrel rustling through the underbrush, a passing bird, or car tires as you approach the Garden State Parkway overpass.

The red-blazed trail offers picnic tables tucked among sweet gums and holly. Lichens on tree bark make interesting patterns, while laurel stands at least eight feet high in places. Tread lightly and you may surprise a turtle as it sunbathes on a log. The Manasquan River, traversing the picnic area, is bordered by paper birch.

Allaire is perfect for a day's outing, and especially nice for a weekend or longer in the spacious, shaded campground. A favorite with young and old alike is a ride aboard the Pine Creek Railroad. Organized as a club in 1951 by three men interested in steam railroading as a hobby, this was the first operating steam train exhibit in New Jersey and one of the earliest in the United States. In 1963 it was moved to Allaire State Park as a nonprofit museum. Today the operating railroad is the museum's principal exhibit. The gauge is three feet, and the mainline is a loop 0.75 mile long. All locomotives and cars used in the train were previously operated by railroads in various parts of the Americas, from Newfoundland to Hawaii.

NOTES: For information on camping at Allaire State Park write to Box 220, Farmingdale 07727, or call (732) 938-2371. A state-operated 18-hole golf course is nearby. Bring a picnic lunch or, if you prefer, try the snack bar (open the same hours as the village) or a nearby restaurant. Canoe rentals are available at Algonquin Adventures on Yellow Brook Squankum Road, (732) 938-7755, for a delightful trip on the Upper Manasquan River and through part of Allaire State Park.

5. Batsto Village

LOCATION Burlington County
In Wharton State Forest (off Route 542 west of the Garden State Parkway), Washington Township 07675
(609) 561-3262

SEASON Year round

HIGHLIGHTS Restored 19th-century Pine Barrens village, guided tours, fishing on scenic Batsto River, woodlands, nature center

ADMISSION Fee for parking Memorial Day–Labor Day and for mansion tour; no admission for walking grounds

HOURS Village grounds: dawn–dusk daily
Visitor's Center: 9 A.M.–4:30 P.M. daily; interpretive programs, daily Memorial Day–Labor Day and Thursday–Sunday Labor Day–Memorial Day. Closed New Year's, Thanksgiving, and Christmas. Hours subject to change; call first to check schedule.

FACILITIES Rest room, refreshment stand Memorial Day–Labor Day, children's playground

EVENTS Craft demonstrations daily April 1–October 31

THE INDIANS ARE GONE. SO ARE THE TIMBER CUTTERS, IRONWORKERS, GLASSMAKERS, and iron barons. All that remain besides a furnace foundation are a few houses and the echoes of history. Yet Batsto Village, located deep within the heart of southern New Jersey's Pine Barren area, lives on. Here, on a portion of a 111,000-acre tract within Wharton State Forest, far away from shopping centers and the roar of traffic, visitors can learn the key role that Batsto played in the industrial development of the United States over two centuries ago.

It all began with the Indians, who never realized that the reddish deposits they dug from surrounding creek beds and streams would be valuable for any other purpose but face paint. They had no way of knowing that the Europeans would later identify this substance as bog ore or that they would make a fortune smelting it down for its iron. Nor could they predict that Batsto Village would develop into a thriving bog iron center as well as a producer of glass and brick.

A sawmill stands beside scenic Batsto Lake in the restored village.

Bog ore, abundant in the Pine Barrens and rich in iron, is formed by the high vegetable content in the waters. As water percolates through the marl beds, eventually reaching the surface, a chemical reaction takes place and causes oxidation. Then, mixed with mud and deposited along the banks of streams, swamps, and pools, this sediment hardens into thick ore beds.

Recognizing the tremendous ore supply, the abundance of trees (necessary for fuel), and the supply of water that could be harnessed for power, entrepreneurs made this area a mecca for the manufacture of bog iron. Charles Read, a distinguished lawyer and Supreme Court justice, was the first of many to realize this potential for wealth and, at the age of 51, acquired the rights to thousands of acres. Prior to his purchase in 1766, the land had been sold numerous times for sawmill operations.

Read cut timber, dammed streams, and built several forges and furnaces, including Batsto Furnace. The area was well known, particularly to smugglers, even before Read opened his ironworks. Its remoteness, dense forests, and the Mullica River made this location ideal for illicit traders and privateers. It was a place where ships could dock and unload supplies of sugar, rum, tea, and various other staples to be quickly transported through the woods to safety.

Due to overinvesting, Read was forced to sell the ironworks in 1768. It was resold a couple of years later to John Cox, an ardent revolutionary. While continuing to produce iron pots, kettles, stoves, pestles and mortars, and pig iron, Cox began manufacturing new items to be used for war. These included iron fastenings and fittings for caissons, wagons, and ships. The shallow pans he produced were invaluable, for these helped evaporate ocean water so that the troops could preserve their food with salt. General George Washington appreciated Cox's efforts so much that he bestowed upon him the rank of colonel, declared Batsto's workmen exempt from service, and sent 50 men and 2 lieutenants to Batsto to protect the village from invaders. Realizing they might be captured while voyaging the winding Mullica River, the British wisely never attempted to invade Batsto.

In poor health, but all the richer for Batsto's profits and the privateering trade, Cox sold out in 1778. Only six months later the new owner made a handsome profit selling the property again to Joseph Ball, who had been manager of the ironworks under Cox. Ball eventually became one of America's richest men, mainly from his profits as one of the principal speculators in captured vessels and cargoes.

Batsto was sold yet again six years later to William Richards. Once he acquired full rights, Richards initiated various additions and improvements, including building a mansion high atop a hill where he was said to reside in baronial splendor. After Richards retired in 1809 his son, Jesse, assumed management. When William Richards died in 1823, Batsto was bought at auction by his nephew, Thomas S. Richards, who retained Jesse as manager. Jesse purchased a half-interest in Batsto in 1829, rebuilt the furnace, and saw production rise to an average of 800 tons of iron annually.

Although records indicate over 3,000 boatloads of cargo were handled at the village during the 1830s, the end was near because coal had been discovered in the Allegheny Mountains of Pennsylvania. While this meant ease of operation for the iron forges in Pennsylvania, those in New Jersey still had to depend on finding vast acres of timber for fuel. In an attempt to save Batsto, Jesse began manufacturing window and flat glass for municipal gas lamps in 1846. When he died in 1855 his son, Thomas H. Richards, took over for a brief period, but because his interests were in politics and public life, Batsto's long, rich history came to an end. Foreclosure proceedings were held in 1876, when Batsto was sold to Joseph Wharton, a Philadelphia industrialist and financier, for $14,000.

Wharton had new ideas for Batsto. At first he experimented raising sugar beets and cultivating cranberries, while acquiring huge parcels of adjoining land. Noting the abundance of fresh water, he devised a way to divert the supply to Philadelphia and Camden, where he planned to sell the clear drinking water. However, neither city expressed much interest, and before he was able to proceed further, the New Jersey Legislature passed a law forbidding the export of water from the state. This defeat didn't stop

Wharton from thinking about other enterprises. He continued to purchase more land, enlarged the mansion, built the sawmill and underground silo, and raised cattle.

After his death in 1909, Wharton's heirs offered the estate of nearly 100,000 acres to the state for $1 million. Voters rejected this referendum, and the land and village—which in its heyday had a huge furnace, two glass factories, a brickmaking establishment, sawmills, and a gristmill—lay idle for 45 years. The state, finally recognizing its value, eventually bought it for $3 million.

Listed on the New Jersey and National Registers of Historic Places, Batsto Village and Wharton State Forest are also part of the Pinelands National Reserve, created by Congress in 1978 to protect the unique cultural and natural resources found in the Pinelands. Today, Batsto Village lives on in peace and seclusion. It's best to start your tour at the Visitor's Center, where you can obtain a map of the village and view the exhibit gallery. An ore boat, rescued from the bottom of Batsto Lake in 1957, and a bog ore exhibit showing the raw material used in the furnace can be seen outdoors adjacent to the Visitor's Center.

The General Store displays products of the 19th century. The Post Office, established by Jesse Richards in 1852, is located on the second level of the store, and outgoing mail is sorted on the original sorting racks and hand-stamped for cancellation as it was in the old days. Because of its historical significance, no zip code is required.

One of the treasures often overlooked by visitors is the short nature trail along the lake. Some of its highlights include the tiny scarlet lichens known as "British Soldiers," named after the "redcoats," and the pitcher plant, which traps insects inside its pitcher-like leaves. Sphagnum moss bogs can also be seen. This light green moss, capable of absorbing many times its own weight in water, is thought to have been used by American Indians as the first disposable diaper! Batsto played an important role in our history, and it's still playing an important part in our appreciation for the industries and agriculture that once thrived here, as well as for the scenic beauty of the surroundings.

NOTES: The Visitor's Center is handicapped accessible. Other areas of the village are partially accessible to the handicapped. A food concession operates daily Memorial Day weekend through Labor Day. A picnic area is available; fires are not permitted. Fishing is also available on Batsto Lake; a license is necessary for those 14 and over.

6. Wheaton Village

LOCATION	Cumberland County Glasstown Road (off Route 55), Millville 08332 (856) 825-6800; 1-800-998-4552
SEASON	Year round
HIGHLIGHTS	Demonstrations of glassblowing in Wheaton Glass Factory; pottery, woodcarving, tin, and flame-working demonstrations; historic schoolhouse and Down Jersey Folklife Center; quaint shops; rides on ½-scale model of C. P. Huntington train
ADMISSION	Fee
HOURS	April–December daily 10 A.M.–5 P.M.; January–March closed Mondays and Tuesdays; also closed Easter, Thanksgiving, Christmas, and New Year's Day
FACILITIES	Rest room, drinking water, snack bar, adjacent PaperWaiter Restaurant & Pub, picnicking
EVENTS	Antique fire and auto shows, a glass lover's weekend, antique fair, craft fair, Christmas exhibition, and various other events throughout the year; for free calendar of events write Wheaton Village, Glasstown Road, Millville 08332

DESPITE THE INTENSE HEAT GENERATED BY A 2,100-DEGREE FAHRENHEIT FURNACE, visitors to Wheaton Village remain riveted to their seats. And no wonder, for the glassmaking demonstrations are fascinating. Inside this replica of the glass factory founded by Theodore Wheaton in 1888, attention is focused on the artisans as they scoop up blobs of molten glass, shaping and oozing fiery balls into magnificent colored shapes.

Southern New Jersey, with its abundance of silica sand, timber, and waterways, is an ideal place for glassmaking. The first factory was the Wistarburg works in Alloway, established in 1739. Master craftsmen from Germany, who were called "gaffers," were attracted to the area, and by 1900 dozens of glass factories had sprung up. The T. C. Wheaton Glass Company became the most famous of all.

Wheaton, born in Tuckahoe, New Jersey, was one of five sons. He earned money in his youth by clamming and oystering in local bays, and he spent a year sailing before he began working in a South Jersey pharmacy.

After graduating from the Philadelphia College of Pharmacy and Science in 1876, he enrolled in the Medical College of the University of Pennsylvania, receiving his M.D. degree in 1879.

Wheaton successfully managed his medical practice while owning two drugstores but, sensing that there was great potential in the glass industry, purchased a fledgling glass factory and renamed it the T. C. Wheaton Company. The enterprise quickly grew from the 25 people originally engaged to make pharmaceutical bottles and scientific glassware to over 3,000 people employed in Millville at the present time and thousands more working in factories in other areas.

Buildings along the main street reflect architectural styles from a bygone era, creating a feeling for what life was like here long ago. Wear comfortable shoes, and begin the self-guiding tour through Wheaton Village at the Museum of American Glass, one of the few museums in the nation devoted entirely to American glass.

Housed within this blue-and-white Victorian building are 6,500 glass objects, with an emphasis on items manufactured in southern New Jersey. The building's four wings encompass an open central court. Each room contains glassware created during various eras of history, and the architectural style of the room corresponds to the period of the glass on display. Objects are exhibited typologically.

Illuminating the lobby are the impressive chandeliers rescued from Atlantic City's famous Traymore Hotel before its destruction. The lobby is furnished with pieces taken from old homes in this area.

Room Two features decorative and utilitarian items from the earliest period of American manufacturing. Bottles, which were the most important product made by early glass houses, can be examined in Room Three. Free-blown or mold-blown, these include carboys, whiskey bottles, and flasks to hold strong drink; bitters bottles used to hold "aids to health" and pharmaceutical products; figurals or whimsies, developed for advertising and as an inducement to buy certain brands; and household and personal types such as pickle and fruit jars, soda bottles, and those for snuffs, inks, hair dyes, and scents.

The art of making paperweights is explained in Room Seven. Originally sold in Europe at stationery stores for practical use, paperweights appeared in the United States in 1851 for advertising and floral design displays. Here you'll see the famous "Millville Rose" created by Ralph Barber. Glassworkers competed with one another during their lunch hours to make the perfect rose, and Barber's is considered the most valuable today. In the South Jersey Room are many "end-of-day" items, as the lunch-hour pieces were referred to, including canes, decorative fish, hats, and turtles.

The works of Tiffany, Steuben, Fry, Fostoria, Durand, and others are displayed in Room Nine, and Room Ten offers information on the change to automation in the early 20th century. When you're finished admiring the beautiful glass, walk over to the Glass Factory, where demonstrations are offered three times daily. The schedule is available at the admission booth. The exterior of the factory was duplicated from photographs, but the interior is made of steel and concrete block to protect the building from fire, which was the cause for the demise of the original building in 1889.

The furnaces and stack, copied from the original blueprints, are now fired by natural gas while the originals used wood and coal. The "glory hole"—the square box with several ports in front of the furnace—is used to reheat the glass at the end of the glassmaker's blowing rod or punty. Several types of wares are produced here, and during the demonstrations, explanations are given for each of the six main styles of work used in 1888.

Paperweight-making is one of the most colorful to watch. Paperweights are not blown but made through a series of "gathers" of glass that are first shaped and then encased in additional gathers. If you didn't read about the procedure in the glass museum, the text and photo panels hanging below the visitor gallery will provide the details. You can learn even more by signing up to make your own paperweight under the supervision of one of the glassblowers. The charge of $55 is well worth it, but reservations are necessary.

If you can pull yourself away, stop by the exhibit cases on the way out. These contain illustrations of tools and related products, with an explanation of the "annealing" process, a procedure used to finish the rough bottoms of glass pieces where they were snapped off the blowing rods.

Spend some time browsing along Crafts and Trades Row, where craftspersons demonstrate their specialties. Watch as a flameworker manipulates cold glass in a hot flame to fabricate decorative objects, and talk with the wood carver, who'll be happy to explain the environment of New Jersey's tidal marshes. Take a peek at the salt-glazing kiln (located behind the pottery building), which enables the potter to reproduce the traditional salt glazes used in the 19th century. The authentic Tin Shop, where (on weekends) a tinsmith will acquaint you with his occupation, has a three-hole indoor privy. The Down Jersey Folklife Center, the first of its kind in the state, displays examples of artistic and cultural traditions maintained by residents of New Jersey's eight southern counties. You'll learn how diverse ethnic, regional, and occupational groups make up the living culture of "Down Jersey," as well as discovering traditions ranging from lifeguard shore boat races to split-oak basket making in the Jersey Pine Barrens. The Centre Grove School dates from 1876, while the Brownstone Emporium boasts an oak fireplace from an 1895 Massachusetts hotel and an oak cupboard, circa 1900, rescued from the Lydia Pinkham building in Boston. Bring lots of money; you may not be able to resist the blown glassware, jewelry, and lamps for sale in this building.

Wheaton Village's main street offers quaint shops and a glimpse of architectural styles from a bygone era.

You can also shop for housewares, yard goods, soaps, lanterns, black iron, and other old-fashioned goodies at the General Store. If you don't have time to make a paperweight, you can purchase beauties made in Wheaton Village as well as in the United States and Europe at the Paperweight Shop. The General Store was the official town hall in many communities; this one has a tin porch roof and cedar siding, which was common to this era.

Before walking to your automobile and returning to the present century, complete the day with a ride on a mini-version of the 1863 C. P. Huntington of the Southern Pacific Railroad. As this Iron Horse puffs smoke from its balloon-shaped stack in a scenic 0.75-mile trip along the edge of Wheaton Village Lake, you can spend a few minutes savoring yesteryear.

NOTES: Lunch and snacks are served at the adjacent PaperWaiter Restaurant & Pub; if you prefer, bring along a picnic. You can also stay overnight at the immaculate and comfortable Country Inn, adjacent to the village (reservations, 856-825-3100 or 800-456-4000) to spend more time at Wheaton, or visit Bridgeton (see the next chapter) and Cape May, which are both close by.

7. Historic Bridgeton

LOCATION	Cumberland County
	At the junction of Routes 49 and 77, Bridgeton 08302
	(856) 451-4802, (856) 455-3230, ext. 262
SEASON	Year round
HIGHLIGHTS	New Jersey's largest historic district, Nail Mill Museum, Cohanzick Zoo, Swedish Farmstead, George Woodruff Indian Museum, Old Broad Street Church, Potter's Tavern, riverfront promenade
ADMISSION	Fee to the Swedish Farmstead
HOURS	Museum hours vary; call before going Bridgeton-Cumberland Tourist Association open Monday–Friday 9 A.M.–4 P.M. and weekends May–Labor Day 10 A.M.–4 P.M.; closed major holidays
FACILITIES	Picnicking, rest room, drinking water, playground, jogging and fitness trails, beaches, boating
EVENTS	Special events throughout the year; for free calendar write Bridgeton-Cumberland Tourist Association, 50 East Broad Street, Bridgeton 08302

For a trip to yesteryear, plan on spending an entire day exploring Bridgeton's history-laden neighborhoods. In this unique town, where 2,200 houses and buildings are listed on the National Register of Historic Places, you'll find architecture spanning the centuries, including the Colonial, Federalist, and Victorian eras. Many of the historic buildings are still in use today.

In addition to being New Jersey's largest historic district, Bridgeton boasts the only municipal zoo in the state; one of the best-preserved 18th-century churches in the nation; a recreated Swedish homestead from the 1630s; and a lovely 1,200-acre city park.

The Lenape Indians, who settled here originally, were New Jersey's first farmers. Establishing villages close to streams, they burned sections of the forest to create open fields for farming; this is known as the "slash-and-burn" method. In 1638 the Swedes and Finns arrived, lured to southern New Jersey by Dutch promises of wealth from the fur and tobacco trades.

Unlike other settlers before them, the Swedes and Finns enjoyed a peaceful coexistence with the Indians. Not only did the primitive environment resemble that of their homeland, but both groups employed the same farming methods, traveled by water, and believed that sweating had spiritual and physical benefits. In addition, the Indian method of pouring boiling water over rocks was similar to the Swedish sauna.

Stop in at the New Sweden Company Farmstead Museum (Mayor Aitken Drive, Bridgeton City Park, 856-451-4802) for a look at the way Swedish settlers constructed their 17th-century farmsteads. The seven log structures consist of a blacksmith shop, where metal tools, hardware, and implements were made from local bog iron; a storage shed for storing grain, seed, food, and items to trade with the Indians; a threshing barn for storing tools; a stable; a residence; a barn with an outhouse; and a smokehouse and bathhouse combination, which was the first shelter built by an arriving pioneer family. Craftspeople in native costumes are on hand throughout the year to demonstrate old-time crafts.

When the first settlers arrived from Sweden, they erected log cabins low to the ground because they were accustomed to paying a tax if their cabin was more than six logs high. They also kept their tradition of taking a weekly sauna, but according to the curator, when the English came, they discouraged the Swedes from this practice because they believed that taking a bath was as deadly as night air. During their lifetimes, the English took two full baths: one at birth and the other when laid out for burial.

Most of the metal hinges, tools, and furnishings within the buildings are original period pieces donated by the Swedish government. Many hex signs are displayed, including a butterfly-shaped sign in the Store House used to ensure that only good spirits entered the building. Considered the most important building on the entire homestead, the Store House held seed, grain, all the smoked meats, and whatever articles that the Swedes brought with them to use in trading with the Indians. Supposedly a house fairy lived inside, and bits of food were usually left on the doorstep so he wouldn't go hungry.

The Blacksmith Shop was the only building with a sod roof; small animals would be placed there so they could graze without fear of being attacked by larger animals. Sod was also an inexpensive means of insulation.

The Residence House contains a wealth of interesting objects, including elegant cooking tools, betrothal gifts, and an unusual oven. The guides explain how it was possible for the Swedes to erect buildings without nails, and they describe the lifestyle of the settlers. This homestead is typical of land owned by a family with as many as 10 children.

Bridgeton's history formally began in 1686, when Richard Hancock arrived and built a sawmill and workmen's houses here. In 1716, when a bridge was placed across the Cohansey River, the town was named

You'll find architecture spanning centuries in Bridgeton, where 2,200 houses and buildings are listed on the National Register of Historic Places. This group of buildings, now used as stores, is known as the "Seven Sisters" and is reputed to be among the oldest commercial structures in the state.

Cohansey Bridge. At this time it served as the county seat, but locals preferred to call it Bridgetown. This name stuck until 1816, when a local bank officer ordered stationery. When the printer omitted the letter "w" from the name in error, legend tells that it was less expensive to rename the town than to return the letterhead. In any case, the name Bridgeton stuck!

By 1838, Bridgeton's population totaled 2,387. With 475 buildings in town, including a nail and iron factory, a woolen mill, two gristmills, a sawmill, and over 30 cargo-carrying coastal schooners and sloops based here, it was a self-sufficient, thriving community.

In the latter half of the 1800s, Bridgeton became an industrial center, and wealthy families built fine homes in grand styles. Atlantic Street and Commerce Street have the greatest concentration of the remaining Victorian houses, and the best way to explore the town is on foot, starting from the Tourist Information Center (50 East Broad Street, 856-451-4801). Housed in a Queen Anne–style building, originally home to the Pennsylvania Reading Seashore Lines in the late 1800s, the center offers travel information, a slide show, and a free guide entitled "A Walking Tour of Historic Bridgeton."

If the center is closed, park in the lot and begin by turning left one block to Laurel Street; then go right onto Laurel, proceeding downtown for two blocks. Victorian architecture is evident in many of the shop facades, brick sidewalks, and attractive landscaping. From here, cross Laurel Street, turning left onto Commerce Street, and continue toward the bridge spanning the Cohansey River. At the traffic light, to the left, is a group of stores known as the "Seven Sisters," reputed to be among the oldest commercial structures in New Jersey.

Bear right at the traffic light to the Nail Mill Museum. In the early 1800s this was the office of the Cumberland Nail and Iron Company, the town's largest industry until the 1890s. The Nail Works, powered by a hand-dug raceway, employed 300 people to produce wrought-iron nails used not only in the construction of most of the local houses but throughout the country. Fortunately, when the company closed, the city set aside over 1,000 acres of woodland for recreational use.

After examining the Nail Company Museum's collection of relics, including an unusual two-faced clock, Civil War flasks, turn-of-the-century bottles, East Lake pottery, and a collection of 18th-century lanterns, go around back to the one-room Dame Howell School. Built in 1830 primarily for the very young, its emphasis was on religious instruction. Tuition was a few pennies a week, and schools like this, run by an educated woman or "dame," remained until public education became prevalent throughout the country around 1850.

The Cohanzick Zoo, the only municipal zoo in the state, is nearby. Although small, with old-fashioned heavy iron cages, it houses an interesting assortment of animals, including the rare golden lion tamarin, the smallest of all primates.

Return to the traffic light at the corner of Commerce Street and Mayor Aitken Drive for a look at the Federal-style Sheppard house (31 W. Commerce Street), the oldest mansion in town. Sheppard, a prosperous farmer who owned most of the land in the area, spent a fortune building this three-story house, which was completed in 1791. After his death, his wife turned it into a boarding school for girls; later it served as a nursing home.

From here, turn left, and go uphill to Commerce Street and Franklin Drive. Along Franklin Drive is a large white Italianate house built in 1850 by the owner of the Cumberland Nail and Iron Company. An unusual feature is the main stairway, made of iron. Turn left onto Lake Street, where you'll come to a huge tree in the middle of the road. Rather than chop it down, the town built the street around it. The massive Gothic Revival house at 25 Lake Street is known as "Seven Gables." Now a complex of apartments, it was built in 1872 to serve as a school and later as a maternity hospital.

Construction of the Old Broad Street Church (Route 49 and Broad Street) was begun in 1791, but when funds ran out halfway through the project, progress halted. Money was raised through a local lottery, and the Georgian-style church was completed in 1795. The bricks were handmade at the site and laid in Flemish-bond style. Inside, the pulpit is in the shape of a wine glass and stands beneath a massive Palladian window.

On the way back you'll pass "Potter's Tavern" (49–51 W. Broad), a prime example of a typical New Jersey frame house built during the 17th and 18th centuries. Built in 1767, the tavern served as the hub of the town's social life. It was here that people discussed liberty and separation from British crown rule, voicing their opinions in the *Plain Dealer*, one of the state's first newspapers. On Christmas Day, 1775, the paper was posted outside the tavern in a protest, and Matthew Potter, owner of the tavern, is thought to have marched off to fight the British a short time after. The paper's first editor was Dr. Ebenezer Elmer, a member of Congress; contributing writers included Joseph Bloomfield and Richard Howell, both serving as governors later on.

You'll pass an 18th-century stone warehouse, along Broad and Atlantic streets, which stored goods brought in by ship along the Cohansey River. Before crossing the bridge you'll come to Bridgeton's original bank, the one allegedly responsible for the misspelling of the town's name. On the opposite side is the town's landmark, a red diner. It's a good place to stop for a snack.

The George J. Woodruff Museum of Indian Artifacts (Bridgeton Free Public Library, 150 East Commerce Street, 609-451-2620) contains an excellent collection of 20,000 Indian artifacts found within a 30-mile radius. Among the finds are arrowheads, bone awls, axes, copper and clay beads, a dog skull, spear points, and shards.

Inside the Cumberland County Courthouse (Broad and Atlantic) is the bell that rang out and drew everyone together when the Declaration of Independence was signed on July 7, 1776. The Engine House (Bank and Orange streets), erected in 1898, houses steam engines and other horse-drawn apparatus. It is one of the oldest working firehouses in southern New Jersey. Inside is a drying tower for hoses, a bell, a brass sliding pole, and a steam fire engine dating to 1876.

Bridgeton may not have the manicured look of Cape May or wide expanses of white sandy beaches, but it is definitely worthwhile if you want to take a walk through time in New Jersey's largest historic district.

NOTES: Many charming shops line the historic downtown area. Enjoy a picnic lunch in the park, or try one of the local restaurants for well-prepared food.

8. Red Bank Battlefield

LOCATION Gloucester County
100 Hessian Avenue (off Route 295), National Park
08063
(856) 853-5120

SEASON Year round

HIGHLIGHTS Remains of Fort Mercer, Whitall House, and scenic view of Delaware River

ADMISSION Free

HOURS Park: dawn–dusk
Whitall House: Wednesday–Sunday, Memorial Day–Labor Day, 1–4 P.M; call before going; hours subject to change

FACILITIES Rest room, gift shop, picnic pavilions, playgrounds

EVENTS Battle of Fort Mercer reenactment; Jonas Cattell 10-kilometer run each October, call for date and time

NOT MANY PEOPLE WOULD STICK AROUND IF A CANNONBALL WAS SHOT THROUGH their wall, but Ann Cooper Whitall did. According to legend, she picked up her spinning wheel, carried it down to the cellar, continued spinning, and announced, "I will not leave; I'll be needed after the battle is over." Her bravery earned her the nickname "The Angel of the Battle of Red Bank." That was in 1777.

Before this, life had been peaceful for Ann and James Whitall. James, a wealthy farmer and merchant, had inherited his grandfather's 411-acre plantation, named Red Bank. Here in 1748, on a secluded bluff overlooking the Delaware River, James built a brick mansion. The location, less than five miles by river to Philadelphia, was ideal.

Then, in 1777, part of Whitall's house was commandeered as military headquarters, and Fort Mercer was built on the strategically situated apple orchard. Named in honor of Brigadier General Hugh Mercer, and manned by Continental forces on October 18, 1777, Fort Mercer stood opposite Fort Mifflin on the Pennsylvania side of the river. These two forts were built to protect Philadelphia from enemies approaching from the water. When the British won the Battle of the Brandywine on September 11, 1777, and overtook Philadelphia, they realized that in order to move their warships and supply boats down the Delaware to the fallen capital, they would have to destroy both forts.

Ann and James Whitall built this house on a secluded bluff overlooking the Delaware River in 1748. In 1777, when a cannonball was shot through their wall, Ann declared, "I will not leave; I'll be needed after the battle is over."

British General William Howe, in command in Philadelphia, assigned this task to Carl Emil Kurt von Donop and his 1,228-man brigade of Hessian soldiers. At the same time, General George Washington ordered Colonel Christopher Greene, who had served successfully under General Benedict Arnold, to hold down Fort Mercer at any cost. With only 400 men, Greene apparently came up with a few good ideas on how to defend the fort. He and his men gathered over 200 huge logs supplied by Whitall and local farmers. Then, tying them in sections with two to four timbers ranging 65 feet long and 20 inches square, they added iron sheaths extending outward at an angle of about 45 degrees. When finished, these stockades, known as chevaux-de-frise, were floated out across the river, sunk with stone cribs, and anchored down so that the points of the protruding timbers rested about four feet below the water's surface between the two forts. They were designed to destroy the wooden bottoms of any enemy ships trying to get down the river.

Greene also followed the advice of a French engineer who had been sent to assist him. Chevalier de Mauduit du Plessis suggested building an inner wall between the outside of the fort and the inner redoubt to reduce the size of the perimeter that the men had to patrol. The northern section of the fort was then evacuated before the battle began, but a few sentries were left in place to deceive the enemy.

Jonas Cattell, a young blacksmith, had been keeping an eye on the enemy. As they left Haddonfield on the morning of October 22, he ran through the woods to alert Greene that the soldiers were headed toward the fort. When they arrived at 4 P.M., the Hessians began their attack at the northern section of the fort but were shocked after climbing the walls to find themselves in front of the newly built 10-foot wall and sharpened tree trunks and branches. This was the opportunity Greene's men had been waiting for, and they charged, killing and wounding hundreds of men, including Donop, who was seriously wounded.

On the Hessian side, casualties in the Battle of Red Bank amounted to 514, while the Americans fared much better with 23 wounded and 14 dead. And, as she thought, Ann Whitall was needed; her house was turned into a hospital where she treated friend and foe alike.

Although the victory didn't keep the British supply ships from reaching Philadelphia, it did cause tremendous financial and manpower losses for the enemy. It also gave Washington and his men, who had endured defeat for the previous nine months, renewed hope. The real turning point in the Revolution came when France, discovering how well the Americans had fought, decided to enter the war against Great Britain.

The Whitalls remained in their house for a month after the battle; they fled when the fort was evacuated and the British looted the property. The damage to their land and house was so great that they eventually submitted a bill to the United States government for repairs, but they never received a settlement. They returned six months later, and records indicate that five generations of Whitalls lived here from 1748 to 1862.

In 1872 the property was taken over by the federal government until Theodore Roosevelt transferred it to Gloucester County in 1905. Today visitors can visit the Whitall House and stroll through shady groves leading to several monuments denoting the historical events that took place here, including a 75-foot monument erected by the state in 1905.

The Whitall house was enlarged three times over a period of 100 years as the property descended from generation to generation. There is a stone addition, built during the third quarter of the 18th century, containing a bedroom and a large kitchen. The main brick section consists of a spacious keeping room, which was the center for everyday life. At the front of the house, facing the river, is a small receiving parlor, an exhibit room, and James Whitall's farm office. The formal parlor has an ornate mantel and woodwork. Most of the furniture, rugs, and paintings are contained in this room, which was used on formal occasions such as weddings or for receiving important guests.

NOTES: On display in a long shed near the Whitall House are the remains of one of the chevaux-de-frise, recovered in 1936 after having been submerged for at least 170 years. A staircase leads to the beach. Bring a picnic lunch to enjoy in one of the groves, or try one of the numerous restaurants in National Park and Woodbury.

9. Double Trouble State Park

LOCATION	Ocean County On Keswick-Pinewald Road (west of Route 9), Berkeley Township 08721 (732) 793-0506
SEASON	Year round
HIGHLIGHTS	Historic sawmill, remnants of logging village, one-room schoolhouse circa 1890s, cranberry bogs
ADMISSION	Free
HOURS	Park: dawn–dusk
FACILITIES	None
EVENTS	Cranberry harvest in September–October; call for dates

How Double Trouble State Park acquired its intriguing name is still a mystery. One idea is that an elderly preacher and his wife gave it this name in the 1840s after muskrats had dug holes in their dam twice in one week.

The other version, told by Mickey Coen, a naturalist with the Ocean County Parks System, attributes the name to Thomas Potter, a minister and founder of the Universalist Church in America. Potter built the first mill before 1765 along the Factory Branch of Cedar Creek, and after learning that spring floods had washed out the dam above his mill for the second time, Potter is said to have remarked, "Now we have double trouble; go back and repair the dam."

While Double Trouble State Park doesn't offer camping, picnicking, or even rest room facilities, it does offer a bit of history and easy hiking along sand trails. With the exception of the 1890s schoolhouse, located at the park entrance at Keswick-Pinewald Road, the village buildings date from the early 1900s. The sawmill, in operation until recently, is being restored and contains a machine from 1883 capable of cutting 1,000 shingles an hour.

When the village was in its heyday, the surrounding stands of cedar, oak, and maple produced high-quality lumber for shipbuilding and home construction. Some of the earliest houses in the area still have the original cedar shakes produced from Double Trouble's mills. The first known mill and surrounding land were purchased by William Giberson in the early

1830s. With his son, Captain George W. Giberson, he operated a little community and mills on these grounds from the middle to late 1800s. The Gibersons built housing for their year-round mill hands and the seasonal workers who worked on the cranberry bogs they owned.

Thomas Hooper operated five other bogs here in the 1800s, in addition to cultivating cranberries and making charcoal from cut timber. The charcoal was then used in bog iron furnaces and forges in Ocean, Burlington, and Atlantic counties. Hooper supposedly had as many as 100 charcoal fires burning here simultaneously in the 1860s.

After he bought the village in the early 1900s, Edward Crabbe formed the Double Trouble Company and raised cranberries commercially. Crabbe, commodore of the Toms River Yacht Club and the Cruising Club of America, succeeded in turning Double Trouble into one of the state's top cranberry producers. In addition he rebuilt a burned-out sawmill and continued lumbering operations. However, cranberry cultivation wasn't new to the area. The Indians had been eating these delectable wild red berries, besides using them for medicinal purposes and to dye clothing, long before sailors discovered that munching on berries could prevent scurvy during long sea voyages.

Cranberry localities in New Jersey have always used unusual names. In addition to Double Trouble, there's Ongs Hat, Mount Misery, Calico, Friendship, Penny Pot, and Hog Wallow, with the bogs incorporating unique names such as Boo Coo, Cold Water Run, and Half-A-Dollar.

The Crabbe family played an important part in launching the cranberry business. New Jersey ranks third in production today after Massachusetts and Wisconsin; in 1981 over 22.8 million pounds of cranberries were produced.

Perhaps "Peg Leg" John Webb was also responsible for the cranberry industry's success. He's credited with inventing, by accident, the first mechanical berry sorter. Missing one leg, Webb had a great deal of difficulty getting sorted berries down from his barn loft to the marketplace. One day, probably out of frustration, he allegedly dumped the berries down a staircase. As the story goes, the soft ones surprisingly got stuck while the juicy, plump ones bounced down to the bottom of the steps. This accident was the basis for a much needed invention. Commercial cranberries are still sorted based on this simple "bounce" test.

A lovely short walk awaits on the trail at the first left turn near the park entrance. White pine—recognizable by bundles of five needles growing three to five inches long—line this wide sand road. Pass by the fire road on your right, turning at the next right to the Crabbe family graves. The Crabbes owned this land until 1964, when it was sold to the state. When you're ready, return to the path, turn right, and continue to an abandoned sluiceway and bog. Water inside this former bog was regulated by lowering or raising wooden boards. In a short distance you'll reach an old dam along Cedar Creek.

From here, face the creek and head for the narrow trail bearing to the left along the water's edge; this leads back to the parking area. On the way back try to visualize what this area looked like when trees from the cedar swamp were cut and floated downstream to the mill. Water from the stream was harnessed behind the dam to operate the saws in the mill, but individual mills never lasted over 20 years because the friction of the turning wheels would ignite the sawdust and set the building ablaze. In order to cope with this problem, construction would begin on a new mill as soon as one was completed.

The mill where you started will appear shortly on the left. At this point cross over the canal, make a right on Double Trouble Road along the side of the mill, and walk until you come to a wide road known as the Ocean County Nature and Conservation Trail. (The sign may be missing.) This is a 1-mile loop with a wide variety of flora and fauna, including a cranberry bog.

Many of the surrounding cedars died when this bog was flooded, but because the wood is so resistant, the trunks remain intact. When the sun shines, the cottonweed in this area glistens, and nearby you can see a stand of huge, healthy Atlantic white cedars. It was considered a criminal act to cut down and keep any cedar for private use during colonial times if the tree measured over 12 inches in diameter, since the King of England claimed them for his ship masts.

If the bogs are empty when you visit, you'll still probably find a few handfuls of cranberries the pickers missed. It's exciting to be here during September and October, when the cranberries are harvested. Two methods are used for gathering cranberries: dry harvesting and wet harvesting. In dry harvesting berries are combed off the vines by a machine that sucks them into a burlap bag. Wet harvesting—the method used here—is accomplished by flooding the bog with a couple of feet of water. Then workers dressed in waders get into the bog and use a machine with rotating bars to knock the berries off the vines. As the berries float to the top, forming a crimson sea, other workers use floating wooden booms to haul them out.

It takes 45,000 cranberries to fill one barrel, and one acre of bog yields 150 barrels of berries! As you walk back to the parking area using the wide trail to your left, you'll pass more bogs, which, some people say, are mind-boggling!

NOTES: Sneakers are fine. Pack a picnic lunch and enjoy it along the trail. The combined walk is approximately 3–4 miles.

10. Historic Kingston

LOCATION	Middlesex County
	Main Street (Route 27), Kingston 08528
	(609) 520-1776
SEASON	Year round
HIGHLIGHTS	Historic sites, antique shops, canal, canoeing
ADMISSION	Free
HOURS	Shop hours vary
FACILITIES	Restaurants, rest room
EVENTS	Holiday sales in shops

SETTLED BY QUAKERS ON LAND WILLIAM PENN PURCHASED IN 1693, PRINCETON'S lush tree-lined streets beckoned dozens of wealthy people, including Grover Cleveland, at the turn of the century. When it was still a village consisting only of small houses and the college, George Washington and his soldiers marched down Nassau Street.

Princeton is still a popular place to visit, and no wonder. Besides Princeton University's beautiful campus, historic buildings, and modern University Art Museum, the town offers dozens of fine shops in addition to those at Palmer Square. But unknown to many is Princeton's next-door neighbor, the historic town of Kingston.

General George Washington led his troops along the Old Indian Path through the center of town, now called Main Street. No doubt he was in a hurry trying to elude the enemy, but he might have taken time out to stop at the Presbyterian Church, established in 1723. Or he might have visited the house built by Jedediah Higgins, who in 1814 was Kingston's earliest recorded settler. These two landmarks still stand and can be seen while exploring this charming town.

Drive to the Higgins House first; it's located on Main Street at the intersection with Raymond Road. The wing with the lower roofline is believed to be the oldest part of the house. Hopefully, at the time you visit, you'll be allowed inside.

In the center of town you'll find antique shops, restaurants, and parking. Visitors interested in antique furniture won't be disappointed. Shops carry an excellent assortment of china, pressed and cut glass, inkwells, handsome oak chests, jewelry, paintings, and oriental rugs.

At the time I wandered through town, there was also a fabulous mix of specialty shops: One sold all different shaped balloons, another had unusual

This stone bridge was built in 1798 as a replacement for the one Washington destroyed when he was eluding the enemy. It overlooks the Millstone River and the impressive Kingston Mill, which operated through the early 1940s.

plants and handmade gifts, and one catered to equestrians who fancied English and western riding equipment.

You can't miss the bell tower atop the Italianate-style Presbyterian Church, which seems to almost touch the sky. The church, completed in 1852, has narrow, arched windows and is surrounded by a cast-iron fence adorned with Greek designs. A bit farther south is the Presbyterian Cemetery, which contains unusual tombstones, many dated to the 1700s, now shaded by towering sycamores. It's a great place to make rubbings, but take care not to deface the stones.

When the Delaware and Raritan Canal opened in 1830, people came from miles to attend the celebration. Governor Vroom acknowledged this great occasion by riding on a barge past onlookers who stood at every lock and on every bridge.

The 43 miles of canal, hand-dug by Irish immigrants using pick and shovel, was once vital for the transport of coal between Trenton and New Brunswick. Although mules no longer pull the heavy barges along the waterway, visitors can now use this scenic area—part of the Delaware and Raritan Canal State Park—for strolling along the towpath, fishing, bicycling, or canoeing on the canal.

Spend a few minutes at the stone bridge built in 1798 as a replacement for the one Washington had destroyed when he was eluding the enemy; the expression "burning your bridges behind you" may well apply to Washington's military tactics. It overlooks the Millstone River, the dam impounding Carnegie Lake, and the impressive Kingston Mill, which operated through the early 1940s. The building previously housed a sawmill, a wool manufacturing plant, a gristmill, and a flour mill.

At the southern end of town are Carnegie Lake and the adjoining Stony Brook. These are both wonderful places for easy canoeing, where you can drift on a calm, scenic lake or get some exercise paddling from the lake over to Stony Brook. The 3-mile-by-0.25-mile man-made lake, a gift from Andrew Carnegie, was created by damming the Millstone River in 1906.

Geologists have determined that the Millstone, one of the few streams in the country flowing north, once flowed in the opposite direction but had its course reversed during the Ice Age. The lake is surrounded on the east by the Delaware and Raritan Canal towpath and on the west by wooded shores of the edge of Princeton. Princeton University's boathouse is at the upper end of the lake; visitors are welcome to park there to launch their boats or watch many of the school's boat races.

Begin your adventure by paddling the lake; then head over to the southern end where Stony Brook comes in. Occasionally you'll see fishermen trying to catch dinner, but you're more likely to spot or hear birds as they fly through the thick tangle of overhead trees. Continue along, stopping wherever you please, but be careful of the poison ivy that grows profusely on the banks.

Peaceful, shaded Stony Brook is the ideal place to learn the basics of canoeing if you've never done it before. After a short distance you'll reach a suspension bridge, a favorite docking spot for those who enjoy the challenge and thrill of walking across a swinging structure.

At one time a historian noted that 49 stagecoaches and over 400 harnessed horses stopped in Kingston at the same time. The horses and stages are gone, but the town still retains a blend of history and simple charm.

NOTES: Take a picnic lunch to enjoy at the water's edge, or try one of the eating places in town. If you'd like to go canoeing, contact Princeton Canoe Rental at Turning Basin on Alexander Road, Princeton, (609) 452-2403.

11. Howell Living History Farm

LOCATION Mercer County
Valley Road (off Route 29), east 1.5 miles to
Woodens Lane, left to parking lot, Titusville 08560
(609) 737-3299

SEASON Best during spring, summer, and fall

HIGHLIGHTS Farm restoration in progress; children and adults
help with farm chores; animals; tranquil scenery

ADMISSION Free; donations appreciated

HOURS Mid-January–March, Saturday 10 A.M.–4 P.M.; April–
July, Tuesday–Friday 10 A.M.–4 P.M., and Sunday
self-guiding tours noon–4 P.M.; mid-July–early
August, Saturday evening hayrides 5–8 P.M.;
September–December 1, Tuesday–Friday 10 A.M.–
4 P.M., Sunday self-guiding tours noon–4 P.M.;
schedule subject to change, call before going

FACILITIES Portajon, drinking water, picnic grove

EVENTS September Plowing Match; October Fall Festival;
Traditional Christmas Celebration; Sled Day in
January; special programs Saturdays throughout the
year (except August); maple sugaring, sheep
shearing, nature walks, arts and crafts, hayrides,
spring gardening demonstrations; for free calendar
write Howell Living History Farm, 101 Hunter
Road, Titusville 08560

SEVERAL YEARS AGO, INEZ HOWELL DONATED 126 ACRES OF LAND TO MERCER County in memory of her husband, Congressman Charles Howell. According to her stipulation that it be developed as a living history farm, the Park Commission has created Howell Living History Farm. Still a restoration in progress, Howell Farm transports visitors back to the year 1900, a time when horse and buggies traveled the lanes of Pleasant Valley and when farms were bordered by snake fences and osage orange trees.

Today the farm uses the same methods that were handed down by previous generations of farmers to crop the acres, while keeping animals that are modern-day descendants of breeds raised in the area almost 100 years ago. Visitors are not only free to watch the farmers drive a team of horses or use old-fashioned walking plows, they are encouraged to pitch in and help prepare a loaf of bread from home-grown wheat, gather freshly laid eggs, lend a hand sweeping the barn, make soap, or churn butter and ice cream. If you prefer, you can pick and shuck corn, shell and grind it, and bake corn bread.

Howell Farm is a throwback to an age that depended on physical labor and horse power. When the gasoline engine and multirow implements were introduced, these new inventions revolutionized cropping methods and tripled the average farmer's productivity. Small-farm extension agents participate in Howell Farm's Intern Program so that they, in turn, can teach thousands in Asia, Africa, and India how to introduce or upgrade similar animal-powered farming systems.

After parking, follow the snake fence to the various sites. Snake fences were popular with farmers at the turn of the century because they were stronger and easier to build than rail fences. An example of a Virginia fence is on the left. Similar to the snake type, it's easier to build because instead of pounding in two upright posts to hold the rails, a farmer used diagonal braces.

In a couple of minutes you'll come to a large grassy area known as the round pasture. Exactly as it was in 1900, it still provides good grass and a natural water supply for the animals, and it is sheltered from the wind. The sheep barn, to the left, was moved here from another property and is home to a flock of 12 Suffolk ewes that supply the farmer with wool and lambs. Spun wool is for sale to visitors, while the lambs are sent to market as they were in earlier days.

Families relied on chickens for their meat and eggs, and they sold the surplus to bring in cash. The chicken house, a reproduction of a common design, houses a flock of Plymouth Barred Rock hens, a cross between Rhode Island Reds and White Rocks. If you arrive early in the day, the farmer is usually delighted to have visitors help collect the eggs. Ducks, geese, guinea hens, and turkeys were also part of circa 1900 farms; these animals can be seen scurrying in the barnyard, around the pond, or near the chicken house.

The hog pasture behind the main barn usually attracts a crowd, especially on a hot day when the pigs get hosed down. Raised for market, they're bought as weanlings and fattened to 220 pounds before shipping. Bear right; you'll come to a corn crib designed to hold a one-year supply of corn and an apple orchard with over 15 old varieties of apple trees. The nearby wagon house dates to the mid-1800s, when expanding farm operations required additional storage space for equipment.

A visitor center occupies the lower level of the farmhouse. This is a good

Visitors to the Howell Living History Farm can go back in time to see how farmers operated in the 1900s.

place to sample apple cider and a cookie (nominal charge) and to pick up a calendar of upcoming events. A small garden displays the typical flowers, herbs, and vegetables that were grown for family use, while the large truck garden was used for growing grain for bread and baked goods, plus vegetables for cooking and canning. Scarecrows were often placed in this area to keep deer, raccoons, and rabbits away. When all else failed, the farmer resorted to firing his gun.

The main barn—built in four sections with the earliest dating to the beginning of the 19th century—usually holds everyone's interest. You may even get to see a huge purebred Belgian draft horse. These were especially bred in the Middle Ages for use as war horses. They had to be large and strong in order to carry their own heavy armor plus that of the knight.

King Henry VIII decreed that every horse in his kingdom shorter than five feet at the shoulder be put to death to ensure that future generations would be large and strong. This breed, as well as the Clydesdale, were later used to pull heavy wagons and plows. They're oddities today, used in exhibitions such as the Budweiser Team or in pulling contests.

The farm's additional work horses provide the power for the various chores such as plowing, fertilizing, planting, harrowing, cultivating, mowing, reaping, and transportation. Ranging in weight from 1,400 pounds to 1 ton, they are Percheron and Belgian crosses. At the beginning of the 20th century, farm horses were lighter, multipurpose workers used for field work, buggy power, and occasional riding. Two or three were usually sufficient to supply a 100-acre farm with power.

Should you grow to love the hard-working but peaceful life on this circa 1900 farm, volunteers are more than welcome to pitch in. And, if you have children between three and five, they may participate in "The Hatchery," a 12-week spring or fall program. While you're out in the field leading tours, carding wool, grinding corn, or doing other chores, they can help raise a baby chick, plant a garden, or care for lambs, piglets, and other baby animals.

Watching farming the old-fashioned way is a step back in time definitely worth coming for.

NOTES: Dogs are not allowed. Handicapped persons and senior citizens may park in the field to the right of the bridge barricade on Hunter Road; it's a short walk from here to the rear gate. Severely handicapped persons can drive directly to the barnyard area by traveling down Hunter Road from Route 518 and entering through the double wooden gates. Special assistance is available if you call ahead. Bring along a picnic lunch to enjoy in the grove. The Belle Mountain public ski area, (609) 397-0043, and Washington Crossing State Park (see chapter 38) are nearby.

12. Liberty State Park

LOCATION Hudson County
Morris Pesin Drive (off Exit 14-B, New Jersey
Turnpike), Jersey City 07305
(201) 915-3400

SEASON Year round

HIGHLIGHTS View of Statue of Liberty, Liberty Science Center,
fishing, crabbing, swimming, tennis, boat
launching, interpretive center, nature trails, bird
watching, ferry service to the Statue of Liberty,
historic Central Railroad of New Jersey terminal

ADMISSION Free

HOURS Park: April–October, 6 A.M.–10 P.M.; other times,
6 A.M.–8 P.M.; since hours are subject to change, it's
best to call before going
Ferry service to the Statue of Liberty is year round
except on Christmas; for ferry service information
call (201) 435-9499

FACILITIES Rest room, snack bar, picnic area, boat launch,
tennis courts, bathhouse, swimming pool

EVENTS Special events and performances summer months;
write to Liberty State Park, Morris Pesin Drive,
Jersey City 07305, or call for complete schedule

LIBERTY STATE PARK OFFERS MAGNIFICENT VIEWS OF NEW YORK'S SKYLINE AND THE Statue of Liberty. Established in 1964, New Jersey's first urban park contains 1,114 acres of which 300 are currently developed.

In the late 1800s, the Central Railroad of New Jersey (CNJ) and the Lehigh Valley Railroad developed this site for railroad freight and commuter operations. During the early 1900s, the CNJ Passenger Terminal, located at the north end of the park, served as a major transportation center in the New York City metropolitan area, with over 28,000 people passing through each day. This was also where thousands of immigrants first stepped on United States soil after being processed at nearby Ellis Island. During World War I, the southern area of the park served as a munitions depot for the armed forces.

With the growth of truck and auto traffic during the 1950s and the use of bridges and tunnels connecting Manhattan, there was a major shift in

Even a helicopter seems to be dwarfed by the majesty of the Statue of Liberty.

commerce and transportation from the waterfront to New Jersey's suburban areas. Pier facilities quickly became obsolete as railroad-related activities in the Liberty State Park area were no longer necessary, and this led to the abandonment of the land and facilities.

Fortunately, with Green Acres Bond Funds and Jersey City's generosity in donating the first 144 acres, the state began to acquire the land in 1970. After cleaning up the harbor, the 35-acre site opposite the Statue of Liberty was completed in 1976.

The park entrance is impressive: Lining the path are 50 state flags, in order of the states' induction into the Union, along with the 13 flags of the original colonies and various historic flags representing the revolutionary war era.

Looking straight ahead from the visitor center, you'll have another impressive sight—one of the most famous ladies in the world, whose steady gaze and outstretched arm have greeted thousands of people who have come to our country looking for freedom and gold-paved streets. Created by Frederic Auguste Bartholdi, and presented to the United States in 1886 by the French government to commemorate the alliance of France and the United States during the American Revolution, the statue's real name is "La Liberté Eclairant," meaning "Liberty Enlightening the World." Later shortened to "Liberty," most people now refer to the lady as the "Statue of Liberty."

Many visitors arriving at Liberty State Park to view the Statue of Liberty are surprised to find they're facing her back, but this unique angle makes it even more inviting to hop on a ferry to Liberty Island to experience her from all sides. It's best to take an early ferry before it gets too crowded on the island; then plan on completing the rest of the day at Liberty State Park—a great place to fish, bird watch, sightsee, walk, visit the Liberty Science Center (see chapter 59), and enjoy an unusual view of the statue and Manhattan's skyline during sunset.

The ferry route takes passengers past two of the same sites that approximately 14 million emigrants gazed upon between 1886 and 1924 on their way into America through New York Harbor—Ellis Island and the Statue of Liberty. Ellis Island still stands as a living memorial to those who passed through its doors. Over 5,000 people each day were examined at this final inspection point after arriving in our country. About 2 percent were rejected and returned to their country of origin, thus earning Ellis Island the nickname "Isle of Tears."

Have your camera ready for unusual close-ups as the ferry passes in front of the Statue of Liberty. Her flaming torch symbolizes liberty, dignity, and authority, while the seven spikes in the crown represent liberty radiating to each of the seven continents and seven seas. The broken shackles at her feet signify freedom from tyranny, and to further the link with the American republic, Bartholdi sculpted a tablet bearing the date July 4, 1776, when the Declaration of Independence was signed.

Not only is her size impressive—she stands 151 feet tall on a pedestal 89 feet high—but so are the words fastened to her base. Written by Emma Lazarus in 1883, "The New Colossus" reads:

> Give me your tired, your poor,
> The wretched refuse of your teeming shore.
> Send these, the homeless, tempest-tost to me,
> I lift my lamp beside the golden door!

Once on the island, the size of the statue is even more surprising. Although she was given to us by France, it was agreed that we would design and pay for her pedestal. However, in 1885, the committee in charge of collecting donations realized that while businesses were donating, individuals were not. Many people thought the statue was sheer folly, but thanks to the efforts of publisher Joseph Pulitzer, Americans changed their minds. Pulitzer began a fund-raising campaign that appealed to our pride, promising that he'd publish in his newspaper, the *World*, the name of every donor no matter how small the gift. Contributions poured in—dimes, quarters, and half-dollars. Schoolchildren helped tremendously; finally one day the paper announced that over $100,000 had been collected from 120,000 people. The pedestal was completed in 1886.

Liberty stands on an island previously used as a fishing ground, quarantine station, hospital base, fort, farm, gallows, military prison, and dump. First named Minissais (lesser island) by the Indians, colonists called it Great Oyster Island. When the Statue of Liberty was placed upon it, it was known as Bedloe's Island after Isaac Bedloe, its first owner, but Congress renamed it Liberty Island in 1956.

If you're feeling energetic and there isn't too long a wait to climb the 168 steps to the crown, it's the best way to appreciate the interior's fragile copper skin. On a clear day you can see almost forever from each of the 25 windows in the crown, in addition to having the best view of the 23-foot-by-13-foot tablet that the lady holds in her hand. Unfortunately, because of structural weaknesses, only park maintenance employees are allowed in the torch. In season, the wait to reach the crown is often at least two to three hours, but for those who don't want to risk a heart attack climbing the steep stairs or simply don't want to wait, the outside balcony also offers excellent views.

Don't miss exploring the American Museum of Immigration; it houses interesting objects and photographs acknowledging the arrival of the immigrants. Once inside the statue, you'll learn historic facts about the hardships incurred in transporting the statue, depicted through models, films, and artifacts; how the statue was built using 19th-century technology and ancient methods, including how models of each part were transformed from small to larger scales and how the copper skin was molded. You'll also be able to examine many of the tools used in restoring the statue in 1984, which are surprisingly similar to the original tools.

Videotapes describe the statue's arrival in the harbor in 114 separate crates, as well as the dedication parade through New York streets. Over a million people attended, along with a colorful 300-vessel salute in the harbor.

After returning to Liberty State Park, head over to the CNJ Station for a start of an enjoyable 4.1-mile walk on a paved trail. Time the walk just before sunset to watch Manhattan's skyline reflect the sky's vivid colors, and watch the lights go on in the statue's crown and torch.

Begin by walking away from the water at the station; in a couple of minutes the statue appears to your left. Turn left at the sign to Liberation Point; as you walk you'll have excellent views of the statue and Ellis Island.

After about 30 minutes, you'll reach a good spot for viewing passing boats and shorebirds. The visitor center is just ahead; turn left to enter it. Sailboats are usually off to the right, while the Verrazano Bridge is aglow straight ahead. This is a good area to stop, rest, buy a drink, and take a walk around the perimeter for a look at the jetty, War Memorial statue, and noisy sea gulls. The smell of the sea air usually starts the juices flowing, and if you have a fishing rod along, it's a good place to try to hook some dinner. When you're ready, and before it gets too dark, continue back to the visitor center, turn right at Freedom Way, and return to the start of your walk.

Liberty, originally reddish-brown, has oxidized over her lifetime to a pale green. After all these years she still looks trim and terrific. Facing her back from Liberty State Park is exhilarating; even more so the closer you get to this important symbol. Liberty State Park definitely is a special place to reflect upon the hope and freedom symbolized so proudly by Lady Liberty.

NOTES: It's best to bring a picnic lunch to enjoy at your leisure, but the visitor center has a snack bar, pretzel vendors abound near the ferry entrance, Liberty Island has a cafeteria, and the Liberty Science Center (see chapter 59) has an excellent cafeteria offering spectacular views of Manhattan's skyline.

13. Edison Tower and Museum

LOCATION Middlesex County
Christie Street (off Middlesex Avenue), Menlo Park
08837
(732) 549-3299

SEASON Year round

HIGHLIGHTS Many of Edison's numerous inventions displayed, including the tinfoil phonograph and the light bulb he illuminated in 1929, which still is aglow today

ADMISSION Free

HOURS Memorial Day–Labor Day, Tuesday–Friday 12:30–4 P.M., Saturday and Sunday 12:30–4:30 P.M.; rest of year, Wednesday–Friday 12:30–4 P.M., Saturday and Sunday 12:30–4:30 P.M.

FROM THE BEGINNING, HE WAS DIFFERENT AND EXTREMELY INQUISITIVE. HOW MANY children would try to figure out the mystery of hatching eggs by sitting on them? When he began school, many of his teachers thought he was "slow." Later in life, Thomas Alva Edison often chuckled as he recalled how he "was usually at the foot of the class." Fortunately his mother knew where the problem was, and she wisely removed him from school and taught him herself. Apparently she did a terrific job, for at the age of 11 Edison had learned his lessons well enough to read college-level books and to set up a chemistry laboratory in his basement.

Of the 1,093 patents Edison received during his lifetime, over 400 were for inventions developed in Menlo Park, New Jersey. From 1876 to 1886 he experienced the most productive years of his life here, having invented the phonograph, the light bulb, an experimental electric railroad (a prototype of the modern subway system), and a method of power distribution that eventually grew into the Consolidated Edison Company and included hundreds of individual machines.

Few people realize that his major contribution to science was in research and development, the basis of the modern research laboratory. Today thousands of companies maintain their own facilities, employing hundreds of thousands of scientists, all engaged in research and development. This

Rising 131 feet above the ground, the Edison Tower and Museum stand at the site of the laboratory where Edison spent his most productive years. Each night a huge light bulb atop the tower is lit as a tribute to his genius.

system had never been used before Edison devised it in his Menlo Park facility. The idea is simple enough: First a phenomenon is discovered through research, then it is developed until something of practical use has been invented.

Great amounts of supplies and instruments, not to mention a storehouse of scientific knowledge, are required for research and development work. Edison had used both. Unique in his day, Edison kept heaps of chemicals and ordinary substances, such as carbon scraped from smoking kerosene lamps, hydrogen dioxide, and potassium hydroxide. When he didn't have a required substance or chemical, he sent out expeditions in search of them. During his famous search for the proper filament for the incandescent lamp, he sent many men to Africa and South America to find a special type of bamboo. The search paid off; it was found in Japan, and the rest is history.

The Edison Tower and Museum are a tribute to this man's genius. Rising 131 feet above the ground in the town of Menlo Park, the Edison Tower and Museum stand at the site of the laboratory where he spent his most productive years. Each night a huge light bulb atop the tower is lit as a tribute to this genius. The tower commemorates the invention of the first practical incandescent lamp and the Edison phonograph, the world's first sound-reproducing machine.

Designed to withstand a wind speed of 120 miles per hour, the tower required 1,200 barrels of Portland cement—another of Edison's discoveries—and 50 tons of reinforced steel. The bulb, made by Corning Glass Works, stands 13 feet 8 inches high, is 5 feet in diameter, is composed of 2-inch-thick amber-tinted Pyrex glass, and weighs 3 tons.

At the age of 13 Edison had been taught telegraphy by a train-station agent as a reward for having saved the agent's boy from death under a moving freight car. It was the beginning of his fixation with electricity. After many years of working at odd jobs, he created his first patented invention—a machine to electrically record and count the "Ayes" and "Nays" cast by legislators. However, when he discovered that politicians wouldn't use it regularly because they preferred to postpone voting by filibuster, Edison decided never again to invent anything unless there was a demand for it.

By 1869 he had invented the Universal Stock Printer, for which he received $40,000. With this he opened a factory in Newark, and by the age of 23 he was working 20 hours a day thinking of new inventions.

In 1876 he established his laboratory at Menlo Park, a simple two-story, wooden barnlike structure 100 feet long by 30 feet wide. Boxes of chemicals, rolls of wire, books, a Brown steam engine, and a gasoline converter were brought in. Here he surrounded himself with scientific apparatus and trained assistants to take care of the drudgery, thereby leaving himself time for thinking and inventing. Newspaper stories predicted doom for his new venture, saying that his lack of education would prevent his success. He immediately proved them wrong by inventing the phonograph.

No other invention seemed to make such a hit, and within a short time word spread throughout the world. People journeyed by carriage, train, or wagon to see this remarkable invention and the man who had created it. Foreigners flocked to New York by transatlantic steamer, finding their way to Menlo Park. At first glance, many were disappointed. Menlo Park couldn't be considered a park or a town; a mere flag station on the railroad, the area consisted of only six houses and a laboratory. However, upon meeting the man and his machine, all held Edison in high esteem, and because the phonograph seemed to contain mystical powers, Edison was dubbed the "Wizard of Menlo Park."

Though it is usually considered impossible for one person to come up with a second great idea, Edison went on to light the way for everyone with the invention of the incandescent light. It was the most massive example of research and development up to that time. Edison worked long hours, demanding that his men keep the same grueling pace. But they were honored to work for such a fair person, for Edison initiated a profit-sharing system that enabled workers to be paid royally if one of his inventions was patented by an Edison company.

Another reason for employee loyalty was Edison himself. He diverted and cheered his employees with practical jokes when times were slow, and he never let anyone get depressed over a lack of success—especially not himself. He showed this quality during the search for a proper filament for the incandescent lamp after testing hundreds of chemicals, only to find that they were all unsuitable. When someone asked him if he was sad that he had no results, Edison replied, "I've got a lot of results. I know several thousand things that won't work!"

After only 10 years, Edison outgrew the Menlo Park laboratory and moved to larger quarters in West Orange. Here he came up with a long list of inventions that improved conditions for everyone, from the fluoroscope to the acidless battery, the first moving film, and countless others.

Though the Menlo Park museum is tiny and can be seen in a couple of hours, many inventions are on display. Curator George Campbell is most willing to explain many of the items displayed and will tell the story of Edison's full-sized electric railway, a first in the United States. Pictures throughout the museum show what Edison, his associates, his laboratory, and the machine shop looked like. Other items on display include various light bulbs and his tinfoil phonograph, demonstrated before the National Academy of Sciences meeting held in Washington, D.C., while President Hayes was in the White House.

Before leaving the museum, ask for permission to view the tower at close range. Outside, seven sides of its octagonal base bear inscriptions on bronze tablets. The seventh tablet identifies the tower as a gift of the late

William Slocum Barstow on behalf of the Edison Pioneers, former associates of Edison.

At the base of the platform is the light that Edison lit on October 21, 1929, during the Jubilee celebration of the invention of his bulb. The light has burned continuously ever since, as amazing as the man who continued working and inventing until his death at 84 in 1931, 52 years after making his successful carbonized filament lamp. On December 8, 1979, the Edison Tower was declared a historic site and is listed in the National Register of Historic Places.

NOTES: A small gift shop is located inside the museum where books and other memorabilia on Edison may be purchased. Afterward you may wish to drive over to the Woodbridge Shopping Center, one of the largest indoor shopping malls around. Menlo Mall, New Jersey's first indoor mall, has recently been renovated and enlarged and is a couple of minutes away off Parsonage Road. Nearby restaurants abound: McDonald's is on Route 27, the Parsonage Diner is two minutes farther along Route 27 south, numerous restaurants are on Route 1, or enjoy a picnic at Roosevelt Park off Parsonage Road and Route 1.

14. Wild West City

LOCATION	Sussex County
	Off Route 206, Netcong 07857
	(973) 347-8900
SEASON	May–mid-October
HIGHLIGHTS	Authentic reproduction of Dodge City, Wild West action shows, audience participation, hayrides
ADMISSION	Fee
HOURS	Hours vary depending on the season; call before going
FACILITIES	Rest room, drinking water, restaurant, picnic area
EVENTS	Daily events: cowboy competition, art of bullwhips and dancing ropes, stage holdup, gunfight, bank holdup, and other activities

BROUGHT UP IN HOUSTON, MIKE ANZELLOTTI ENJOYED STORIES ABOUT COWBOYS AND the old West since he was a kid. He dreamed of life as a cowboy but earned a living driving a tractor-trailer truck across the country—that is, until he visited Wild West City a few years ago.

Wild West City, a reproduction of Dodge City in the 1880s, impressed him so much that he applied for a job there. Today Mike, who plays a "bad guy" (naturally, dressed in black), gets shot off horses and loves every minute of it. He especially likes tearing down Main Street, pursued by the posse, while firing blanks from an original 1871 Colt .22 pistol.

Many movies and commercials have been filmed at Wild West City, no doubt because of its many realistic settings. The Indian museums, authentic-looking buildings, and dusty atmosphere appeal to just about everyone, but the shows are where the real thrills are. Over 22 live-action shows are presented daily, each depicting an event that took place over 100 years ago. A gunslinger may bring up his six-shooter in a lightning-fast draw against the Marshall, or the Sundance Kid (a reformed outlaw leader) may suddenly spring into action. If you see clouds of dust rising, it is probably the Pony Express rider coming through, changing horses and galloping off with a mail delivery without missing a beat.

Not many people can resist the excitement as the Jesse James gang holds up a passing stagecoach. Stick around and watch the marshall form a posse of children. If you care to, go over and volunteer; you'll even get a free,

"Bad Guy" and one of the stars of Wild West City, Mike Anzellotti stands beside his Palomino horse; it's one of the shortest horses here so Mike can "fall" off when he's pursued by the sheriff.

shiny deputy's badge to take home! Then, once the outlaws are captured, you'll see how fast a western judge and jury can pass judgment on the desperadoes.

Lots of lawbreakers pass through town each day, and the Wild West City bank is held up on a regular basis, just as fists fly and bullets ring out during fights at the O.K. Corral. The sheriff and his men can't do a thing about it, either, because they're usually on the train protecting the gold shipment. If the outlaws don't stop the train, the Indians will! If you don't mind risking your life and perhaps catching a stray bullet, hop aboard for a pleasant 0.75-mile trip to wild outlaw and Indian territory to see them in action.

And, if you can stand absolutely still and have nerves of steel, volunteer to hold a piece of rolled-up paper between your lips; a cowboy who is an expert handling a bullwhip will quickly cut the paper down before your very eyes. Before leaving, you may want to take a short pony ride, or sit back and relax on the stagecoach. A petting zoo is also on the grounds for the children, and you may be lucky enough to arrive on a day when there's a square dancing show at the Golden Nugget Saloon.

NOTES: Dress in jeans and comfortable shoes, and wear a hat, since most activities take place outside. Fast food is available at the Golden Nugget Saloon, and while numerous eating places can be found outside the grounds, it's best to bring along a picnic lunch and enjoy it in the shaded picnic area.

15. Watchung Reservation

LOCATION	Union County Coles Avenue and New Providence Road (north of Route 22), Mountainside 07092 (908) 789-3670
SEASON	Year round
HIGHLIGHTS	Museum, nature trails, stables, planetarium, Deserted Village, Trailside Nature & Science Center
ADMISSION	Free, except for planetarium and stables
HOURS	Nature trails: dawn–dusk Planetarium: Sunday shows at 2 and 3:30 P.M. Museum: 1–5 P.M. daily, except most holidays
FACILITIES	Rest room, drinking water, handicapped access
EVENTS	Planned nature walks, planetarium and craft shows; family programs; call for schedule

ONCE UPON A TIME THERE WAS A KING NAMED DAVID FELT, WHOSE KINGDOM, CALLED Feltville, consisted of a small village with a mill and about 400 residents. Living under a king's reign in the 1800s wasn't very unusual, but to be a subject of "King" Felt certainly was: This kingdom wasn't in a foreign country, it was right here in the Garden State.

Felt's kingdom, now known as the Deserted Village, is part of the Watchung Reservation, a 2,000-acre woodland located only 35 miles from New York City. Here you can enjoy the remains of Felt's Village, cross-country ski, bird watch, view a planetarium show, visit a museum, watch nature films, and explore lush woodland.

Nestled between two ridges the Lenape Indians called the "Wach Unks," meaning "high hills," and now known as the Watchung Mountains, the area is rich in beauty and history. Dutch settlers pushed the Indians aside in 1736 so that their leader, Peter Wilcox, could erect a gristmill and lumber mill and dig a quarry for sandstone. During the American Revolution and during the War of 1812, the mill was converted to a powder plant for making ammunition.

David Felt, a stationery dealer from New York, bought about 700 acres here in 1845. He quickly established a paper mill and "kingdom" where he believed "the inhabitants would be removed from the temptation and sorrows of city life and would enjoy goodness, peace, and plenty."

Felt's kingdom included thirteen double houses, two dormitories for

Children love to explore the rocks within the Watchung Reservation, a 2,000-acre woodland area.

single men and women, a manor house, a school, a barn, and a blacksmith shop. There was also a building combining a general store on the lower level with a church on the upper level. As the village prospered, Felt was dubbed "king" because of the strict way in which he ruled. Not only did he force his workers and their families to shop in his general store, but he also required that they attend church. Several times daily Felt would sound a bell to let his workers know when to begin work, when to leave for lunch, when the day was over, and even to let them know when it was time to retire for the evening!

This paper manufacturing and farming venture thrived until 1860. Rumors abound on what happened after that. One theory is that Felt plain retired and closed up shop; another is that he was forced to put more time into his New York manufacturing business and couldn't handle the two ventures at once. Over a period of time, his workers vacated their homes and also left. For a while the site served as a resort, but today it's known as the "Deserted Village," and the original two-story general store and church building, once occupied by the Union County Outdoor Education Department, is no longer in use.

The Deserted Village, now part of the Watchung Reservation, can be reached by car directly or via a circular five-mile walk from the visitor center. The original buildings still stand. Many of the trees found in this area are said to have been brought over by early settlers from England, Wales, Scotland, and Ireland. Ailanthus trees surround the remains of what historians believe is either an old mill wall or part of the former water storage system. Earning the nickname "stinkweed" because of the offensive odor of its crushed leaves or the bruised bark, this tree's compound leaves may grow to 2 to 4 feet in length with up to 31 leaflets.

Near the old mill stands the remains of a former "sluiceway," once used to carry water from the dam site to the mill, and a small cemetery dating to the 1700s. The entire area is interesting to explore, so plan on leaving enough time to enjoy one of the fine walking trails. Start inside the Trailside Nature and Science Center (adjacent to the entrance parking area), where you can examine mineral and fossil displays and obtain a free map of the trails.

If you like rocks, take the Orange Trail. You'll walk on an outcrop of dark rock resembling brain, called basalt. It was deposited by rapidly cooling lava from the Newark Basin's first fissure eruption. In addition, you'll find large boulders of sedimentary rock, known as "pudding stone," containing large, rounded quartz particles surrounded by hard reddish-brown cement.

The trails traverse easy terrain with some gentle, rolling hills. They range in length from a couple of miles to the 11-mile Sierra Trail.

NOTES: Tree and bird identification books will enhance the experience. Sturdy walking shoes are recommended. Bring along a picnic lunch; there are also many fast-food places and restaurants along Route 22.

16. Museum of Early Trades and Crafts

LOCATION	Morris County
	Main Street at Green Village Road, Madison 07940
	(973) 377-2982
SEASON	Year round
HIGHLIGHTS	Hands-on view of the past tracing the legacy of 18th- and 19th-century artisans; interactive exhibits, workshops, demonstrations
ADMISSION	Fee
HOURS	Tuesday–Saturday 10 A.M.–4 P.M.; Sunday 2–5 P.M.
FACILITIES	Rest room, classroom
EVENTS	Discovery days, craft demonstrations, treasure hunts for all ages, guest artists and speakers, educational programs; write or call for schedule

GEORGE WASHINGTON COULD VERY WELL HAVE BEEN THE REASON FOR TODAY'S medical malpractice insurance. And, had he lived to tell the tale of his doctor's incompetence, he probably would have been the first on line to file a claim.

Washington's problem began when he came down with a simple cold after he'd been outdoors riding his horse for hours in a snowstorm. Deciding that Washington's cold was getting far too serious, his doctor began a "bloodletting" procedure that involved piercing a vein to allow "bad" blood to drain out so that, theoretically, new blood would form to take its place. The only problem was that 96 ounces of Washington's blood poured out and he bled to death! While today's physicians still make many mistakes while "practicing" medicine, and a cure for the common cold still hasn't been discovered, they wisely acknowledge that bloodletting can be hazardous to one's health.

These bloodletting implements and other horrors used in medicine in "the good old days" are part of the Edgar Law Land Collection, housed at the Museum of Early Trades and Crafts, which was founded by Agnes and Edgar Land in 1970. In addition, the small but fascinating museum contains countless artifacts dating from the 18th and early 19th centuries.

Hands-on exhibits bring to life a time machine of situations in the home, on the farm, and in the shop as our state was settled, and they clearly

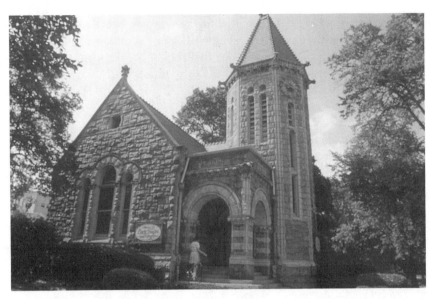

The exterior of the Museum of Early Trades and Crafts is a magnificent example of turn-of-the-century Romanesque Revival architecture.

convey what it was like to live in a world that relied on craftspersons, homemakers, and farmers for survival. Best of all, visitors of all ages are encouraged to participate using the tools of yesteryear to get a first-hand feeling for life and work during this period.

The building in which the collection is housed is listed on the National Register of Historic Places and is a magnificent example of turn-of-the-century Romanesque Revival architecture. Although the exterior resembles a church, the building was originally a library. Today, the bell tower, wide doorways, and cruciform layout inspire photographers. Inside, brick-tiled walls are decorated with stencils; ornate ironwork is found along the stairs and balcony; and the windows, adorned with stained glass, are decorated with quotes and images from Shakespeare, Coleridge, and Benjamin Franklin.

Permanent exhibits include a recreated kitchen, typical of a Morris County house between 1790 and 1821, which features a huge hearth. Kitchens were the focal point of the early-American home, rooms where cooking, learning, and Bible lessons took place. Usually there was a garden outside with vegetables, herbs, and flowers used as a source of food, drink, garnishes, sweeteners, dyes, cosmetics, medicines, and insect and rodent repellents. Although the settlers brought a few plants with them from Europe, Native Americans instructed them on how to grow and cook other staples, such as pumpkin, which was enjoyed dried, boiled, baked, roasted, or stewed, along with squash, potatoes, and corn. Berries were important, too, for making pies, jam, and wine. Plantings were grown in raised soil beds, and bees kept nearby helped pollinate as well as provide honey.

Displays are changed frequently and include a shoemaker's shop, plus everyone's favorite, a one-room schoolhouse. In the 1800s, the lifestyles of urban and rural people were quite diversified. While wealthy children attended schools regularly, children of poor families did so infrequently or not at all since it wasn't compulsory and farming responsibilities kept them away. Also, it was difficult to raise the tuition. Often, when it was paid, it was in what was known as "country pay"—corn, eggs, cheese, or firewood. Children are encouraged to ring the class bell or, during "schoolhouse discovery days," take penmanship lessons using old-fashioned pens and inkwells.

After visiting this winning museum, I returned home counting my blessings, knowing that in this century our cups runneth over. Also, after studying the excellent displays, I changed my view concerning the children of yesteryear. Life was definitely difficult in the 18th and 19th centuries, a time when only half the children born during this period survived past the age of five. For this reason, baptism was a parent's first and foremost concern.

Before my visit, I thought that children of days long gone had too many chores. However, Director Elaine Zopes pointed out that "just as a child of that period learned how to milk a cow or spin, so does a child of today learn the basics of cooking by using the toaster or microwave. Our concept of work has changed dramatically in the last hundred years. Throughout the centuries, work was a part of life. There was very little division between work time and leisure time since people lived and worked in the same place. Often work would be shared or done together. Think of quilting bees and barn raisings. Women would also carry their spinning wheels to each other's houses to spin together and socialize."

Furthermore, "with the industrial revolution came factories and time clocks. Suddenly time was divided into work time and leisure time. Our concept of time is only a hundred to a hundred and fifty years old. For a child living in the early 1800s, work, life, and play were combined, just as it was for their parents. We're judging by our standards, not theirs. Unlike our standards of teaching a child how to cross the street and learning how to use a computer, they taught their children to cook, sew, spin, mend fences, and care for the animals."

Many of these children grew up without learning how to write their names, and, even if they could, paper was so scarce they couldn't keep records. At this time, tools were extremely important and craftsmen were the pride of every community.

Not only is a trip to this museum educational, it's food for thought!

NOTE: Madison is a charming town filled with interesting shops and many places to eat.

GLORIOUS GARDENS

17. Reeves-Reed Arboretum

LOCATION Union County
165 Hobart Avenue (near Route 24), Summit 07901
(908) 273-8787

SEASON Year round

HIGHLIGHTS Geological formations, rose and azalea gardens, wildlife habitat garden, perennial border, magnificent tree collection, library devoted to botany and horticulture

ADMISSION Free

HOURS Arboretum grounds: daily 10 A.M.–sunset
House and office: Monday, Tuesday, Thursday
9 A.M.–3 P.M.

FACILITIES Education Center, well-marked nature trail, library, rest room open during office hours, gift shop

EVENTS Sunday series of lectures; poetry readings, concerts, adult education programs year round; children's "Elephant Tree Nature Camp" during summer; Family Harvest Festival and bird seed sale in October; Holiday House Tour in December

VIEWED FROM THE AIR, THE REEVES-REED ARBORETUM RESEMBLES A TINY OASIS IN THE heart of a busy town. Occupying 12½ lush, green acres of natural hardwood forest, open fields, lawns, and formal gardens, it is a place where one can sit, relax, paint, read, stroll, and smell the roses. It is also where one can see the remarkable geological formation known as a "kettle."

The grounds, originally part of a revolutionary war–period farm, were purchased in the late 19th century by the Wisner family, who built the Colonial Revival mansion and planted the first daffodils on the property.

In 1916 the Reeves family purchased the home, laid out gardens based on plans by prominent New York architects, and planted thousands of daffodils in the kettle (depression) existing in front of their home. The kettle was formed when a large chunk of the melting Wisconsin Glacier broke free, became buried, and then melted completely, leaving the huge depression now seen in the ground. A similar kettle lies along the East Trail

A nymph statue stands at the center of the rose garden at the Reeves-Reed Arboretum, an oasis in the midst of a busy town.

in the woods. Later, a herb garden was added on the grounds.

If the house is open during your visit, ask for a trail booklet and try the delightful self-guiding walk through the property. Figure on spending a couple of hours leisurely walking; if you bring along tree or bird identification books, you'll want to spend a morning, afternoon, or a whole day here.

The native trees are typical of the Eastern deciduous forest and include many specimens from colonial times as well as imported trees. There are also numerous shrubs and wildflowers, as well as collections of ferns, herbs, and roses.

An impressive Atlas cedar *(Cedrus atlantica)* stands at the corner of the house. A fragrant evergreen, it is native to the Atlas Mountains in Algeria. To the left of the house is a Canadian hemlock *(Tsuga canadensis)*. One of the easiest of all the evergreens to identify, its needles are dark green on the upper side and pale gray or silvery on the lower side. Near a Colorado blue spruce *(Picea pungensi)*, you'll see the showy saucer magnolia *(Manolia soulangeana)* cluster, easily recognizable during winter by its fuzzy, insulating buds and during spring when its flowers put on a spectacular show before the leaves are out.

The ginkgo *(Ginkgo biloba)* trees, easily recognized by their fan-shaped leaves, are known as the "living fossil" tree, because fossil prints of its leaves have been found, indicating that it existed millions of years ago. The male ginkgo is preferred for planting because the yellowish plum-like fruits produced by the female trees have a bad odor. The ginkgo, meaning "silver fruit" in Chinese, was once cultivated on temple grounds by Chinese monks, and its nut is still used in China on special occasions.

When you see it you'll know why the European beech *(Fagus sylvatiea)* is nicknamed the elephant tree. The bark is wrinkled and silvery, just like an elephant's hide. Once a favorite food among early settlers, today its three-sided fruit is a popular food for wild animals. The aptly named silver bell tree *(Halesia carolina)* produces lovely white bells during spring.

Look closely inside the fence that borders the kettle hole. Here stands a tall tulip tree *(Liriodendron tulipifera)*. Straight as soldiers, tulip trees can often obtain a height of 80 feet before first branching. For this reason they were prized by the Indians, who would carve the trunks into long, straight canoes. If you visit during the summer, you'll see the beautiful tulip-shaped flower it produces. Also in this area are perennial beds planted in nooks along the rock wall. They're aglow with color through the fall months.

The various species of fern identified along the Fern Walk reproduce by means of spores. The dark bumps, called "sori," hold the spores. Opposite this walk are stands of mountain laurel, Carolina hemlock, and rhododendron, all delightful during spring.

The rose garden reaches its peak during mid-June. Each year in early June the arboretum sponsors Rose Day, an afternoon to enjoy the special beauty of a formal rose garden and learn about rose selection and care. During September many of the roses put on their final showing, along with colorful asters, chrysanthemums, and sedums.

By October the last of the chrysanthemum peek out amid the autumn foliage, but winter is a great time to visit, too. That's when visitors can see the contrast of lovely red holly berries against a white blanket of snow and when one can experience new sounds in a beautiful, peaceful setting.

When you walk back to the parking lot, check out the huge trees towering overhead. Mainly black oaks, with a sprinkling of white oaks, these are typical of the oaks from America sent to England to supply her shipbuilding industry in the 1700s.

NOTES: Write or call for a schedule of adult and children's education programs, including lectures on horticultural and cultural topics, crafts, horticulture-related workshops, and day and weekend trips to museums, gardens, and historical and cultural sites. Restaurants and fast-food places are in town and along Route 22.

18. Duke Gardens

LOCATION	Somerset County
	Route 206 (1.25 miles south of the Somerset Shopping Center), Somerville 08876
	(908) 722-3700
SEASON	Fall, winter, and spring; winter is best
HIGHLIGHTS	Eleven garden displays from around the world
ADMISSION	Fee
HOURS	Reservations necessary; October 1–May 31, daily noon–4 P.M. except Thanksgiving, Christmas, New Year's, and summer months
FACILITIES	Rest room

THERE'S NO NEED TO SET OUT FOR AFRICA, FRANCE, ITALY, OR EVEN ARIZONA WHEN you can explore plantings from all these places at nearby Duke Gardens. Amid 11 individual gardens—one of them under an acre of glass—you'll find the lush foliage of a tropical jungle, an English summer garden, and the stark beauty of an American desert, each offering distinct floral backgrounds.

Duke Gardens offers visitors an unbelievable vista of flowers and is literally a winter paradise under glass. Even on the coldest day, the aroma and sights inside will keep you warm.

Tobacco magnate James Buchanan Duke purchased this land in 1893, for the then huge sum of $32,680 and, over the next 20 years, added many more land parcels to his holdings. At first, having been raised on a North Carolina farm before becoming president of the American Tobacco Company, Duke was happy to spend his time being a gentleman farmer and raising one of the largest and finest herds of dairy cattle in the country on this land. He also bred horses and even built a half-mile-long racetrack.

It is estimated that Duke spent over 10 million dollars to have his large staff of landscape gardeners and horticulturists level the land to transform it into a magnificent estate. Laborers toiled for months to create a chain of nine lakes on the property while building 200-foot hills with the dirt they removed. This wasn't an easy task, but with the help of a narrow-gauge railroad built on the grounds, soil was carried from one area to another. In addition, 32 miles of roadway was laid throughout the property, including many twisting roads that crept over the newly formed man-made hills.

Water drawn from the Raritan River filled the lakes and 35 ornamental fountains, while stone walls were erected by Italian immigrants to encircle the estate. During this time Duke imported over two million shrubs and specimen trees from all over the world to be planted on the grounds.

Married for the first time at 48, Duke divorced his first wife to marry Nanaline Holt Inman, widow of a Georgia cotton merchant. After returning from their honeymoon, Duke became involved in a battle between union bricklayers and nonunion brick carriers when they stopped working on an extension of the mansion. At his request the police arrested the bricklayers, but when the bricklayers agreed to resume work the next day on his terms, Duke had them released from jail and rehired them.

After seven years, when the estate was finally taking shape the way he envisioned it, Duke began inviting people onto the grounds to stroll and admire his creation. However, after he discovered picnickers had dropped refuse on his lawn and trampled flower beds, Duke limited these visits to one day a week only.

Following his death in 1925, Duke's estate ceased to be maintained in the same grand style. Several years later his only child, Doris, married James Cromwell, a Canadian minister, and took over the property. This was during the depression, when people would frequently show up seeking jobs. At one time 400 people were employed on the estate. Over the years an indoor skeet shoot, a Japanese garden, a boxwood garden, and an 18-hole golf course were built.

Similar to a tiny village, the estate was self-contained, with its own mechanical and construction crews, a shop for overhauling trucks, and even a fire engine in case a brush fire broke out from a spark from one of the coal-burning locomotives that ran through the grounds. With a pair of seals in one of the lakes and strolling peacocks free to roam on the lawn, the Duke estate was certainly an exciting place to visit.

When World War II broke out, many of the staff entered the army. This, combined with the Cromwells' divorce and Doris Duke's subsequent move to Hawaii, led to the closing of the estate. Slowly, as the gardens deteriorated, the land again reverted to a livestock farm, producing crops for the war effort. As weeds took over, the golf course disappeared, and silt filled in the lakes and ponds. However, in the 1960s Ms. Duke had the gardens restored, opening them to the public.

Upon arrival you'll be whisked by bus up a hill for the start of a one-hour, one-mile walking tour through the interconnected greenhouses, beginning with the Italian Garden, very romantic and in vogue in Europe during the 19th century; a Colonial Garden, with dazzling camellias, azaleas, magnolia, and crepe myrtle, similar to gardens found in South Carolina; an Edwardian Garden, a replica of the English home conservatory established in our country in the gay nineties housing rare tropical plants and orchids; and a French Garden, with 1700s-style latticework.

Farther along is the English Garden; it's divided into five sections, each in a different style, including topiary, a rock garden, herbaceous borders, the

Duke Gardens is particularly beautiful to visit during bleak winter days when the splendor of a tropical orchid brightens the spirit.

Knot Garden containing herbs, and a succulent garden. The Desert Garden, with its huge century plant and blooming prickly pear and jade, is striking, as is the Chinese Garden, containing bold rock formations, bamboo, and golden carp that swim lazily beneath visitors' feet in a small pond. There is also a peaceful Japanese Garden.

A fantastic aroma of orange blossoms greets you in the Indo-Persian Garden, while the Tropical Garden induces the feeling one would experience upon entering a rain forest. The last garden, under glass, is the Semi-Tropical Garden, containing tree ferns from the volcanic high-plateau regions of New Zealand and Hawaii, and dozens of eye-catching bird-of-paradise plants.

Ms. Duke died in 1993 but, hopefully, the gardens will remain for all to enjoy.

NOTES: Cameras and high-heeled shoes are not permitted. The tour is not suitable for handicapped persons, and visitors must follow the tour guide and cannot linger to savor the beauty of the gardens.

19. Leonard J. Buck Garden

LOCATION	Somerset County
	11 Layton Road (off Route 202), Far Hills 07931
	(908) 234-2677
SEASON	Year round; excellent in spring for wildflowers
HIGHLIGHTS	Rock outcroppings, native and imported plants,
	ponds, meadow, bird watching, variety of trees
ADMISSION	Free; donation requested
HOURS	Monday–Saturday 10 A.M.–4 P.M., Sunday noon–
	5 P.M., summer, and noon–4 P.M., winter; closed on
	major holidays
FACILITIES	Rest room, drinking water, visitor center, reference
	library
EVENTS	Plant sale in April

AFTER PURCHASING A HOUSE AND APPROXIMATELY 50 ACRES OF LAND IN THE 1930s, Leonard J. Buck discovered that his property was geologically unique. Dominated by oak, beech, maple, ash, and a few hemlocks, it contained not only a deep valley but also many rock outcroppings. Fascinated, Buck, a mining engineer, researched further and found that the valley, located at the outlet of ancient Lake Passaic, was formed approximately 11,000 years ago after the Wisconsin Glacier retreated.

Determined to find a way to landscape the grounds while blending in the natural surroundings, Buck began to read about horticulture. He visited flower shows and attended numerous horticulture society meetings in addition to exploring the relationship of plants and mineral deposits. He believed that a garden should be "ecologically correct and visually appealing...a place where one area moves naturally into the next, making it as pleasant to walk through as to sit in."

At a flower show, Buck met Swiss-born landscape architect Zenon Schreiber and invited him to see his magnificent property, which had a huge variety of trees and habitats, including a brook, grassy meadow, bog, and rock ledge.

Both men agreed that the garden should retain its natural look, and they began building upon the many rock outcroppings found on the palatial

The Leonard J. Buck Garden is not only visually attractive, it is an instant stress-reliever. Plan on taking a leisurely stroll, and bring lots of film to capture the rock formations and flowers.

country estate. First, high-pressure hoses were used to clear the outcroppings of glacial rubble. Later, dynamite was employed to create miniature pockets and terraces for plantings. The first rock outcropping discovered was named "Little Rock." Slowly others were found and developed, and a few were partially removed and reconstructed to conform to the surroundings.

Many native plants were chosen for their adaptability and significance, and according to Andrew Burnett, former gardener, "plants from many corners of the globe, rare as well as commonplace, were introduced to inhabit this unique microclimate." In addition to the rock outcroppings, Moggy Brook was dammed to create a habitat for bog and water plants.

Leonard Buck died in 1974. Two years later, his widow donated the garden to the Somerset County Park Commission and, in 1984, the visitor center was opened to the public. Visitors can spend a delightful morning or afternoon strolling through the grounds. Most of the plants and shrubs are labeled, making it an educational experience as well as an aesthetic one.

After arriving, stop in the visitor center, which previously served as the carriage house, and ask for a map and brochure. Begin your walk by heading straight ahead on the entrance path. Nearby is a flat, grassy prominence known as Big Rock. Rising about 20 feet above the lower meadow and pond, this ledge hugs the north wall of Moggy Hollow. Here, dazzling pink-flowering lungwort and saxifrages poke up through the cracks.

Take the path back up the slope, keeping Big Rock in view along the valley wall until you come to Ivy Rock, sitting off in a recess. Comprised of basalt, it has fractured into vertical columns, an indication that this formation is close to the top of a former lava flow. Just down the path is Reno Rock, said to be named after Mrs. Buck threatened to divorce her husband if he didn't stop blasting. In this area is the Azalea Meadow, a beautiful sight during spring. New Rock and Horseshoe Rock are summit exposures with crumbling surfaces.

The map includes meandering walkways traversing wooded paths winding gently past the ponds, creeks, and meadows on these peaceful acres, where you'll find the formations Buck sculpted to fit into his garden. Since he truly admired the natural beauty of the rock formations, modifications were made only to enhance their beauty and create pockets and beds to accommodate plants. The heather collection is outstanding and particularly colorful during the fall and early winter months.

NOTES: Bring binoculars if you're a bird watcher; warblers, Canada geese, ruffed grouse, scarlet tanagers, sparrows, finches, and pileated woodpeckers have been spotted here. Smoking and pets are not allowed.

20. Leaming's Run Gardens and Colonial Farm

LOCATION	Cape May County
	1845 Route 9 North, Cape May Court House 08210
	(609) 465-5871
SEASON	Gardens: May–October
	Cooperage: May–Christmas
HIGHLIGHTS	Twenty acres of individual gardens in a picturesque setting, a reconstructed whaler's log cabin, and ruby-throated hummingbirds in August
ADMISSION	Fee
HOURS	Gardens: daily 9:30 A.M.–5 P.M. May 15–October 20
	Cooperage: May 15–Christmas, may be visited apart from gardens at Route 9 entrance 10 A.M.–5 P.M.
FACILITIES	Rest room, water, gift shop
EVENTS	Special guided tours are offered June–October in addition to Hibiscus Week in July, arrival of the hummingbirds in August, and picnicking in October; write Cape May Court House 08210 or call for schedule

W HEN HE PURCHASED HIS WHITE STUCCO HOUSE OVER 30 YEARS AGO, JACK APRILL knew that it had been built by Christopher Leaming in 1730 and that it was named "Leaming Run." But Aprill didn't find out until later that it is one of the oldest houses in Cape May County or that it is the last remaining whaler's home in the state.

For years after buying the house and 50-acre property, Aprill worried about losing the land because of rising taxes. Fortunately, he found a way to preserve the land in its natural state and, at the same time, create an oasis for those who appreciate outdoor beauty. By keeping 30 acres in their natural wooded state and designing 27 individual gardens on the remaining 20 acres, Leaming's Run Gardens and Colonial Farm was born.

Visitors come from all over to see what Aprill has successfully accomplished. They come to stroll along a 1-mile meandering path he built joining the gardens together. They also come to enjoy the visual splendor of thousands of flowers blooming in every color, as well as to relax. Many leave

For those who love the outdoors and natural beauty, Leaming's Run Gardens and Colonial Farm features 27 individual gardens to stroll through.

inspired to find new ways to transform their own home gardens.

Aprill has placed these garden areas along bends in the walkway, in nooks, near a gentle flowing stream, in dense woods, and next to a pond. Thanks to the natural flow of Leaming's Run Brook, which traverses the property, its tea-colored cedar water has become a central feature of the entire garden. It is viewed sometimes as a sylvan pond and at other times as a moss-banked woodland stream or a curving river. When Aprill refers to his creation as "an island of peace in South Jersey," it's true. After spending three leisurely hours strolling through the grounds, I left feeling calm and relaxed.

There are a great variety of environments to see. Rustic bridges follow over lowland marsh, leading to water-loving wildflowers, scarlet cardinal flowers, and cattails. Throughout the garden, annuals grow profusely from May through October. Annuals were selected by Aprill not only for their vivid color but also for their marvelous fragrance. Here and there swamp azaleas, sweet pepper bushes, and magnolias provide a delightful natural backdrop for the annuals.

Each garden has a theme. The Yellow Garden, first on the walk, was designed as a quiet and restful garden during all seasons. It contains various textured plants including gladiola, banana pepper, and yellow squash, with yellow gourd vines draping the rustic fence. The lush green lawn makes the yellow appear even brighter, and in autumn this area is aflame with huckleberries and sumac.

The Evening Garden is best seen during morning or evening hours. Early in the day the blue morning glories cast a bright blue hue over the garden, but as the sun goes down these merge into darkness and the white and light-foliaged plants beam. During September and October the chrysanthemums and asters bloom profusely.

One of the nicest places to linger is at the Reflecting Garden, where water lilies blooming en masse are mirrored in the pond. The Red and Blue Garden is perhaps the most colorful, for it contains a kaleidoscope of brilliant flowers. Here royal blue lobelia and plum-red celosia mesh together beautifully against a backdrop of tall trees.

Eventually you'll reach the Colonial Farm section, an area which has been recreated to appear as it was when Leaming settled here. Cedar and oak logs were used in building the cabin, which also has oak shingles to form a watertight roof and a fireplace and chimney made of brick, mud, and twigs. Leaming had used the cabin as a temporary shelter until mills were erected and materials assembled to build the main house.

Tobacco, cotton, and herbs grow as they did in the 18th century. Using herbs was very important for the colonial housewife, since they added flavor to an otherwise bland diet. The sheep, geese, chickens, and other animals roaming nearby are also historically correct.

The red barn at the end of the path, built by Leaming as a work shed for the barrels he made to contain whale oil, has been converted to a gift shop known as The Cooperage. It contains a wealth of floral arrangements, barrels, furniture, and gift items made by Aprill's wife Emily.

You're bound to run into Jack Aprill or his son, Gregg, somewhere on the grounds tending the garden. They're usually happy to take a break and answer any questions you may have.

NOTES: During October picnicking is allowed anywhere in the garden. If you prefer, bring your own lunch the rest of the year, and enjoy it at nearby Cape May County Park (609-465-5271) on US 9, where you'll also find a children's zoo, bike trail, and, during summer months, concerts.

21. Ringwood State Park

LOCATION Passaic County
Route 511, Ringwood 07456
(973) 962-7031, (973) 962-9534

SEASON Year round

HIGHLIGHTS Skylands Botanical Garden, Skylands Manor, Ringwood Manor, swimming, boating, fishing

ADMISSION Parking fee Memorial Day–Labor Day

HOURS Grounds: dawn–dusk
Ringwood Manor: Tuesday–Sunday 9 A.M.–4 P.M.

FACILITIES Rest room, drinking water, snack bar in season, beach

EVENTS Victorian Christmas celebration at Ringwood Manor first two weekends in December; annual Plant Sale first weekend in May; Crabapple Festival mid-May; bird walks, hikes, gardening programs, bus trips, and lectures; write for free program of events: Skylands Association, New Jersey State Botanical Garden, Ringwood State Park, Box 302, Ringwood 07456, or call (973) 962-9534 for a recording of latest events

RINGWOOD STATE PARK IS NESTLED IN THE GENTLE, ROLLING RAMAPO MOUNTAINS OF northern New Jersey. In addition to Skylands, the state's official botanical garden, the park includes Ringwood Manor, Skylands Manor, a lovely swimming beach, lakes, and—according to some accounts—a number of ghosts.

Little physical evidence of Ringwood's important role during the revolutionary war remains today. After iron was discovered here in 1740, a forge was built and the Ringwood Company was established. Word of this successful operation reached the London-based American Iron Company, which sent Peter Hasenclever across the Atlantic to purchase the business and more land. After his takeover, Hasenclever added more furnaces and forges and built a large house at Ringwood in 1765.

Ringwood served as General George Washington's headquarters on numerous occasions; Washington would frequently have his horses shod in the blacksmith shop. In a brochure about the park written in 1987, park

Though little evidence of Ringwood's important role during the revolutionary war remains today, the mansion and gardens are interesting to explore.

officials note that Robert Erskine, manager of the Ringwood Mines and Surveyor General for the American Army, "prepared many maps here which aided Washington in his military campaigns. Following Erskine's death on

October 2, 1780, his remains were buried in the cemetery on the property overlooking the lake. Washington and his wife planted a tree at his grave in 1782."

After it had been sold a number of times, Martin J. Ryerson purchased Ringwood in 1807 and built a 10-room Federal-style house. He produced iron during the War of 1812. His descendants sold the property to Abram S. Hewitt, secretary of Cooper Hewitt & Company, who added 68 rooms in addition to continuing the mining operations. Today the rambling mansion, which has served as park headquarters since Hewitt's heirs donated it to the state in 1936, is open to the public. A fascinating eclectic collection of belongings covering the period from 1810 to 1930 are displayed inside.

Outside the mansion, a variety of interesting relics from the iron-making days can be seen. These include an anvil and trip hammer from Long Pond Ironworks; a deck gun from the frigate *Constitution*, commonly known as "Old Ironsides"; and a Civil War mortar, the bed of which was made under a "rush order" issued by President Lincoln. On the terrace are several massive links representing the chain Washington had placed across the Hudson River at West Point to prevent British vessels from reaching the upper Hudson.

For over 150 years Ringwood was the center of North Jersey's iron industry, operating 100 years after the bog iron industry collapsed in southern New Jersey. Wisely, Ringwood had adopted the "Scotch blast" method developed in Scotland in 1828 in which the heated air was recycled through a series of coiled pipes. This saved energy and made the process more efficient.

The formal gardens in back of the house are delightful. In addition to lush plantings there is an assortment of columns, gateposts, a fountain, millstones, statuary, and other items gathered by the Hewitts from their travels throughout the world.

Stop at Ringwood Cemetery, about a 15-minute walk from the mansion. (Ask at the office for directions.) Although many of the names on the tombstones have eroded, some quotations can still be deciphered; one reads:

> Ye friends who live to mourn and weep,
> Behold the grave within I sleep;
> Prepare for death, for you must die,
> And be entombed as well as I.

Dating to the late 1700s, it's located along part of the original Continental Road connecting Morristown and West Point.

Ghosts, according to museum curator Elbertus J. Prol, are rumored to haunt the cemetery. The spirit of Robert Erskine supposedly sits upon his tomb waiting to help those who wander here late at night by holding a lantern to light their way to a nearby bridge. Some visitors have reportedly heard "Mad Mag," another ghost, moaning loudly while perched upon a boulder along an old mining road. Unfortunately, she always disappears within the rock before anyone can reach her.

When you're finished here, drive over to Skylands Botanical Garden at the other side of the park. You can also ask for a trail map at the office and walk around four to five miles to the garden. The land in this section was amassed from surrounding pioneer farmsteads by Francis Lynde Stetson in the mid-1800s. A prominent New York lawyer who incorporated railroads and the U.S. Steel Corporation, Stetson maintained a stylish mansion and working farm with 30 outbuildings. He frequently entertained friends here, including Grover Cleveland, Andrew Carnegie, Ethel Barrymore, and J. P. Moorage.

In 1922 Clarence McKenzie Lewis, an investment banker and trustee of the New York Botanical Garden, bought the property. Determined to make it a botanical showplace, Lewis tore down the Stetson mansion, built a Tudor manor house, which he named "Skylands Farms," and hired the prestigious landscape firm of Vitale and Geiffert to design the gardens on his property.

Lewis, who collected and planted trees and plants from all over the world—including New Jersey roadsides—kept meticulous logbooks of every plant. Although he traveled to Afghanistan, the Azores, Kashmir, and many other exotic places, one of his collecting spots was the Pine Barrens of New Jersey. The property was sold to Shelton College in 1956, and in 1966 the state purchased the 1,117 acres.

Approximately 5,000 species, varieties, and horticultural forms exist at Skylands. There are many unique specimens, such as a climbing hydrangea, a golden form of oriental spruce, and a dwarf iris. Governor Thomas Kean officially designated Skylands as the New Jersey State Botanical Gardens in 1984.

Opposite the manor you'll find several small gardens, including the formal annual garden featuring seasonal exhibits. One of the focal points is the half-mile "Crab Apple Vista" consisting of 166 trees marking the boundary between formal gardens around the manor and the informal and wildflower gardens at the foot of the Ramapos. It's spectacular during spring. The Winter Garden is a beautiful evergreen collection surrounding a century-old weeping beech. During spring the laurels, viburnum, and azaleas add brilliant color.

The Terrace Gardens contain a series of five spaces: the Octagonal Garden with miniature perennials and shrubs on a waist-high wall circling the pool; the Magnolia Walk, filled with a southern species of magnolia and an impressive ground planting of hosta; the varied Summer Garden; the Peony Garden; and the Azalea Garden stretched along the reflecting Lily Pond. Fragrant lilacs have also been planted along the vast lawns.

The Wet Meadow, filled with wildflowers, includes the rare fringed gentian, and the Wildflower Garden is surrounded by towering white pines. Here you'll find the native trailing arbutus, insect-eating pitcher plants, and 30 varieties of fern.

A willow tree grown from a cutting taken at Napoleon's tomb in Paris stands at the Bog Pond and Garden. At the Heather Garden, set among glacial boulders, you'll also find the Rhododendron Garden. Bluebirds can usually be spotted nesting in the nut trees nearby.

In season, don a bathing suit and enjoy a cool dip in Shepherd Lake, or rent a canoe or paddleboat. No matter when you visit, you'll find the trip worthwhile.

NOTES: A picnic lunch is the best bet since restaurants are a distance away. A snack bar is open during the summer season, from Memorial Day to Labor Day.

22. Deep Cut Gardens

LOCATION Monmouth County
Red Hill Road (from Garden State Parkway, Exit
114), Middletown Township 07748
(732) 671-6050

SEASON Year round

HIGHLIGHTS Rockery, perennial gardens, greenhouses filled
with spectacular orchids, orchard, walking paths

ADMISSION Free

HOURS Garden: every day 8 A.M.–dusk
Main building: until 4 P.M.

FACILITIES Rest room, classes, horticultural reference library,
Horticultural Hot Line (732) 671-6906 staffed by
trained horticulturists daily 8:30 A.M.–4:30 P.M., and
gift shop

EVENTS Plant sales, garden-related seminars.

As LORD CORNWALLIS RETREATED FROM THE BATTLE OF MONMOUTH, HE TRAVELED through farmland now known as the Deep Cut Gardens. Over 100 acres of this land remained in the Taylor and Osborn families until 1890, when the sheriff took it over for nonpayment of taxes. After changing hands several times, it was eventually deeded to Vito Genovese, one of organized crime's most notorious bosses, in 1935.

Genovese renovated the old farmhouse, built extensive stone walls, and had Italian stonemasons begin the hillside gardens. These included an Italian-style rock garden on the steep slope below the house, an English boxwood garden with roses and annuals, and a series of ornamental pools with water supplied by a deep well. At the bottom of the garden he not only built a huge swimming pool but had workers erect a cone-shaped replica of Mount Vesuvius that could spew smoke. Genovese fashioned his estate after similar ones at Nola, near Naples, Italy, where he was born.

Although these were the depression years, Genovese spared no expense to live well. Many of the rare plants and trees he imported can be seen today, including the gnarled Sargent's weeping hemlocks shading the terrace gardens, which are the oldest in the state.

In 1937 Thomas E. Dewey, then a special prosecutor, began singling Genovese out as an organized crime boss, and the family left for Europe.

Later that year a "mysterious" fire swept through the mansion. When World War II broke out Genovese fled to Italy to work with dictator Benito Mussolini. He later switched his loyalty to the American government when the Allied victory ended power for the Fascists. Finally, Genovese's past caught up to him. It was discovered that he was wanted in New York City, where he had been indicted for murder. Genovese was returned to the United States from Italy to stand trial, but the case against him was dropped when a key witness was poisoned, and Genovese was soon back in business again. His dubious profession won him the title "King of the Rackets" by New York Governor Thomas E. Dewey.

Genovese sold his property for $35,000 to Mary Gladys Cubbage of Rumson in 1949, but it was sold again to Karl and Marjorie Wihtol four years before Genovese was finally sentenced on narcotics charges. The Wihtols built the present house, which now serves as the visitor center, and they planned the gardens and greenhouses surrounding the house as a living plant catalog.

Wear comfortable shoes so you can stroll down the path to the hillside gardens in comfort. These contain a large variety of exotic trees and shrubs currently in the process of being tagged. The 11-foot Alberta spruce and the weeping hemlock, measuring 35 feet across, are particularly impressive. The beautiful walkways eventually lead to the meadow, where the swimming pool Genovese had built lies buried. Nearby is his pergola, now overrun with magnificent kiwi and wisteria. A tiny brook runs along this garden, a paradise for white-throated sparrows, titmice, quail, cardinals, chickadees, and downy woodpeckers.

Each spring nodding daffodils sprout in huge clumps beneath the lush green evergreens along the path leading to the gazebo and at the entrance to the park. It is during this time that the magnolias burst with rich color, and the columbine creeps along the ground following the azalea walk. Here too are rhododendrons and stands of birch, black pine, oak, and dogwood. In May thousands of tulips poke their way up through the ground.

Don't leave without going into the greenhouse to see the succulent collection, which Ms. Wihtol obtained by purchase or barter from places throughout the United States, South America, South Africa, and Britain. The collection includes miniature Haworthias and large varieties of vining Hylocereus. One of the most amazing sights in the greenhouse is the huge cactus sprouting up from the cement floor. If you can't figure out how it was planted, the naturalist will be happy to explain.

At the age of 71, Genovese died of a heart ailment while in prison in 1969. The property he loved so much was in ruins when he sold it to Mary Gladys Cubbage, but it was lovingly restored by the Wihtols, who willed half of it to the county with the provision that they purchase the rest. When

The grounds at Deep Cut Gardens, a collection of exotic trees and shrubs and beautiful rose gardens, were once owned by one of organized crime's most notorious bosses, Vito Genovese.

the county park system took it over in 1977, the house was converted to classrooms, a garden gift shop, a library, and offices.

NOTES: The Elvin McDonald Horticultural Library, located in the main building and reputed to be the largest horticultural library on the East Coast, has 3,000 books and catalogs available for instant reference. Pack a picnic lunch and enjoy it in the park opposite Deep Cut, or try one of the many nearby restaurants.

23. Well-Sweep Herb Farm

LOCATION	Warren County
	317 Mount Bethel Road (near Route 57), Port Murray 07865
	(908) 852-5390
SEASON	Best during July and August
HIGHLIGHTS	Herbs, dried flowers, perennials, Knot Garden, old-fashioned well-sweep
ADMISSION	Free
HOURS	Tuesday–Saturday 9:30 A.M.– 5 P.M., closed holidays; call before visiting October–April
FACILITIES	Rest room, drinking water
EVENTS	Open House, June and September; Christmas shop; call in advance for hours

OVER 250 YEARS AGO JOSEPH PITTON DE TOURNEFORT WROTE THE *GREAT HERBALL.* In this book he warned readers about the dangers of "sniffing herbs," stating they may be dangerous to one's health. He reported that "a certain gentleman of Siena being wonderfully taken and delighted with the Smell of Basil, was wont very frequently to take the Powder of the dry Herb and snuff it up his nose; but in a short time he turned mad and died; and his Head being open by Surgeons, there was found a Nest of Scorpions in his Brain."

That was in 1719. Fortunately we now recognize the medicinal and aesthetic benefits of herbs. A trip to the Well-Sweep Herb Farm is not only absolutely safe but is educational and relaxing as well. Established by Cyrus and Louise Hyde over 20 years ago, the farm reflects Cyrus Hyde's lifelong interest in herbs. "Herbs were a way of life with us," says Hyde. "When we were sick, my mom treated us with a lot of old herbal remedies that had been passed down from my great-great-great-grandmother, who had fed and treated a lot of Washington's troops. In gratitude, he presented her with a pair of silver knee buckles, one of which I still have."

After the Hydes married, they started raising basic herbs, including rose geranium, rosemary, lemon verbena, lemon balm, mint, lovage, and basil. Hyde says he follows the Bible's teaching—"Give and you shall receive"—

Cyrus Hyde stands next to the well and sweep for which he named Well-Sweep Herb Farm.

and plants something in the ground each year. His reward, he says, is "nice black soil instead of the original hard packed clay we found when we moved here."

Visitors to the 120-acre farm are free to wander and sniff any of the herbs they wish to; most herbs are marked. Self-guiding tours begin at the house, where many basic herbs are planted. Here you'll find feverfew, used for migraine headaches; rose geranium, great in apple jelly; summer savory, delicious in beans; tansy, supposedly good when dried for keeping ants away from food; apple sage, treasured for its fragrant aroma on breezy evenings; garlic chives, an essential ingredient in most Chinese stir frying; thyme, a flavoring in clam chowder and a replacement for salt; chervil, similar to parsley; and miniature basil.

And that's not all. You'll find borage, known for its cucumber flavor and pretty star-shaped flowers used in decorating drinks and cakes; rosemary, good on lamb, chicken, and pork; lovage, stronger in flavor than celery and excellent in potato salad; miniature impatiens, used as a border; rosebud impatiens; Spanish peppermint adorning a bell; and the unique Yesterday, Today, and Tomorrow plant, which turns three colors depending on the time of day.

Myrtle, traditionally used in Polish bridal wreaths, can be seen on the grounds, along with tea and coffee plants. Hyde, who is a collector of unusual plants, is usually on hand to show his outstanding basil collection gathered from all over the world, with interesting specimens from Puerto Rico, Greece, Mexico, Portugal, and Thailand.

The rosemary plantings are intriguing. Hyde takes these plants, which normally grow as bushes, and changes their growth patterns to make them into a form of topiary known as "standards."

Check out the Knot Garden, typical of those seen in England, and the 80 varieties of scented-leaf geraniums. If you come in September, you'll be treated to a showing of more than 40 varieties of rosemary along with lush lavenders.

If you're wondering how the farm acquired its name, look at the stone well in front of the house. A long pole, with a bucket attached, stands above this well. The pole, called a "sweep," lowers the bucket into the water; when it's filled up, the weight at the other end of the pole pulls the bucket out from the water automatically. Hyde named this farm for the same type of "well-sweep" that he used to know as a child.

Bring extra cash; you'll probably go home armed with herbs, seeds, standards, herb books, and other items from the attractive gift shop. Before leaving, ask for a free catalog listing hundreds of herbs and plants you can purchase by mail.

NOTES: Bring along a picnic lunch to enjoy at the farm; the nearest restaurant is about 15 minutes away in Washington.

24. Colonial Park

LOCATION	Somerset County
	Mettler's Road, East Millstone 08873
	(908) 234-2677, (732) 873-2459
SEASON	Year round; the Rose Garden at its peak June–September
HIGHLIGHTS	Rose Garden, Fragrance and Sensory Garden, arboretum, nature trail, bicycle path, ponds
ADMISSION	Free
HOURS	Year round, sunrise–sunset
FACILITIES	Par course fitness circuit, picnicking, children's playground, ponds for fishing, open play fields, ice skating, tennis, rest room, and drinking water
EVENTS	Rose Day in June; call for exact dates

SHAKESPEARE RECOGNIZED THAT THE BEAUTY OF THE ROSE TRANSCENDED ANY NAME we might give to it, but he wasn't the first person to admire this beautiful perennial. Laura C. Martin points out in *Garden Flower Folklore* (Globe Pequot Press, Chester, CT, 1987) that while roses have been cultivated in Greece and the Orient for over 3,000 years, it's believed that all cultivated roses originated from the dog rose, *R. canina*, which dates back 35 million years. This theory has been substantiated by fossils found in Montana.

The rose, crowned the queen of all flowers by Chloris, the Greek goddess of flowers, is not only attractive but useful. In the days of the Roman Empire, legend tells how beautiful Rhodanthe had so many suitors that she had to hide in the Temple of Diana. However, when her suitors broke down the gates to see her, Diana became so angry that she turned Rhodanthe into a rose and her suitors into thorns. Supposedly, it was after this incident that the rose became a symbol for love and beauty.

In medieval times compressed rose petals were used for making rosaries. The rose was also valued for its medicinal qualities; it was used for curing hemorrhages, stomachaches, toothaches, and excessive perspiration. "Sub rosa," a term meaning "confidential" today, meant "under the rose" in Roman times. When the Romans hung a bunch of roses over a table, the gesture ensured silence; it was understood that nothing said there would be repeated to others.

Samuel de Champlain introduced roses from France to North America in

The geometric beds in the Rudolf W. van der Goot Rose Garden in Colonial Park are filled with hundreds of roses. Nearby, the Fragrance and Sensory Garden is home to more than 80 varieties of annuals, herbs, perennials, flowering shrubs, and vines.

the early 17th century. Through the centuries this flower has been displayed as a symbol, appreciated for its nutritional value, used in perfumes, made into rose water for use in cooking, and displayed in gardens. In 1986 the rose was chosen as the national flower of the United States.

One of the best places to see, smell, and admire roses is at the one-acre Rudolf W. van der Goot Rose Garden in Colonial Park, where more than 271 species are displayed. Over 4,000 rose bushes are represented, including hybrid teas, grandifloras, floribundas, climbers, miniatures, old-fashioned, and botanical roses. Recently the display garden received an award of excellence from the All American Rose Selections Society.

Whether you're looking for ideas for your garden or just want to appreciate the flowers, this is the place to find out what Shakespeare was talking about. For an overall view of the three garden areas, walk to the gazebo a bit past the entrance gate. The gardens were designed and developed by Rudolf W. van der Goot, Somerset County Park Commission's first horticulturist, for whom the garden was named in 1981.

When the formal garden of the original Mettler estate was redeveloped, its best elements were retained, such as the reflecting pool, the brick-edged paths, and hedges. Miniature roses are at the base of the fountain; the geometric beds surrounding it are filled with hybrid tea roses, and the area known as Grandmother's Garden contains hybrid perpetual and hybrid tea roses, many of which date back to the 1820s. The Center Garden has beds of polyantha roses; these are flanked by a brick path on either side. Known as the Millicent Fenwick Rose Walk, this section honors the late Ms. Fenwick, a Somerset County resident who had served in Congress, as Director of the New Jersey Consumer Affairs Department, and the U.S. Ambassador to the United Nations Agencies for Food and Agriculture.

Interesting garden specimens include heritage roses, which often bloom only once but are capable of reaching 15 feet; modern hybrids, dating from the mid-1800s and known for their long bloom period and wide color range; and the polyanthas, low-growing plants ranging from one to two feet in height with numerous clusters of tiny flowers.

The Fragrance and Sensory Garden, home to over 80 varieties of annuals, herbs, perennials, flowering shrubs, and vines, is at the western portion of the Rose Garden. Many of these plants are noted for their fragrance or varying textures, and since many must first be touched in order to release their fragrance, touching and smelling are encouraged. The barrier-free sunken garden has a wheelchair ramp and guide rail for the handicapped and visually impaired, as well as attached plant labels printed in Braille and script for easy identification. This is a good place to sit and sniff the fragrant flowering vines overhead and to listen to birds.

In addition to the beautiful garden, Colonial Park offers much more to see and appreciate on its 467 acres, which were acquired in 1965. A visit to the arboretum is always a treat. Known as a "living tree museum," the large collection of trees is labeled for easy identification. You'll find dwarf conifers, lilacs, and Japanese cherries, as well as hollies, dogwoods, and viburnums. One of the most unusual fruiting shrubs is the sweetleaf, which sports bright sapphire-blue berries until frost.

For exercise, try the par course fitness circuit. After the heart check and a few exercises to limber up, you'll be on your way. The circuit takes about 25 minutes to complete; to ensure you won't strain yourself, there are several heart check stations en route.

Colonial Park offers family and group picnic sites and paddleboats during the summer months. If you like bicycling, the level 1.4-mile path is perfect for a short ride, or bring skates along. Resident Canada geese line the path and usually make tempting models for photographers. During winter months the park offers ice skating on Powder Mill Pond and Mettler's Pond.

NOTE: Bring along a picnic lunch; restaurants are a distance away.

25. Cora Hartshorn Arboretum and Bird Sanctuary

LOCATION Essex County
324 Forest Drive South (off the Garden State
Parkway, Exit 139), Short Hills 07078
(973) 376-3587

SEASON Year round

HIGHLIGHTS Arboretum, bird sanctuary, wildflowers, small zoo,
nature center, walking trails

ADMISSION Free

HOURS Grounds: daylight hours year round
Stone House: Tuesday and Thursday 2:45–4:45 P.M.
September–May

FACILITIES Rest room and drinking water available when
Stone House open

EVENTS Guided trail walk on first Sunday in May; Open
House and birdseed sale on second Saturday in
October; maple tapping January and February;
various activities during year; for free calendar
write Cora Hartshorn Arboretum, 324 Forest Drive
South, Short Hills 07078

FEELING STRESSED AND PRESSED FOR TIME? THE CORA HARTSHORN ARBORETUM AND
Bird Sanctuary may be just the ticket for a refreshing, mind-clearing walk.
The easy, meandering trails, which spread over 16.5 acres, offer a peek at
some of Mother Nature's best work. If the house is open, visit the tiny
nature center inside that's filled with local critters.

This arboretum is particularly impressive during the winter months. Plan
on visiting during a light snowfall, when a hush falls upon the forest,
making it possible to actually hear the snow land and swish beneath your
feet. With a magnifying glass you'll discover that no two snowflakes are
alike. Surrounding trees seem to have a voice of their own; the slightest
breeze causes one branch to rub upon the other, creating supernatural
sounds.

Strolling through the arboretum is a delight year round.

When temperatures fall, sharp eyes may uncover animal tracks atop freshly fallen snow. The few remaining green plants include the Christmas fern, which usually can be spotted poking up through the snow as it reaches toward the sun. This is also a good season for tree identification, which presents a challenge once the leaves have fallen. Each species has individual characteristics, but by comparing the silhouette and bark, the mystery can be solved. The white oak with its thin, gray scaly bark is an easy tree to identify, while the dogwood hides its flowers and leaves in tiny reddish buds tucked neatly into forks and prongs. The holly oozes warmth during freezing weather by sporting glossy evergreen leaves, and the female produces bright red berries throughout the winter. If you spot a few prickly balls clinging stubbornly from branches, you've found the sweetgum.

A wildflower lover should come during spring, when over 80 species set the forest floor ablaze in striking colors. You'll also hear a wonderful chorus of delightful sounds during this season. The longer days are believed to trigger the release of hormones in many animals and birds, who begin their mate-seeking and territory-marking. You'll hear the sweet melodic twitter of a robin, the shrill cry of the blue jay, and, walking through the damper areas, you might even hear the high whistling sound of the spring peeper, a tiny tree frog. Sometimes you may hear a few different songs from only one bird, the mockingbird, who is an excellent mimic.

If the Stone House is open, step inside to see and pet some of the creatures, including a rabbit, ferret, garter snake, lizard, and cricket. The house itself, designed in 1931 by architect Bernardt E. Muller, is built of fieldstone and trap rock from a nearby quarry. The rafters are made of hewn oak trees from land the Hartshorns owned in Short Hills.

The Arboretum, planned by artist and naturalist Cora Hartshorn, sits on land her father Steward Hartshorn (the founder of Short Hills) had owned. Ms. Hartshorn recorded 72 varieties of birds on her property and created three miles of paths within the hills and gullies skirting terminal moraine holes. In 1958 she bequeathed her land to Millburn Township.

NOTES: Bring along bird and tree identification books and a pair of binoculars. Restaurants are located in town.

THE GREAT
OUTDOORS

26. Mount Tammany

LOCATION	Sussex County
	Exit off Route 80 west to first rest-area sign right after town of Columbia; park and walk short distance into second parking lot; the trail begins at the white blaze. For further information contact Worthington State Forest, Old Mine Road, Columbia 07632. (908) 841-9575
SEASON	Year round
HIGHLIGHTS	Magnificent views of the Delaware Water Gap; trout fishing; a wide array of trees, plants, flowers, geologic formations
ADMISSION	Free
HOURS	24 hours a day
FACILITIES	Parking area

MOUNT TAMMANY IS THE PLACE TO BE IF YOU'VE EVER LONGED TO BE "KING OF THE Mountain." Those who take this strenuous hike are rewarded with spectacular vistas of the Delaware Water Gap, Mount Minsi, and the Pocono Mountains.

Situated within the 70,000-acre Delaware Water Gap National Recreation Area, Mount Tammany is part of the rocky, wooded mountain ridge known as the Kittatinnys, an Indian name meaning "Big Mountain." According to archeological evidence, Indians were living in the valley around Mount Tammany hundreds of years ago. Later—long before William Penn founded Philadelphia—Dutch explorers settled in the area, which eventually served as an important link in communications between New York and Philadelphia.

After parking, walk to the path marked with white blazes, part of the Appalachian Trail. Cross the wooden bridge. Dunnfield Creek, a swift-moving brook, will be on your right. After heavy rains its roar is almost deafening. Rhododendrons are lush during spring, and the beauty of the surrounding oak and hickory forest makes it hard to believe that civilization is not far away.

After about 0.5 mile, watch for another trail marked with blue blazes, and make a right turn at the double blue blaze where another bridge crosses

One feels like "king of the mountain" atop Mount Tammany, overlooking the Delaware Water Gap.

the creek. (A double blaze always indicates a turn.) Nearby, a small but lovely waterfall is a good spot to rest, especially on a hot day. The effect of water cascading through large boulders and logs on its way down to the Delaware River is almost hypnotic. Hemlocks abound in this area, providing a pleasant sound as breezes rustle through their branches.

The blue-blazed trail is extremely rocky, winding past oak, maple, and beech trees, and after about two hours you'll reach the crest of the trail. Once atop Mount Tammany, cars traveling on the highway 1,527 feet below resemble tiny toys. Mount Minsi, named for the Minisink Indians, stands on the opposite side. The almost unspoiled beauty of the Gap, where the Delaware River cuts through the mountains, is a memorable sight. Geologists believe that originally, when flat-lying rocks folded, erosion beveled the deformed rocks. Uplifting then caused the streams to cut downward, and as the land rose, the main stream may have been able to maintain its old course, thus cutting the valley into bands of both resistant and nonresistant rock. Tributary streams then etched out the easily eroded materials, adjusting their course to go around the tougher rocks of emerging ridges. The master stream eventually cut a ridge and formed the notches or "water gaps" that we now see.

The summit is an ideal place for a lunch break. It's also perfect for observing red-tailed and broad-winged hawks as they soar gracefully with the wind currents. Songbirds often frequent the woods during spring and fall, but if you hear boisterous honking in the fall, the Canada geese are making their presence known.

When you're ready, continue following the blue blazes until you come to the Mount Tammany trail, indicated by red dots on a white background. From here it's a steep, 1.5-mile hike back to the parking lot, with more spectacular views and lots of places to rest. It isn't unusual to see people in their seventies and eighties, or families with young children, on this somewhat difficult trail. Everyone seems to enjoy the experience of scrambling over the rocks.

If you've come during fall, the striking bush bearing yellow flowers is the witch hazel, so-named by settlers who thought its leaves looked similar to European hazel. Supposedly, witches made their brooms from this plant and claimed they could even ride them. Several hundred years ago those who proclaimed themselves witches also raved about their powers of witchcraft or magic. They would often hold meetings around a huge fire and drink potions. When they drank enough, they imagined they were actually flying, and with brooms near the fire to sweep it clean no doubt they actually did see themselves flying high on their witch hazel brooms.

At these higher elevations, you'll probably come across shadbush as well. A common underbrush plant, it remains inconspicuous year round until late April, when it bursts open producing white blossoms, each having five narrow petals resembling ribbons. It blooms the same time that the frisky shad fish swim up the Delaware to spawn. It's also known as the Juneberry because its fruits ripen in June.

Don't dismiss the thought of hiking here during the winter. Not only are the white-tailed deer easier to spot, but the bare trees offer unusual shapes and are a challenge to identify. Then, too, the forever-green rhododendrons brighten the trail. When the temperature drops, their leaves curl to conserve water and droop to expose less of their surface to the air.

You might want to take fishing gear with you; Dunnfield Creek is loaded with native brook trout. But don't forget your license.

NOTES: The round trip, approximately 4 miles, takes about 4 hours with time to enjoy a leisurely lunch and the views. A backpack is a good idea, as is a camera, binoculars, and bird and tree identification books. Pack lots to drink and a towel in case you want to take a dunk in Dunnfield Creek.

27. Round Valley Recreation Area

LOCATION Hunterdon County
Lebanon–Stanton Road (off Route 22), Lebanon
08833
(908) 236-6355

SEASON Year round

HIGHLIGHTS Fishing, boating, camping, hiking, hunting, swimming, sledding, cross-country skiing, ice-skating, iceboat sailing, scuba diving (April 15– October 31), and bird watching

ADMISSION Fee Memorial Day–Labor Day except on Tuesdays

HOURS Memorial Day–Labor Day, 8 A.M.–8 P.M.; rest of year, 8 A.M.–4:30 P.M.

FACILITIES Rest room, drinking water, campsites, fishing, boat ramp

EVENTS Iceboating races during winter months

IN 1958 A NATURAL HORSESHOE-SHAPED VALLEY IN THE ROLLING HILLS OF HUNTERDON County was dammed, and today 55 billion gallons of water fill this area, known as Round Valley Reservoir. Not only is the water a valuable resource, but the reservoir provides year-round recreation for the entire family. The land surrounding the reservoir, Round Valley State Park, offers an abundance of facilities as well.

The cool, clear water of this 70-foot-deep lake—the deepest in the state—makes it a fisherman's paradise. In addition to rainbow trout, 19 species of fish are found here, including brown trout, smallmouth bass, and sunfish. Even if you're not "hooked" on fishing, the underwater life can be observed by scuba diving, for the reservoir is reputed to be one of the best sites in the state for this activity.

One way to savor the beauty of this man-made lake is to hike along a portion of the 9-mile trail. Ask for a free trail map when you sign in at the visitor center. A few minutes after starting out you'll come to a marvelous view of the narrow reservoir, one mile wide and three miles long. Eventually, after traversing open fields, the trail leads to thick woods before heading up a hill following the ridge line toward Cushetuck Mountain, a scenic spot to have lunch or a snack.

In about 3 miles the southern side of the reservoir comes into view. Here you can peek in on the wilderness camping area. Return another time if you're tempted to experience backcountry camping at one of the 116 rustic campsites. Surrounded by trees, with two-thirds of the sites near water, privacy from your neighbor and cars is assured—the only way to the campsites is by hiking or boating in. Fires are permitted in provided rings, but always carry a stove in case a fire ban is in effect. There aren't any picnic tables, but water is available from nearby wells, and on a warm day a dip in the lake is ideal.

Boating enthusiasts love it here, and no wonder, for they're surrounded by 2,000 acres of water! A free boat launch is provided north of the day-use area; sailboats, motorboats up to 10 horsepower, and canoes are permitted.

Things don't come to a halt during winter months either. Ice skaters can perfect their footwork at the east end of the beach from early morning into late evening hours, while iceboaters and skate-sailors quietly glide over the frozen surface. Heated rest rooms are provided.

Iceboats can sail six times faster than the wind, and watching captains practice for upcoming races is a sure way to beat the winter blues. This fascinating sport may have started as long ago as the mid-1600s, when sailboats were fitted with runners and used for moving cargo around bays and canals along the North Sea. By the 1800s, descendants of Dutch settlers built large, stern-steering iceboats just for the joy of racing them along the Hudson River north of New York. The hulls of these boats were 30–40 feet long, and they could attain a speed of 60 miles per hour.

Iceboats are highly specialized. They have to be extremely strong to withstand the force of wind and ice while traveling at tremendous speeds, and they also must be capable of being quickly assembled and disassembled in subfreezing weather. The sail resembles an airplane wing on edge more than the sail of a boat.

In the 1900s the sport was one of the fastest means of travel, beating trains, cars, and airplanes of that era. Although today they go slower in comparison, iceboats can attain speeds of 100 miles per hour. and are a thrill to watch as they gather speed. The way they work is simple; the hull, known as a fuselage, is similar to that of a small plane. A steering runner is attached to the hull, as is a runner plank and the mast. The hull also holds the cockpit for the skipper and passenger, if it is a two-person boat. The steering runner may be controlled by any number of methods. On a stern-steerer boat, which has the simplest steering, a shaft on the steering runner pivot is directly connected to a tiller operated by hand.

On certain iceboats steering is accomplished by a triangular wooden tiller mounted on a rotatable vertical shaft that extends from the deck through the hull. Beneath the hull on the shaft is a cross arm that drives a similar cross arm on the steering runner by rods or by two parallel cables.

No matter which season you visit Round Valley, you'll be guaranteed an exciting day. Winter sports played in this huge hole in the ground include ice-skating, ice fishing, and iceboating.

The tiller is then used to steer by hand or can be held between the captain's legs, freeing the hands. Newer boats are steered by the feet.

An iceboat can be stopped using a hand brake pivoted on the runner plank on the side of the hull. Its lower end has one or more sharp joints that are forced against the ice, but the brake is used only when traveling at slow speeds. When you walk out on the ice, look for marks the brakes have left.

If the beauty of these boats has aroused your curiosity, you may be tempted to build or purchase one. Before proceeding, ask to ride as a passenger, observe, and beg a turn at steering. It's quite an experience. There are an estimated 1,200–1,500 people throughout the country today who are devoted to this sport; they are a good-natured group and usually willing to explain the elements of iceboating to spectators while they rest up for the exciting ride.

Should you wish to come only to admire the fantastic scenery here, bring along a pair of binoculars, sit high on a knoll overlooking the reservoir, and watch the activity below you. Two picnic areas are located at tree-covered plots at either end of the beach, while the third is on a hill overlooking the park and reservoir. Each provides handicapped access, and all have tables and grills.

Wherever your perch, you'll no doubt see many of the birds common to Round Valley. These include the catbird, a slate-gray bird with a black cap known for the "meow" call; the mockingbird, light gray, often imitating the songs of other birds; and the quick-darting barn swallow, often spotted along the bay shore searching for eel grass to build its mud nest. Barn owls, loons, hummingbirds, and Canada geese, wild turkey, and a variety of warblers have also been known to frequent the area.

If you hear loud chattering, it's probably a red squirrel. This jolly half-pound creature, covered with yellowish or reddish fur, measures about a foot from head to tail. As cold weather approaches, it rushes about toting pine cones, hickory nuts, walnuts, chestnuts, and acorns. Then in a comfortable hideaway it shucks off the scales in one pile, while storing the seeds elsewhere for the dead of winter. Some shucking sites stand as high as nine feet!

Round Valley is very popular not only during summer months, when hundreds of swimmers and sun worshipers use the facilities, but during winter months, when the trails are frequented by cross-country skiers. It's sometimes difficult to believe that Round Valley is one of the state's largest and deepest man-made lakes when not too many years ago it was merely a hole in the ground.

NOTES: Visitors must register at the visitor center to obtain a parking permit. Lists of birds and animals found on the trail are available here. Pack a picnic lunch; restaurants are a distance away.

28. Tillman Ravine

LOCATION Sussex County
Stokes State Forest (turn left going north on Route 206 at the 4H sign), Branchville 07826
(973) 948-3820

SEASON Year round

HIGHLIGHTS Geological formations, waterfalls, lush woods, wildflowers

ADMISSION Free

HOURS Dawn–dusk, except from December 25 to the end of March or April (depending on the weather), when the auto road is closed at the 4H sign. From this point, it is one mile (walking or skiing) to Tillman Ravine.

FACILITIES Outhouse

STANDING IN TILLMAN RAVINE, BENEATH TOWERING HEMLOCKS AND HEARING ONLY THE music of a flowing stream and tiny waterfalls, brings what I can only describe as a feeling of complete serenity. Each time I visit this wondrous place it's a happy experience and a spiritual reawakening.

Although the self-guiding circular trail is only about a mile long and can take as little as 45 minutes, plan on spending several hours here. The temperature is always cooler inside the shaded ravine, and on hot summer days you can dip your feet into the stream. During winter months, when the streams are frozen a milky white, the deep emerald glow of the evergreens against the snow is like a magic elixir.

At the beginning of the trail, which begins to the left of the trail map sign in the parking lot, is a stand of red and yellow pines planted over 50 years ago as part of a Civilian Conservation Corps project. Both these pines produce needles in bundles of two; however, the yellow pine has three- to five-inch needles and a prickly cone, while the red pine has smoothly edged cones and six-inch needles.

Next come the magnificent hemlocks, graceful evergreens shaped like pyramids with needles about a half inch long spreading out on either side of the branches. You can easily identify this beauty by turning over the flat needles and checking for two silver stripes on the underside. Also look for tiny cones hanging on the tips of the branches year round. Until recently the

Walking beneath towering hemlocks and hearing only the music of a flowing stream brings a feeling of complete serenity.

acid soil and humid air have nurtured these specimens: Hemlocks can live over 150 years, grow to 46 inches in diameter, and reach 112 feet. A new disease is suddenly threatening their health. Photographing them presents a challenge, because it's always so dark in these woods. A tripod is the best way to get good photos.

After crossing a small wooden bridge, you'll hear and see the Upper Falls, where the roar of the bubbling water beckons. Tillman Ravine is a relatively young geologic feature; about 20 feet down the trail, adjacent to the Upper Falls and to the extreme right, you can see a fold in the rock known as an anticline.

The ravine developed when the last glacier began to melt and small streams started flowing from springs farther up on the ridge. The energy of the water flowing downhill eroded the rock and, in time, this new, deep valley will erode into a broad, gentle valley that is characteristic of a mature stream.

Lush stands of rhododendron adjoin the path soon after the second wooden bridge; these remain green year round before bursting with rich color in July.

Examine the fallen hemlocks after the next bridge for the "varnish conk," an unusual fungus. Look at it through your pocket magnifier if you brought one; it appears as though someone has sprayed it with a coat of varnish! Pretty trilliums, with a whorl of three leaves at the top; partridgeberry, a trailing plant known for its scarlet berry, which remains in bloom from July through November; and Jack-in-the-pulpit, with its purple hood arched over a stalk, are often found in this area. During spring they dot the forest floor with bright color.

Near the bottom of Tillman Ravine is a formation called the "teacup," more commonly known as a pothole, which was created by the swirling motion of sand and rock carried by rapidly moving water. As the swirling deepens, it enlarges the pothole, causing a circular shape and smooth wall. A few of the bottom rocks helped to form the pothole.

After the fourth bridge, you'll come to the ridge trail again. Follow it through an oak and maple forest, where in June mountain laurel puts on a colorful show of white and pink in spring and summer and during fall months turns brilliant colors. In May and June other flowers along the walk include the May apple, meadow buttercup, wild indigo, and smooth Solomon's seal. In July hundreds of wildflowers light up the green surroundings.

While the hemlocks are truly special, striking black birch, black cherry, flowering dogwood, hickory, sycamore, and stately tulip trees are also lovely. This is a fine place to learn tree identification. To have a record of each tree, try the art of bark rubbing. All you need is a piece of waxed paper or grease-proof paper, sticky tape, and a supply of crayons. Tape the paper to the bark, rub slowly with all the strokes going in one direction using the flattened side of the crayon, and then compare the pattern of the bark to the ones in your tree identification book.

For a feeling of peace, the sight of majestic trees, or the fresh aroma of pines, Tillman Ravine is definitely the place to visit.

NOTES: Sneakers are fine, but a sturdy walking shoe will prevent your toes from getting stubbed on boulders. A few sandwich shops are along Route 206, but it's more enjoyable to bring a picnic lunch and plenty of water so you can rest along the trail, refuel, and admire the scenery while listening to the sounds of the forest.

29. High Point State Park

LOCATION Sussex County
Route 23, 7 miles north of Sussex
(973) 875-4800

SEASON Year round

HIGHLIGHTS High Point Monument, views, hiking, swimming,
fishing, picnicking, camping, boating, skiing,
snowmobiling, dog sledding, cross-country skiing,
ice skating

ADMISSION Fee on weekends, holidays Memorial Day–Labor
Day, except Tuesdays; fee for camping and
entrance to the monument

HOURS Visitor center: daily 9 A.M.–4 P.M.
Camping: April 1–October 31
Cabins: May 15–October 15
Monument: noon–4 P.M. weekends, daily
Memorial Day–Labor Day (weather permitting),
9 A.M.–4:30 P.M. Monument hours subject to change;
call first.

FACILITIES Rest room, campground, two cabins, bathing
beach, bathhouses, refreshment concession,
playground

THE APPROPRIATELY NAMED HIGH POINT STATE PARK STANDS 1,803 FEET ABOVE SEA level at the highest point in New Jersey. Situated along the crest of the Kittatinny Mountains in the northwestern corner of the state, the park offers breathtaking views, exciting trails, swimming, fishing, picnicking, and other activities the whole year round.

To establish the park, land was donated by Colonel and Mrs. Kuser of Bernardsville in 1923. Avid bird watchers, the Kusers wanted to provide a nature reserve open to the public, to protect wildlife and to conserve clean water.

The Kusers also provided funds to build a 220-foot obelisk in memory of New Jersey's wartime heroes. The monument, faced with New Hampshire granite and local quartzite, stands 34 square feet at the platform and 19 feet at the base of the apex.

Steps within the shaft allow visitors to climb to the top of the monument

High Point State Park affords day hikers wonderful trails to explore as well as overnight camps for those who seek longer walks.

for a panoramic view of the surrounding land. Westward vistas across the Delaware provide an impressive view of Pennsylvania, with the ridges of the Pocono Mountains towering in the distance, while Port Jervis lies in the valley 1,300 feet below. To the north are the Catskill Mountains; to the southeast, the Wallkill River Valley; to the southwest, farms and woodlands and the Delaware Water Gap 40 miles away. From this viewpoint you can also see Sunrise Mountain between the Kittatinny Ridge and the Wallkill River Valley, along with the crystal-clear waters of Lake Marcia, the highest lake in the state.

Stop at the visitor center on the south side of Route 23 for a map of the park and trail information. In addition to a short stretch of the Appalachian Trail that runs through the park, there are nine other trails here. They vary from less than half a mile to over four miles over rocky terrain. Each is marked with colored blazes: white blazes mark the Appalachian Trail.

One of my favorite walks, a true leg-stretcher of 7.5 miles, is along a portion of the Appalachian Trail starting at the parking lot just east of the visitor center on the same side as Route 23. Starting at the wide path with white blazes, take the right fork at the first junction, where you'll begin climbing through a lovely wooded area. Wear sturdy shoes: This makes it easier to scramble over the huge granite boulders along the way. About 0.5 mile after the sign for an overnight shelter, the trail dips, crossing Iris Trail coming in from the left where the main trail swings to the right. Change here to the Iris Trail, identified by red blazes; it's an easier walk that leads back to the visitor center and provides a look at scenic Lake Rutherford, privately owned by the town of Sussex.

Ayer Trail (black blazes, from Sawmill Road), is an easy 1-mile trail cutting through a large hardwood forest of oak, hickory, and red maple. Along the trail you'll see an old farm site and hand-built five-foot stone walls. The Blue Dot Trail (dark blue blazes, across from campsite 15 at Sawmill Lake) is a rugged 0.5-mile trail running through an oak and maple forest, which turns to scrub oak and pitch pine in the rocky areas of the high ridges. You'll find numerous washes spotted with fossilized shells along this trail.

Life Trail (brown blazes, as the group campsite to Ridge Road) is a 0.5-mile walk through an abundance of wintergreen, mountain laurel, and hardwood trees. The Mashipacong Trail (yellow blazes, opposite the junction of Ridge Road and Mashipacong Road) is an easy 1.5-mile walk leading through an oak and maple forest. Huckleberry bushes and wildflowers grow along this trail, and you'll see the remains of an old farm. If you're on this trail during the summer months, look for traces of black-striped larva or the chrysalises of the red and black monarch butterfly in the patches of milkweed near the farm site.

Monument Trail (red and green blazes, at the end of the monument parking lot) is a rugged 3.5-mile hike along a shaled bed that runs up and down ridges. Besides having views of New York, New Jersey, and Pennsylvania, you'll hike through scrub oak and pitch pine, traversing a thick undergrowth of grasses, sweet fern, and huckleberries. Deer frequent these ridges, feeding on grasses near the monument at the end of the trail. Often turkey buzzards and hawks circle these areas, especially during their fall migration. Take along a magnifying glass; it comes in handy if you're searching for carnivorous plants, such as the sundew and pitcher plant, in the cedar swamp.

The Old Trail (brown and yellow blazes) runs from Route 23 at the junction of Sawmill Road to the swimming beach. This is an easy 0.5-mile walk on an old carriage road. Here you'll find outcroppings of slanted rock beds within a wooded area of oak, maple, and small American chestnut shoots. There is also an undergrowth of sweet fern, huckleberries, and assorted wildflowers. Grasses and wildflowers grow in profusion along the parallel stream, and deer can usually be spotted near the Route 23 end of the trail. The large mounds you're likely to encounter to the north of the trail are anthills; they can be up to three feet in diameter and a foot high.

Equally enjoyable is the Parker Trail (light green blazes), a moderate 1-mile hike, from Ridge Road to Deckertown Pike connecting High Point State Park and Stokes State Forest, which winds around many springs. The Steenykill Trail (light blue blazes, from the Route 23 barricade to the Monument Trail) provides a leisurely, moderate 1-mile walk from Lake Steenykill to the top of High Point Mountain through a stand of gray birch trees. Beaver, ferns, and a waterfall can be seen in this area. During summer months, swimming is available on spring-fed Lake Marcia. In season you can also fish for trout and largemouth bass in the lakes and streams within the park.

NOTE: Bring along a picnic lunch; tables, grills, and fireplaces are available.

30. Swartswood State Park

LOCATION Sussex County
Off Route 619, Stillwater Township 07875
(973) 383-5230

SEASON Year round

HIGHLIGHTS Nature trails, boating, swimming, fishing, hunting, cross-country skiing, iceboating, ice-skating, ice fishing, camping, picnicking

ADMISSION Free for day use, except Memorial Day–Labor Day (free on Tuesdays) and for camping

HOURS 8 A.M.–8:30 P.M.; hours vary; call before going

FACILITIES Rest room, campground, picnic tables, showers, snack bar, boat rentals, marked trails

EVENTS Guided nature walks and interpretive programs Memorial Day–Labor Day; call for scheduled times

PEOPLE VISIT SWARTSWOOD STATE PARK FOR MANY REASONS—SOME LIKE TO SWIM, others like to fish, bird watchers concentrate on finding new species, while nature lovers enjoy autumn's bright foliage. There are those who come to hike the nature trails, and many who appreciate camping in the peace and quiet of the woods.

This area wasn't always considered a peaceful or special place to visit. In 1756 conditions were extremely dangerous, especially when an Indian war party burned down a home owned by Anthony Swartout near Swartswood Lake. They scalped Swartout, killed four of his children, and kidnapped two others. After this terrible incident, according to Warren D. Cummings in his book *Sussex County, A History* (Rotary Club, Newton, NJ), the governor "offered rewards for the capture or killing of male Indians over fifteen years of age." And, "when an Indian's scalp was brought in to prove the killing," recounts Cummings, "the state paid one hundred and thirty dollars"—an enormous sum in those days.

A new governor, appointed in 1758, dealt with the situation differently. He had blockhouses erected along the Delaware and ordered patrols with hounds to guard the bank, figuring it wouldn't be difficult for the dogs to pick up an Indian's scent. After a short time it became obvious that a wiser solution would be to make a deal with interested tribes. Eventually all Indian claims north of the Raritan were settled for $1,000. With peace

Trees of all shapes and sizes greet visitors to Swartswood State Park, which in addition to beautiful woods has a lovely campground and lakes.

established by the early 1800s, visitors began flocking to the beautiful Sussex hills area for rest, swimming, fishing, and hunting.

Named for the Swartout family, Swartswood State Park comprises 1,304 acres, including a gristmill at the southwestern tip of Swartswood Lake, Mill Pond, and a dam. Its 70-acre campground, open from April through October, offers large, wooded campsites, picnic tables, fire rings, a dumping station, heated rest rooms with hot showers, and a laundry.

Maps are available at the park office located near the entrance. The beautiful white sand beach, also near the entrance, is ideal for relaxing, swimming, or boating. Rowboats, canoes, and small sailboats are available for rental on Swartswood Lake during the boating season. If you're interested in fishing, you can cast from the shore or take a boat on this lake or on Little Swartswood Lake, both stocked with brown trout, rainbow trout, bass, catfish, perch, sunfish, and pickerel. Live bait is available at the boathouse.

For a good view of the Kittatinny Mountains, try one of the nature trails. The yellow-blazed Mill Trail, an easy 1.3-mile loop starting near Keen's

Gristmill, meanders through fields and a forested area and offers beautiful vistas along the lake's southeastern shoreline. It's a bit tricky staying on the trail at the double blaze where the trail divides. Try to keep the blaze in front of you in sight at all times. If you lose it, turn back to pick up another blaze and then continue on the path.

Walk uphill after the trail divides, bear right crossing over the stone fence, and search for the almost invisible ground-hugging mosses. Moss, which can be found on top of the soil, on the side of a tree, or on a rock, dates back over 300 million years. Without flowers or seeds, mosses reproduce by spores and have played an important role commercially. Years ago these absorbent plants were used to make ropes, blankets, brushes, and doormats, as well as lamp wicks, caulking material, bandages, mattress stuffing, and even as a poultice to treat burns and bruises. Today they're used in floral arrangements and as decorations.

In winter months, skiers use the 2.5-mile Equestrian/Cross-Country Ski Trail, which follows alongside stone fences, fields, ponds, wetlands, forest, and hemlock groves. The rest of the year it's a good trail to spot deer, squirrels, and opossums.

Songbirds are abundant throughout the park. The red-tailed hawk and turkey vulture frequent the open water areas, and as a migratory stopover in spring and fall, Swartswood is a resting place for the ring-neck duck, common loon, and pied-billed grebe among many others. The migratory seasons are good times to watch for osprey as they search the water for dinner or for observing the American coot as it paddles across the lake.

You'll know spring is just around the corner when you hear the musical call of the spring peeper. Awakened from their winter sleep by rising temperatures, these tiny frogs begin their mating choruses while the marshes and ponds are still iced over. In late March the males use a two-note, high-pitched call by gulping air, closing their mouths, inflating a vocal sac under their chins, and driving the air back and forth from their lungs to the vocal sac, resulting in the air vibrating the vocal chords on the floor of their mouths. If the singing stops as you approach, move closer to the water's edge and wait quietly. You'll probably spot a peeper clinging by its toe pads to the grass or brush.

NOTES: The campground is open year round; pets and alcohol are not allowed. Reservations are accepted by mail or in person for 7 or 14 nights from Memorial Day to Labor Day and for a minimum of two nights or more from Labor Day to Memorial Day, with two-thirds of the sites available during summer on a first-come, first-served basis. Write to Swartswood State Park for more information: P.O. Box 123, Swartswood 07877-0123. Bring along a picnic lunch, or if you prefer, try one of the restaurants in nearby Newton.

31. Scherman-Hoffman Wildlife Sanctuaries

LOCATION Somerset County
Exit 26B from Route 287 on Hardscrabble Road,
Bernardsville 07924
(908) 766-5787

SEASON Year round

HIGHLIGHTS Birds, woodlands, streams, fields

ADMISSION Free

HOURS Office, exhibits, bookstore: Tuesday–Saturday
9 A.M.–5 P.M., Sunday noon–5 P.M; closed Monday,
major holidays, end of June, and end of December
Trails: Tuesday–Sunday 9 A.M.–5 P.M., year round

FACILITIES Exhibit rooms, rest room, drinking water, gift shop,
a birding hot line (908-766-2661) reporting rare
bird sightings and local reports of interest

EVENTS Birding, field trips, monthly photo/art exhibit, free
nature/bird walks every Friday and Saturday
morning 8–9 A.M., natural history courses, "Bear
Fair," a day of nature games for children first
Saturday in June, and the "World Series of Birding,"
an annual fund raiser centered around the spring
migration when as many as 25 species of warblers
can be seen

THE NEW JERSEY AUDUBON SOCIETY'S SCHERMAN-HOFFMAN WILDLIFE SANCTUARIES prove that some of the best things in life are still free. With approximately 265 acres of deciduous woodland, floodplain, fields, streams, and ridges of over 600 feet elevation, there is always something new to discover here.

On one winter's walk, the naturalist taught me how to use the color, texture, and shapes of the trees for identification and pointed out the black cherry, dogwood, sassafras, shag bark hickory, hornbeam, and other trees that thrive here. On another walk, he directed our attention to broad-winged hawks, one of over 60 resident species in this area.

The wood frog begins its beautiful song in April, and if you're talented in imitating calls, you'll receive many responses. Even if you don't know how

Along the Dogwood Trail at Scherman-Hoffman Wildlife Sanctuaries stands an unusual boulder known as the "elephant rock." It's surrounded by a large American beech. This boulder was so huge that the trees had to adapt and grew around it!

to whistle, stop for a few minutes to listen to the breeding warblers and fledgling birds during summer months—the chattering, drill-like sound of the field sparrow or an ovenbird's "teacher teacher" call. In addition to birds, many of New Jersey's common mammals, 25 fern species, and 6 snake, 6 frog, and 5 salamander species can be found here, along with hundreds of wildflowers.

Donated by Harry Scherman in 1966 and G. Frederick Hoffman in 1981, the twin sanctuaries are described in the trail guide leaflet as "quiet places where nature is undisturbed except for passive use through trails used for observation, study, and refreshment." The only sound heard along the trails is the chatter of a passing bird, the gurgling of the pristine Passaic River, and the mating calls of birds and frogs. During spring and summer a wealth of flowers brighten the landscape with their lush colors, adding to the tranquillity.

Stop in at the Hoffman House first. Built in 1939, it now serves as the visitor center. Pick up a free trail map, look at the exhibits, watch the birds perched on feeders outside the picture window, and browse through an excellent assortment of books, feeders, and outdoor gifts on sale. Audubon members receive a 10 percent discount on gifts and 20 percent on optical equipment.

When you're ready, take the red-blazed Dogwood Trail in back of the house. This easy trail leading through both sanctuaries can also be reached from the lower parking lot a few minutes past the Hoffman House. The trail takes approximately 1½ hours to complete.

Follow the Dogwood Trail as it winds past red, white, black, and chestnut oaks, tulip trees, red and sugar maples, and American beech. The rebirth of the black birch is fascinating to witness during spring, when its buds burst open. Along this trail you'll also come to an unusual boulder known as the Elephant Rock, surrounded by a large American beech. Usually trees crack rocks and grow up through them, but this boulder was so huge that the tree had to adapt and grow around it.

The hills around you are an outcropping of the Central Highlands; their parallel ridges and valleys, approximately 600 million years old, were formed during the Precambrian period, making this one of the oldest formations in New Jersey. Believe it or not, George Washington camped out in these woods! Since the parallel ridges haven't any natural passes running through them, he took advantage of the situation, setting up camps in the ridge area during the revolutionary war to protect his troops. Messages were safely sent all the way into New England, and supply lines in the valleys were protected as well.

The mysterious pit on top of the hill was man-made, and its use is still unknown. Some think it might have been an iron mine from the revolutionary war, and that the stone used for building Scherman's home was quarried from it. Nearby stands a shadbush tree; it's also known as a shadbush or shadblow, because shad run upriver to spawn at about the same time these trees flower in the spring. Its white or pink flowers come out just before the leaves appear. Another beauty found in the underbrush is the flowering dogwood, especially nice in the spring, when its white or pink blossoms appear, and again during the fall, when its leaves turn bright scarlet.

As you descend, watch for two trees that have merged together to form an "H." It is believed that when this tulip tree fell over, a nearby black birch supported it; miraculously, the tulip tree not only stayed alive but grafted naturally onto the neighboring birch.

Grape, poison ivy, and bittersweet vines hug the path ahead. The grape vine, easily identified by its reddish bark, looks much different from the light gray, bumpy bark of the bittersweet, but all three of these vines work their way along tree trunks in order to obtain sunlight. The poison ivy should always be avoided; it's easy to recognize by its hairy vine, white berries in the winter, and three-leaf clusters during summer. Remember this adage: "Leaves of three, let it be."

Look closely at tree trunks with large holes in them—especially dead trunks—because a pileated woodpecker may show up. As large as a crow, this black-and-white bird with a bright red crest works diligently to dig out grubs or adult beetles from tree trunks with its huge bill. It whacks away with such tremendous force that it can be heard for great distances.

Where the road divides, turn left if you wish to walk along the River Trail adjoining the headwaters of the Passaic River, or turn right if you want to head back along Old Farm Road passing between two fields. Both lead to the Hoffman House. On the way back to the parking lot the River Trail passes marvelous specimens of Christmas fern, so-named because it is one of the few fern species remaining green into December, and numerous ironwood trees, known for their tough bark.

If you've chosen the trail to the right, woodchucks, rabbits, bluebirds, indigo buntings, field sparrows, and numerous other creatures may be spotted, since the fields are an important habitat for them. Butterflies and moths are also common in this area; they feast on the black-eyed Susans, beardtongues, lobelias, and goldenrods.

There's no doubt that these sanctuaries are ideal for the birds, but they're also a sanctuary for people who want to find peace and quiet while observing nature.

NOTES: Wear sturdy walking shoes to protect your toes from rocks. Picnicking and pets are not allowed. Friendly's and the Old Mill Inn are located nearby for snacks or a meal.

LOCATION	Somerset County
	190 Lord Stirling Road (exit at Maple Avenue from
	Route 287), Basking Ridge 07920
	(908) 766-2489
SEASON	Year round
HIGHLIGHTS	Easy, flat hiking trails including a handicapped-accessible trail, cross-country skiing, bird watching from blinds and towers, various plant communities, woodland, wetland, exhibition area within the solar-heated building
ADMISSION	Free
HOURS	Building: daily 9 A.M.–5 P.M.
	Trails: dawn–dusk
FACILITIES	Rest room, drinking water, library, well-maintained trails, excellent gift shop
EVENTS	The Great Environmental Magic Show, February; North American Wildlife Art and Carving Show, May; the Lord Stirling 1770s Festival, October; Festival of Trees, December; plus changing exhibits and classes year round, in addition to archaeological digs; for schedule of events write Environmental Education Center, 190 Lord Stirling Road, Basking Ridge 07920

IF YOU "DIG" HISTORY, HAVE A LOVE FOR THE OUTDOORS, AND ENJOY HIKING ALONG flat, easy trails, you'll love the Environmental Education Center at Lord Stirling Park. Each year, on the third Sunday of October, the public is invited to attend the 1770s Festival—a living-history portrayal of courtyard activity and display of recovered artifacts on the site of William Alexander's (Lord Stirling's) former manor house, stables, and coach house.

Alexander loved his royal British title, although he had to leave New Jersey in 1756 to claim it. For unknown reasons his father had never bothered to apply for the title after an uncle, the Earl of Stirling, died childless.

Having successfully established his title under Scottish law, Alexander insisted on being called Lord Stirling despite the fact that the British House of Lords refused to acknowledge him. After building a manor house suitable for a man of his self-acclaimed importance, complete with outbuildings topped with cupolas and gilded weather vanes and a coat of arms displayed on his carriages, Alexander worked very hard. His reputation quickly grew, not only as surveyor general of New Jersey but as an officer in the revolutionary war. He bequeathed part of Island Beach to Columbia University (see chapter 36).

After living in grandeur, Alexander died penniless in 1783; supposedly, because he believed so completely in the war effort, he lost his money paying for arms and equipment to outfit the entire New Jersey militia. After his death, a succession of owners occupied the property, including a farmer who stored grain in the once elegant dining room and used the courtyard as a pig run. Eventually everything deteriorated, and in 1920 the remains of the manor house burned to the ground. Attempts to drain the swamp and lumbering activities in the area eventually made the land look totally different from the way it did during Alexander's time.

When a proposal to build a jetport arose in the 1950s, threatening to claim the land Alexander once owned, the Somerset County Park Commission purchased the property, creating an Environmental Education Center "to educate people about open space values and public land use management."

Visitors are welcome to hike the 8.5 miles of flat, easy, six-foot-wide trails traversing diverse areas, including marshes, swamps, a river, streams, springs, a floodplain, a natural pond, and a man-made pond. Wooden bridges and two miles of boardwalk allow access over high-water places, which form an important part of the physical makeup of the center.

According to Paul Becker, naturalist at the center, the extreme wetness of the area is "the result of its topography and impervious clay soil." He went on to explain that "the soil here represents bottom sediments laid down approximately fifteen thousand years ago in glacial Lake Passaic, formed when meltwater was trapped between the retreating Wisconsin Ice Sheet and the Watchung Mountains. The park is ideal for the study of wetlands and their value to humans, since water bodies form an important part of the physical makeup here. After heavy rains, the Great Swamp, which is within our boundaries, acts as a huge retention basin, which is slowly drained by the Passaic River."

Pick up a trail map inside the education center so you can plan your walk in advance. Observation blinds are situated on the western side of Branta Pond and on the southern edge of Lily Pad Pond, making it easy to study a few of the 188 species of birds that have been observed in Lord Stirling Park. Among them are the great blue heron, least bittern, wood duck, barred owl, alder flycatcher, bald eagle, bobwhite, great horned owl, ruby-throated hummingbird, tufted titmouse, and a variety of warblers.

If you don't feel like walking too far, take the 1,200-foot trail circling

Even when the ground is snow-covered, the boardwalks at Lord Stirling make walking delightful.

around the pond next to the education center; deer, meadow voles, and rabbits are often spotted here, while dozens of Canada geese create an almost deafening "honk-honk" conversation.

Oak, beech, and hickory are the dominant trees in the park, a delight on hot summer days when their limbs create a lush overhead canopy of shade. These trees provide food and cover for deer, chipmunks, gray squirrels, pheasants, raccoons, skunks, opossums, and fox.

Besides a marvelous array of wildflowers during spring, including lady's slipper, marsh marigold, trailing arbutus, trout lily, trillium, violet, wood anemone, and buttercups, this is the time of year that pickerel migrate from the Passaic River, heading upstream into the swamps and marshes where they spawn.

As you walk through the open areas, especially on a warm day, keep an eye open for any reptiles that may be basking in the sun. Of the six snakes known to live in the park, none is poisonous, although the northern water snake, identified by a dark blotched skin, has a nasty temper and will undoubtedly bite if handled. The northern brown snake, tan to reddish-brown with two rows of dark spots down its back, rarely exceeds 13 inches in length.

On the way back take a closer look at the education center. Completed with the aid of a Department of Energy contract, it operates on a simple solar system. Sunlight is captured by 135 solar collectors located on the roof and is then converted to heat and carried by a liquid through a piping system to a 4,000-gallon solar energy storage tank. The hot water stored in this insulated tank is then pumped through heating units into the building during cold weather to warm the rooms. Heat from the storage tanks is also used to provide domestic hot water, used right from the tap in the rest rooms.

Besides providing a toasty feeling after a day of hiking or cross-country skiing during winter months, the center's library is full of interesting nature books.

NOTES: Picnicking is not allowed. Restaurants are available at Basking Ridge, or pack a picnic lunch and enjoy it at Southard Park two miles away. There is a special trail for the blind and those confined to wheelchairs.

33. Edwin B. Forsythe National Wildlife Refuge

(also known as Brigantine National Wildlife Refuge)

LOCATION Atlantic County
Off Route 9 south, Oceanville 08231
(609) 652-1665

SEASON Spring, fall, and winter

HIGHLIGHTS Atlantic Flyway route, cordgrass and saltgrass tidal marsh, excellent photo opportunities of abundant wildlife

ADMISSION Fee per vehicle

HOURS Sunrise–sunset

FACILITIES Rest room, drinking water, viewing platforms, reporting station for birders, picnic area, partially handicapped accessible

EVENTS Bird migration during spring and fall; January and February, diving ducks, rough-leg hawks, short-eared owls, bluebirds, bald eagles, snowy owls; March 20–April 15, peak of northbound waterfowl migration; April 20–May 30, shorebirds and wading birds—glossy ibis peak about April 28, Canada geese hatching, usually feeding on dikes by May 20; first week in May, warblers best on bright, warm days; May and June, horseshoe crabs spawning, ruddy turnstone migration; about June 20, annual Canada Goose Roundup at sunrise; June 15–July 15, ducks hatching; August, shorebirds and warblers return, wading birds gather; September, ducks gathering in flocks, teal migration, terns and skimmers flocking at Holgate; October, Canada goose migration begins about the 8th and peaks about the 25th, brant arrive about the 19th and peak about the 25th; November 1–10, spectacular concentrations of ducks, geese, and brant, snow geese begin stopping; December, peak snow goose numbers around the 15th, ducks and geese moving south, bald eagles likely

THERE'S NO NEED TO TRAVEL TO CAPISTRANO TO SEE THE BIRDS—NOT WHEN Brigantine Division of the Edwin B. Forsythe National Wildlife Refuge is so readily available. Consisting of over 20,000 acres, this haven is perfect for bird watchers, photographers, and hikers, especially during peak migration periods.

A self-guiding tour through the refuge can be taken by auto, foot, or a combination of the two. By auto, plan about two hours or longer; the well-paved 8-mile trail is one way, with ample space to pull over anywhere en route to observe or take photographs. However, I've always preferred walking; it's a delightful way not only to appreciate the area but to get in some exercise at the same time.

If you're brave enough to dodge the mosquitoes during summer months, you'll be rewarded by the sight of hundreds of flowers. Wisteria vines are ablaze with purple flowers at the entrance, Japanese honeysuckle releases its sweet perfume, open fields shimmer with large yellow black-eyed Susans, and hundreds of butterflies flit from one flower to another.

After you've entered the refuge, head over to the Leeds Eco-Trail; its 0.5-mile walking trail (part is handicapped accessible) is a mini-introduction to the refuge. Raccoons, foxes, and opossums frequent this area, seeking out the persimmon's tasty orange fruit. If you get caught on a thorny branch, you've discovered the greenbriar, a favorite food of deer, grouse, catbirds, and a variety of songbirds.

Follow the boardwalk leading into the salt marsh, an area teeming with life. Here plants and animals are alternately bathed by saltwater flowing in from the sea, and fresh inland water drawn from the ebbing tide. Few plants can survive the continuously fluctuating salt concentrations and water levels found in a salt marsh, but the ones that can include salt marsh hay, which grows at higher elevations and is flooded only during extreme high tides; tall, stiff cordgrass, found along ditch banks; glasswort, which is commonly known as pickleweed; and spikegrass.

Farther along is a fine example of a changing boundary between different plant communities known as an ecotone. The line of marsh grasses changes to a border of shrubs and finally to trees. A wide variety of plants and trees exist in this ecotone, among them bayberry, sumac, red cedar, black cherry, sassafras, and pitch pine—all harboring sparrows, robins, mockingbirds, cedar waxwings, cottontail rabbits, and white-tailed deer, who avail themselves of the tasty berries.

The clapping noise usually heard in the distant marsh is the call of a clapper rail, a common bird of the salt marsh, who builds its nest in the taller cordgrass. Near the ditch you'll probably spot various herons, shore birds, and gulls. Atlantic City's skyline rises along the horizon.

Fiddler crabs make their home along the banks of the tidal creeks and on the mudflats. Males wave their enlarged claws in the air to attract mates, but it's like sending up a red flag to the clapper rail, who relishes and hunts the tasty fiddler.

Head to the main road to begin the 8-mile trail. To the left, at the West Pool, water control structures permit the outflow of fresh water and prevent saltwater on the bay side from entering. This 900-acre area attracts a wide variety of bird life. To the right there's a large salt marsh similar to the one along Leeds Eco-Trail.

Continue to the large observation tower, climb to the top, and enjoy Atlantic City's skyline on one side and the spectacular wildlife on the other. If you walk, you may find enormous quantities of Canada geese droppings on the trail. These majestic creatures—the symbol of national wildlife refuges—are almost always forgiven for their sloppy habits if seen and heard as they fly overhead. The surrounding water supports huge concentrations of ducks, geese, and brant in the fall. During winter the snow geese, resembling soft, white clouds on the water, arrive.

Shortly after the road passes the cross dike, reserved for nesting peregrine falcons, it turns toward the East Pool, a 700-acre prime nesting area of gadwalls, shovelers, and ruddy ducks. Conditions here are so favorable that over 3,000 ducklings are born annually.

At Perch Cove (stop 7), 16,000 acres of salt marsh and bays lure the American brant to stay over during winter. Over 60,000 have been seen here by mid-November; their late-afternoon watering flights are a sight to behold. That "quack, quack, quack" you may hear is the black duck's call; it's the most common puddle duck along the Atlantic Coast. During fall, over 70,000 of this species return to the refuge.

At stop 10, North Dike, the combination of salt marsh on the right and fresh on the left attracts ibis, egrets, herons, and many wading birds. The mute swan, one of the heaviest flying birds in the world—with adults often weighing up to 40 pounds—nests here, and an occasional whistling swan may be seen.

As you near stop 11, look at the trees atop the bluff to your right. Bald and golden eagles have been spotted here during winter; other birds of prey, such as osprey and the marsh hawk, may be seen over the ponds.

If you have enough energy left at the end of the trail, stretch your legs a bit more on the short nature walks where juniper, holly, and scrub pine tree dominate and where 200 bird species have been recorded. Bobwhites and ring-necked pheasants frequent the edge of the woods, while mourning doves, yellow-shafted flickers, downy woodpeckers, flycatchers, catbirds, mockingbirds, red-winged blackbirds, and the American goldfinch dart in and out of the trees.

A day spent taking in the sights and sounds within Brigantine makes it easy to forget about the blackjack tables and slot machines in nearby Atlantic City.

NOTES: Be on the lookout for poison ivy. This plant, found creeping along the ground or growing as a low shrub or hairy vine, is identified by its three leaves growing from one stem or, during the winter, by its white berries. Bring along binoculars or a telescope, a warm jacket and hat to ward off the stiff cross breezes, and a canteen if you walk the trail. Insect repellent is a must in summer. Pack a picnic lunch; restaurants are not in the immediate area. Allow some time to visit the Noyes Museum (see chapter 50), located outside the refuge entrance.

34. James A. McFaul Environmental Center

LOCATION	Bergen County Crescent Avenue (north of Route 208), Wyckoff 07481 (201) 891-5571
SEASON	Year round
HIGHLIGHTS	Woodland trail, outdoor shelters with native mammals and birds, exhibit hall with live native animals, saltwater and freshwater aquariums, natural history displays, herb garden, observatory overlooking a pond
ADMISSION	Free
HOURS	Center: 8:30 A.M.–4:45 P.M., closed Christmas and New Year's; hours seasonal, call in advance Trail: dawn–dusk
FACILITIES	Rest room, drinking water, handicapped-accessible boardwalk with observation deck, picnic tables, nature library, gift shop
EVENTS	Talks, slide shows, films, and walks Saturday, Sunday, and Tuesday 2 P.M.

RAIN OR SHINE, IN EVERY SEASON, THE AVIATION SHOW GOES ON INSIDE THE environmental center's observation area as birds land and take off from the feeders. The big blue jays noisily compete with smaller birds for seed, and it isn't uncommon to spot a finch, dark-eyed junco, black-capped chickadee, tufted titmouse, or white-breasted nuthatch waiting for its opportunity to grab a tasty morsel.

It's easy to spend an entire morning or afternoon here, especially if you allow time to walk the easy 0.6-mile meandering trail, use the handicapped-accessible 300-foot boardwalk with observation deck, and examine numerous informative exhibits located in the main building, where live turtles may be observed swimming and feeding in tanks. The musk turtle, nicknamed "stinkpot" because of the bad scent it emits if disturbed, is carnivorous, sports two light stripes on either side of its head, and carries a smooth olive-brown shell. The snapping turtle, identified by its large head, a small cross-shaped mark on the lower shell, a long tail, and a short temper, is housed in a nearby tank. This creature often eats birds, small mammals, and insects.

Two 600-gallon tanks enable visitors to peek at fish, crustaceans, and reptiles common to New Jersey's coastal saltwater habitat. These animals include blackfish, sea robin, flounder, dogfish shark, starfish, and crab, while those representative of freshwater ponds and lakes include perch, pickerel, largemouth bass, catfish, sunfish, and turtles.

In addition to a natural history display and a rotating art exhibit, the bird identification game is particularly appealing to children. By placing the tip of one wire onto a bird pictured on a board and the other end of the wire onto its description, the bird's eyes light up if the picture and the description match up. It's an effortless way to learn bird identification or to check what you saw on the trail. Don't miss the live frog and toad exhibits or the huge, fuzzy tarantula sitting all alone in a tank.

The center's library, full of informative nature books and a small local mineral display, is a good place to browse or look up any questions concerning trees, birds, or flowers. A trained naturalist is usually on duty.

Walking toward the trailhead, you'll pass an outdoor shelter housing a skunk, fox, and other native animals. Although the cages are poorly lighted, the exhibit enables a close-up view at these elusive specimens. The trail traverses various habitats including an upland forest, streams, and a swamp that's reachable by crossing a footbridge over the brook just outside the center. This area, often frequented by raccoons and birds, is a good place to watch crayfish moving lazily along the bottom of the water searching for a meal. An old American sycamore, recognized by its colorful, patchy, rich brown and creamy white bark, stands along the stream. The sycamore, one of the largest of our native broad-leaved trees, often reaches a height of over 150 feet.

Walking slightly uphill, you'll come to the upland forest, which, because of dry ground, hosts trees such as the white oak, identified by round-lobed leaves and a shaggy light-gray bark; the yellow birch, with a yellowish bark; the black birch, source of oil of wintergreen; and the gray birch, with its lightly colored bark and triangular black markings below the branch junctions.

New Jersey's official tree, the red oak, can be seen at stop 4. There's a bit of controversy on how this, the tallest of our native oaks, was named. Some say it's because of the reddish tinge as the leaves unfold during spring; others believe it's due to the bright red leaf color in the fall.

Another remarkable specimen found a bit farther along the trail is the tulip tree. Standing straight, with a trunk shaped like a Greek column, it produces a beautiful six-petal flower crossed by a bright orange band with yellow borders in May and June. By winter its conical clusters of winged

The pond at the McFaul Environmental Center is a good place to spot an assortment of waterfowl and spend some quiet moments.

seeds, or samaras, hold on tight at the branch tips—an invitation to small mammals and birds who delight in these delicious tidbits. The light wood from this tree, which is also known as a yellow poplar, is used for the manufacture of crates, boxes, and cabinets.

Even on a sunny day you'll feel quite cool in the upland area thanks to the dense canopy provided by this thick stand of trees. Although little sunlight reaches the forest floor, certain plants, such as evergreen laurel, mosses, and the partridgeberry, thrive under these conditions. So do the deer, raccoons, and chipmunks—thanks to the nuts provided by the American beech (stop 6) and the bountiful berry feast from the viburnum (stop 7).

Spend a few minutes at the swampy area near the next footbridge. Few trees grow in this area because of the wet conditions almost year round, but amphibians and insects find it a prime breeding site. The metamorphic rock found here originated as clay deposited by a river or stream and forced deeper into the earth's crust. An upwelling of molten magma eventually heated the mass, turning it into rock.

Lush ferns reach elegantly up to the sky as they sway in the slightest breeze, and if you're here during fall, you'll probably spot birds around the spicebush gathering its red berries. This pretty bush is named for the spicy fragrance it gives off in the spring.

Continue walking slightly uphill again until you come to an opening in the forest canopy. Wild azalea burst into color in early spring here, and during summer months whorled loosestrife and blue-eyed grass edge the path. The low-bush blueberries growing in this area provide a good snack— but make certain you know for sure that's what they are. Never eat anything you can't identify.

Dominating the scene is witch hazel, an underbrush shrub, the same plant used in the manufacture of the soothing witch-hazel lotion sold in drugstores. During the fall, its flower consists of four twisting linear petals resembling tiny yellow ribbons about three-quarters of an inch in length. Its fruits are nutlets contained in blunt, tiny half-inch capsules that take until the following fall to ripen; at that time they contract and "explode" by flinging the tiny nutlets to the ground a distance away.

Flowering dogwood, found at stop 10, bloom in late spring; migrating songbirds flock to it for its luscious red berries. To the left of the trail are pitch pine, identified by their deeply furrowed, reddish-brown bark; squirrels and birds love the seed it sheds in winter.

Soon you'll come to a mixed oak and hardwood forest, home to those seedlings that are sturdy enough to exist among thick layers of decay. One of these tough trees is the ironwood, also known as hornbeam or blue beech. It's recognizable year round by the smooth, tight bark of wavy and twisting blue and gray bands. Supposedly it was named "ironwood" because it's so hard that axes bounce off it. Also found in this area are the pin oak, a producer of tiny acorns enjoyed by resident wood ducks, and the chestnut oak, treasured by the leather industry for tannin contained in its bark.

Leaving the dry forest, go downhill, following the trail into another swampy section consisting of tall ferns and water-loving trees. The cinnamon fern's fronds rise in clusters, visible even in winter months; during spring its cinnamon-colored fronds shed their spores. Stop 19 sports one of the two shrubs native to this wet region, the coast pepperbush. Blooming in July and August with clusters of bell-shaped flowers arranged in spikes, its fragrant flowers attract bees and wasps. The other native shrub is the spicebush seen earlier.

The swampy section is a fascinating area to explore, especially if you've brought along a magnifying glass. As the logs rot in the wet soil, fungi, ants, lichen, and bacteria attack the wood, feed on the stumps, and make them their home. Woodpeckers and skunks break the logs down even more by digging around to trap the insects.

About 10 feet behind the post at stop 22 is an old stone wall erected long ago by a farmer to mark his property boundary and to prevent his cows from wandering off. Many of the stones have fallen down over the years due to freezing, thawing, and erosion, but what's left is still put to good use by shrews, mice, and chipmunks for shelter from snow, wind, and rain.

The shagbark hickory is unmistakable, for the bark appears to peel away from the trunk at the edges, particularly near the lower end. Hickory lumber, noted for its toughness, was used to make wheel spokes when wagons were the common carriers of goods and passengers in this country. It also is used as firewood in the production of hickory-smoked meats.

If you're here during early spring, one of the first plants you'll see and perhaps smell is the skunk cabbage (stop 24). Their flower hoods begin pushing up through the frozen ground in mid-February, and although it looks beautiful in full bloom as it sits in swampy soil, it smells horrible if the plant is broken.

There's a good chance that you'll hear the metallic click-click sound the cardinal makes if you're standing near stop 26. The wild grape, clinging to trunks and branches of trees with the aid of tendrils, is one of this bird's favorite foods. Mourning doves, grackles, and squirrels love it too.

At the end of the trail is a large enclosure, home to the white-tailed deer. Everyone usually lingers here admiring this graceful animal common in dry and wet woodlands. When threatened, it lifts its tail, showing the white patch for which it is named.

The pond is a good place to rest and watch a large variety of wildlife. Snow geese pause here on their way to winter in the Carolinas. The flock looks like fallen snow and is a sight to behold. During summer months and into late fall, the pond is alive with aquatic plants bursting into bloom, baby ducks paddling behind their mothers, and turtles sunning on rocks. Bring binoculars, sit on one of the benches around the pond, and relax.

The mute swan, with its orange bill and S-curved neck, is another frequent visitor here, as are Canada geese and one of the most beautifully colored ducks in America, the wood duck. The pond can be quiet one minute and almost deafening the next as the geese, deciding to fly away in a V-formation aerial act, let out a honking roar.

See the Herb Garden before leaving; it contains plants native to North America as well as those of Asian and European descent. Whether used for culinary, aromatic, or medicinal purposes, herbs are always enjoyable to see and smell. A few grown here include bee balm, used for flavoring wine, fruit cups, salads, jellies, and teas; feverfew, used for colic, indigestion, gas, and colds; lamb's ears, primarily enjoyed as a decorative border; lavender for sachets and perfumes as well as insect repellents; and various mints used as a tonic for ailments and for their oil in medicine and confectionery.

After walking the trail and viewing a film or slide show, you'll no doubt begin planning a return trip to the McFaul Wildlife Center in the near future.

NOTES: Sneakers are fine. Bring along a picnic lunch to eat at the picnic area or by the pond, or try one of the fast-food restaurants in town.

35. Turkey Swamp Park

LOCATION Monmouth County
Georgia Road (off Route 524 west), Freehold 07728
(732) 462-7286

SEASON Year round for trails; campground closes December 1–end February

HIGHLIGHTS Trails, guided nature walks, campground, boating

ADMISSION Free except for campsites

HOURS 8 A.M.–dusk

FACILITIES Softball and football fields; archery range; playgrounds; fitness trails; ice-skating, call in advance; family and wilderness campground, refreshment machines, fishing, boating, picnic areas; rest room

EVENTS Turkey Swamp Park Day, mid-October; special children's events; arts and crafts sale

NATURE LOVERS AND CAMPERS USUALLY ENJOY TURKEY SWAMP PARK, WHICH FOR MY family will always remain quite special. We experienced camping for the first time in this park, and despite a rainy weekend, we had fun playing games, reading, and taking short wet walks. When we returned to our dry camper, we figured that if we could enjoy ourselves during such miserable weather, it had to be the park that helped make it so exciting.

Located on the northern fringe of the Pine Barrens, the park takes its name from the town of Turkey, now known as Adelphia. According to a Monmouth County Park brochure, this area is unique, for "although the soil is very sandy, the water table lies just beneath the surface, giving rise to swampy conditions whenever the surface topography dips to the water line; [hence] the 'swamp' in the name Turkey Swamp."

Whether you camp overnight or come for a day, plan on hiking one of the short nature trails within the park. The terrain is nearly flat and the geologic formations are composed of sands and clays. There is a habitat of scrub oak, young white oaks, and a thick understory of pepperbush, huckleberries, and blueberries. Tall pitch pines are slowly springing up on the fringes of the forest, while white aspen and sweet gum also exist in thick stands.

The orange-blazed trail, following along a small lake for 1 mile, is a

The well-marked trails at Turkey Swamp Park provide peace and quiet for the hiker or casual walker.

good place to hook panfish and bullheads. The red-blazed trail, 1.75 miles long, leads out to the woodsy Wilderness Camping Area. The green-blazed 1-mile trail borders the red-blazed trail and leads to the lakefront area. The 0.5-mile blue-blazed trail guides hikers to the boathouse, where in season canoes, paddleboats, and rowboats may be rented.

Large quantities of sphagnum moss grow in the bog areas. This plant, capable of holding 10 times its own weight in water, spreads so rapidly that it is dense enough for an adult to walk across! Acting like a huge waterbed, the sphagnum moss will "quake" under the weight of a human. Bring a magnifying glass and search for tiny sundews and pitcher plants in this area. If you're patient, you may see an unsuspecting insect fly into the tiny hairs of the sundew or fall into the pitcher plant's well and struggle to get free. However, the insects usually fight a losing battle because, between the plants' hairs and their sticky liquid, it's almost impossible to escape.

Joe-pye weed, a beautiful wine-colored wildflower, blooms during the early days of fall. Growing to a height of four to eight feet, it stands straight showing off its leaves that grow in circles around the stem resembling the spokes of a wheel. It's said that the flower was named for Joe-Pye, an Indian medicine man who helped many early colonists of Massachusetts cure their diseases, including typhus, with the aid of this plant. Supposedly, Mithridates Eurator, a Persian general, used this plant as a magical medicine in important battles against the Romans. The Indians are also reported to have had success with it: Braves courting young women were assured of a favorable response if they stuck a wad of the plant in their mouths before their dates. And the plant was also reported to improve kidney disorders.

Besides the rare and delicate pink lady's slipper, you may see the evening primrose make an appearance. Only one flower blooms each night, but if you return the next day, you'll see another one opening farther down the spike. If you didn't take binoculars to bird watch, rest against a tree and listen to the music of the forest. Early mornings or late afternoons are good times to catch a glimpse of the birds as they fly in and out of the trees, creating a mass of color against the sky. Yellow warblers, rose-breasted grosbeaks, scarlet tanagers, and dark-eyed juncos are only a few of the birds you may observe here.

NOTES: Camping is on a first-come, first-served basis for 32 of the sites. Reservations are accepted for the remaining 32 sites for a minimum two-night stay if prepaid at least two weeks prior to the camping date. All campsites are pull-through with water and electric hookups. For day trips pack a picnic lunch; tables and grills are available. Soda and candy machines are in the main building. If you prefer, restaurants and fast-food places abound on Route 9.

36. Island Beach State Park

LOCATION	Ocean County
	Route 35, southeast of Toms River, Island Beach
	State Park, Seaside Park 08752
	(732) 793-0506
SEASON	Year round
HIGHLIGHTS	Swimming, sunbathing, surf fishing, scuba diving, crabbing, nature trails, bird watching, nature tours by park naturalists, nature museum, interpretive center
ADMISSION	Fee for parking except Tuesday
HOURS	8 A.M.–8 P.M. except for fishermen with permits
FACILITIES	Bathhouse, rest room, barrier-free access to the beach, snack bars Memorial Day–Labor Day
EVENTS	Bird banding in season, nature tours; contact park office for schedule, P.O. Box 37, Seaside Park 08752

WHATEVER YOUR PASSION—WHETHER SUNBATHING, SWIMMING, SURF FISHING, strolling, scuba diving, hiking, or simply listening to the surf—you'll be able to enjoy it at Island Beach State Park. And if you like bird watching, this is definitely the place for binoculars and an identification book.

One of the few natural barrier beaches remaining on the Atlantic Coast, Island Beach State Park is a 10-mile white sand strip boasting one of the largest osprey colonies in the state. Over 240 different birds have been sighted here, including the peregrine falcon, brown pelican, and blue heron. Several endangered species also visit, including the piping plover, least tern, and black skimmer.

The sand-colored piping plover, identified by a distinctive black-tipped orange bill and orange legs, arrives in mid-March and lays eggs from late April to mid-June. New chicks stay along the beach through mid-July. The crow-sized black skimmers nest on the sand in late April, laying eggs from early May to late July. With a black upper side, white breast and belly, and a long, red bill tipped with black, they're easy to spot. The least tern is a robin-sized bird with black cap, black line around the eye, and bright yellow bill. This visitor usually arrives by mid-May and continues to lay eggs through mid-June.

Even if you're not a bird watcher, there is plenty to do inside the Aeolium, the interpretive nature center named after the Greek god of the wind. Here you can learn about the fauna and flora of a barrier island. Located 1.5 miles from the entrance gate, the center houses numerous hands-on exhibits, offers interesting slide presentations on topics related to Island Beach, and is the starting point for naturalist-conducted tours during summer months. An easy nature trail located behind the building meanders ⅛ mile through dunes and marshland. Signs describing the vegetation and dune formations are posted, but use extreme caution—poison ivy thrives here as it does in the rest of the park.

According to park officials the 3,002 acres of Island Beach were "once part of an island created in 1750 when the sea opened an inlet between the ocean and Barnegat Bay near the northern end of the park area." Then known as Cranberry Inlet, it was an important shipping area in Barnegat Bay and was used by the New Jersey Privateers, a group sanctioned by the government to raid British ships.

Many pirates used ingenious methods to lure vessels ashore, such as the use of false lights that simulated a ship at sail or at anchor, or flashing false signals from a lighthouse. Another successful ploy was to tie a lantern onto an animal's back. Then, as someone led the animal along the dunes parallel to the coast, the light would appear to be another vessel to an unsuspecting captain, who would then turn his vessel toward the light. When the vessel ran aground it fell prey to the waiting pirates.

Island Beach was known as Lord Stirling's Isle when it was owned by William Alexander, Lord Stirling in the 1700s. Born in New York, Stirling went to England at the age of 30 to claim his title. After he returned, he served on the New Jersey Provincial Council, fought in the battles of Trenton, Princeton, Brandywine, Germantown, and Monmouth, and served on the Board of Governors of King's College in New York, now Columbia University. Subsequently he bequeathed a portion of Island Beach to the college (see chapter 32).

Except for a few Indians and whalers, the land remained uninhabited after Alexander's death in 1783. Little is known about this period except that a combination of storms and the raging sea closed Cranberry Inlet in 1812, and two farms existed that were owned by the Haring and Phillips families. Each raised livestock and farmed cranberries in the boggy areas on the island.

Haring opened a 20-room hotel in 1815, and its huge dance floor attracted numerous hunters and fishermen. Fifty years later, it's believed that this structure was rebuilt and named the Reed Hotel, which remained standing until the early 20th century. Since shipment of food to the island was expensive, the hotel grew its own produce.

When the Lifesaving Service was established to provide onshore aid to

Sunbathing isn't the only thing to do at Island Beach State Park!

distressed ships, Phillips sold some of his land so that a lifesaving station could be erected. One of these stations is now used as a park maintenance building, while another houses a park ranger.

Once lifesaving stations were erected, speculators tried to attract people to the area. Cottage City was promoted as a dream resort in the 1890s. Its advertising brochure promised 25-by-100-foot lots, the lifesaving stations, and Reed's Hotel, all within reach of Seaside Park's railroad station. However, historians haven't been able to verify whether or not these cottages were ever built.

Around 1910, squatters, attracted by a new "seaweed" industry, erected shacks along the shore and began collecting eel grass. During summer months this grass was gathered by boat from Barnegat Bay to the south, and in fall and winter the men raked what had washed ashore. The eel grass was then hung on racks to dry, picked clean of clinging crabs and shrimp, and air-dried to remove moisture and odor. This was bailed and shipped by railroad freight to the mainland and used as insulation, mattress stuffing, and as upholstery stuffing in the Model T Ford. However, this new endeavor came to a halt when disease wiped out the supply of eel grass. Today the grass is flourishing once again along the shoreline.

Henry Phipps purchased Island Beach in 1926 and—thinking the area had a future as a beach resort for the upper class—built three homes. The Crash of 1929 ended his plans for further construction, and when Phipps died a few months later, Francis Freeman took over management of the estate. Freeman had different ideas. One included preserving the natural beauty of Island Beach. According to a history of Island Beach State Park written by park officials, to enforce his beliefs Freeman allowed only certain visitors to enter, provided they follow his rules of "no berry picking, dune destruction, littering, and reckless plundering of natural resources." He also leased the area to onetime squatters in return for an annual fee to the Phipps estate and allowed a few day visitors to hunt, fish, and stroll on the island.

When the War Department took over the island in the 1940s and declared it a restricted area, everyone was forced to leave. The army and Johns Hopkins University worked here on antiaircraft rocketry, successfully launching a supersonic ram-jet rocket in 1945 that traveled over nine miles at 1.5 times the speed of sound.

In 1953 the state and various fishermen's groups raised $2,750,000 to purchase the property from the Phipps estate, ensuring that the natural beauty of Island Beach would be preserved and used by thousands of visitors.

Today the park looks essentially as it did during the 1700s, despite the fact that over 350,000 visitors use it each year. Now divided into three areas, the park consists of a botanical preserve extending from the entrance gate south for 3 miles to the ocean bathing section, where excellent specimens of rare seacoast vegetation may be seen; a 3.5-mile recreation area, including a 1-mile guarded bathing beach where visitors can swim, surf, picnic, sunbathe, and surf fish; and an inlet area, extending for 5 miles from parking area A-13 to Barnegat Inlet.

The inlet area, reserved as a wildlife sanctuary, is open to visitors for surf fishing, swimming, picnicking, beach strolling, and scuba diving. Fishermen usually have their own favorite spots along the inlet rocks or the shoreline, and the park is well known for an abundance of striped bass and bluefish. Summer flounder, weakfish, and kingfish are also caught, as well as winter flounder in the Barnegat Inlet. Four-wheel-drive vehicle owners can apply for a "beach buggy" permit to drive along certain sections of the beach but only for the purpose of fishing.

Winter is a particularly peaceful season to visit and a good time to treasure hunt. Starfish can often be found on the beach, as well as egg cases from long skates and purple sea urchins, and at low tide thousands of barnacles can be seen clinging to the rocks. If you dig into the sand at the water's edge, you may find sand crabs. Horseshoe crabs are all over the beach in late spring, when they arrive to lay eggs in the shallow water. Blue crabs, highly prized by the shellfish industry, can be found in surrounding bays and estuaries.

Drive to the southern end of the island and walk the rest of the way along the water's edge for a view of Barnegat Lighthouse, built in 1858. Geologists feel Barnegat Bay will eventually become part of the mainland as sand dunes are repositioned. It's odd to think that these barrier islands are temporary!

As you stand at the ocean's edge, you'll feel the salt spray from the waves breaking onshore. As the saltwater hits the atmosphere and rises, the water evaporates, leaving the salt to crystallize as it lands on nearby grasses and plants. The plants are wedge-shaped from years of salt spray eating away at their tops.

The first six inches of sand in this area are bone dry, supporting only those plants that can tolerate these conditions. The dune grass, approximately 60–100 years old, stabilizes the dunes and sports pretty yellow flowers in the spring. You'll also find black cherry in this dry area and the attractive prickly pear cactus, which produces a huge edible fruit that turns bright red when ripe.

Annuals abound at the upper beach and include the sea rocket and seaside goldenrod, while the secondary dunes support lush American holly, red cedar, and magnolia. Rose hips rich in vitamin C, trumpet vine, and beach plum are also found here.

Try beachcombing for jingle shells, mussels, oysters, slipper shells, whelks, or the quahog, which was used by the American Indians as wampum and to create beads. According to *New Jersey Coastwalks* (American Littoral Society, 1981), the Indians, "using stone tools, drilled cylindrical beads out of the purple portion of the shell. By making patterns of these purple and white beads made from whelk, the Indians wove messages into belts which could be sent to neighboring tribes to inform them of a meeting, to declare war, or to announce a marriage."

No matter which season you decide to visit, you'll find lots to do on this barrier beach.

NOTES: Inner tubes, rafts, and other flotation devices are not permitted in the designated bathing area. Surfing on surfboards is limited to Ocean Bathing Unit 2, while scuba diving and underwater fishing are permitted along 2.5 miles of ocean beach north of the Barnegat Inlet. Scuba divers must register at the park office prior to their first dive each year and bring along certification proof. Six miles of open ocean beach in the southern and central portions of the park are available from October to April 30, and while rentals are not available, there is ample space for horse trailers. For further information on fishing permits, the interpretive programs, and the park, write or call Island Beach State Park, P.O. Box 37, Seaside Park 08752, (732) 793-0506.

37. Cheesequake State Park

LOCATION   Middlesex County
Off Route 34 or the Garden State Parkway via Exit 120; turn right on Laurence Parkway, turn right on Cliffwood Avenue to the T; turn right on Gordon Road to the park entrance in Matawan 07747
(732) 566-2161

SEASON   Year round

HIGHLIGHTS   Nature trails, nature center, open fields, salt- and freshwater marshes, white cedar swamp, hardwood forest, swimming, picnicking, camping, fishing, crabbing, basketball courts, cross-country skiing, bird watching

ADMISSION   Fee Memorial Day–Labor Day except Tuesdays and for campground

HOURS   Daily 8 A.M.–5:30 P.M.; 8–8 in summer

FACILITIES   Nature center, rest room, drinking water, picnic groves, campground, basketball courts, softball field

ALTHOUGH CHEESEQUAKE STATE PARK, LOCATED WITHIN 30 MILES OF NEW YORK City, is Middlesex County's only state park, few people realize how much it has to offer.

Cheesequake, which lies in the midst of urban sprawl between New Jersey's northern and southern sections, offers a variety of plant and animal life found nowhere else in the state. On these 1,300 acres bordered by Cheesequake Creek—an estuary of Raritan Bay—you can explore open fields, salt- and freshwater marshes, a white cedar swamp, a pine barrens area, and a hardwood forest.

No one knows for certain where the name "Cheesequake" came from. Park officials believe it may have been a corruption of "Chichequaas," an Indian word meaning an upland village. Also, because Cheesequake is thought to lie on a fault and has had earthquake movement in the past, with the most recent in 1979, some say the earth trembles like cheese! Others feel Cheesequake got its name because the marshes resemble quaking bogs. The

Skunk cabbage, one of the first plants to make its appearance in spring, can be seen along the wet areas on the trails within Cheesequake State Park.

park nature center houses a small display of Lenape Indian artifacts found on the grounds, dating their occupation of the land back 5,000 years ago.

One of the best ways to gain an appreciation for the wealth of flora and fauna here is to hike through the park along three easy trails, which take from 30 to 90 minutes each to complete, the longest being the 3.5-mile Green Trail. Sneakers are fine for the slightly hilly terrain. After driving in, ask for a map as well as a bird checklist. Over 186 species of birds have been sighted here.

Just past the entrance is a parking area on your left where the trails begin. The Yellow Trail, circling Hooks Creek Lake, takes approximately 40 minutes. It offers close views of swamp azalea, mountain laurel, trailing arbutus, and one of the largest displays of the rare pink lady's slippers in the state. This delicate member of the orchid family stands about a foot high, has two leaves at its base, and produces a lovely shoe-shaped pink flower from mid-May to early June.

The odoriferous skunk cabbage, one of the first plants to push up through the snow, is abundant in the wet areas. When examined closely, it can be forgiven for its disagreeable smell because of the fascinating "spathe" or hood it produces beneath its wide leaves in early spring. After discovering this plant in a swamp near his Concord home, Henry David Thoreau wrote, "They see over the brow of Winter's hill. They see another Summer ahead."

The Red Trail meanders around glens and upland in a 30-minute loop traversing dry, sandy sections resembling the Pine Barrens region of southern New Jersey. Pitch pine, named for the sticky pitch oozing out of its buds and branches, grows in profusion. The towering black gums are a delight in September when their leaves turn bright scarlet. If you're here in April, check the ground for trailing arbutus, prized for its fragrance and clusters of tiny five-lobed pinkish flowers.

According to park naturalist Robert F. Sommers, "Early settlers founded the small village of Cheesequake on the bluffs so that the citizens could avoid the tormenting marsh insects. Two graveyards on Route 34, the Methodist and the Baptist cemeteries, mark the location of the early settlement. In the Baptist graveyard, ancient headstones predate the American Revolution. Nearby are also the remains of long-gone pottery industries dating back to the eighteenth and nineteenth centuries. Some of the finest clay in the world was mined at sites around the headwaters of the creeks. This fine-quality clay was used for making stoneware and was shipped to points on the Atlantic coast from Maine to Texas."

At the upper reach of Cheesequake Creek are the remains of pilings from the famous Steam Boat Landing. From the 1800s to 1930, farmers journeyed here during high tide, carrying their crops in flat-bottom boats. Larger boats would then transfer the produce across Raritan Bay to New York City. When the railroad came, however, the boats and the landing were abandoned.

As you walk back on the same sand road you came on, watch for the Green Trail. This stimulating 3.5-mile trail has a series of boardwalks going through a marsh and swamp. Atlantic white cedar rise above the swamp area, which supports an undergrowth of highland blueberry, swamp azalea, and sweetbay magnolia. Because the soil is so acidic, the decay rate is slow, causing fallen cedar logs to remain intact for a very long time. This is also an excellent place to spot owls.

You'll see the remains of white oak stands that were destroyed by gypsy moths. Gypsy moths were brought from Europe to Massachusetts in 1869 to breed a hardier silk moth; the experiment failed, but the gypsy moths unfortunately live on.

The oaks are rapidly being replaced by sassafras, a pretty shrub distinguished by green twigs and mitten-shaped leaves. In the 1500s sassafras was widely used as a medicinal herb; today its oil is used as a flavoring for certain medications and in soft drinks, confections, and tea. When the plant is crushed or bruised, the oil is released, producing the unmistakable fragrance of root beer.

Hawks and owls frequent the stand of white pine in the natural area of the park's southwestern sections; these trees are estimated to be between 100 and 150 years old. Important in American history, the white pine was in demand by the British Crown as early as 1691. The tallest and straightest trees were marked with a broad arrow, the royal navy's symbol, for use as masts. When the American Revolution began, their supply of trees was cut off and the ships were irreplaceable if their masts were broken. After the Revolution, white pine was still in demand for building houses.

When you're ready for a swim, try Hooks Creek Lake. Another interesting walk in this area follows the lake path to Hooks Creek Trail. Spend some time peering into the water beneath the boardwalk, and you'll be rewarded by the sight of fiddler crabs scurrying about. Up ahead, you'll come to a "quaking bog," which took thousands of years to form.

NOTES: Bring along binoculars; opossums, muskrats, marsh hawks, herons, and other specimens usually make an appearance. A picnic lunch is a good idea; there are tables and benches throughout the park. During summer months a snack bar is open at the lake. If you prefer, there are many restaurants outside the park along Route 34. The campground has a bathhouse and rest room; hot showers are available year round. Water is supplied in front of the bathhouse, but the sites do not have water or electricity.

38. Washington Crossing State Park

LOCATION	Mercer County
	Route 546, Titusville 08560
	(856) 727-0609
SEASON	Year round
HIGHLIGHTS	Nature museum, easy trails, woods, and fields
ADMISSION	Free, except for parking weekends and holidays and from Memorial Day to Labor Day
HOURS	Wednesday–Sunday 9 A.M.–4 P.M.
FACILITIES	Museum, gift shop, trails, rest room, drinking water
EVENTS	Family nature walks, hands-on nature program for preschoolers, crafts projects, walking tours during summer months; call for schedule

WASHINGTON CROSSING STATE PARK'S NATURE CENTER IS A GREAT PLACE TO LEARN all kinds of obscure facts. For example, did you know that in Madagascar textile silk is drawn out of the living spider's body and then woven into cloth? Or that in the United States the spider's silk provides the cross hairs for telescopes?

The center also presents interesting facts about common insects and animals found within the park's 807 acres. All the exhibits are educational and entertaining, but the rock section is especially interesting. One rock "rings" when hit with a hammer while others can be "sniffed" or "floated" on water. Accompanying signs describe why the rocks react the way they do.

If you like guessing games, try your skill at matching skull bones to their living species. Samples include skulls of a coyote and various rodents. Once you examine the rodent's skull and feel its two upper and two lower teeth, you'll gain an appreciation for its ability to gnaw through the toughest materials.

Live turtles swim lazily in tanks, and if you are around during their feeding times, you can watch them gulp down insects, crayfish, and other turtle treats.

When you're finished browsing inside, you may wish to stretch your legs on one of the many easy trails, located nearby, which range from 0.2 to 1.1 miles. Several can be combined to make a longer walk, while all have well-

A couple of nature lovers stop to enjoy the sights along one of the easy trails in Washington Crossing State Park.

marked loops. Sneakers will sustain you over this fairly level terrain.

The Sensory Trail, used mostly for educational presentations, is only 0.2 mile but is perfect for a quick walk. Reach out and touch the staghorn sumac's velvet twigs, or relax while listening to the different bird calls. While you hike along any one of the park's trails, you may observe the interesting resident critters, such as white-footed mice, cottontail rabbits, white-tailed deer, red and gray foxes, raccoons, chipmunks, woodchucks, moles, and opossums. A variety of birds are often found eating or playing within sight, but the squirrels can always be counted on for a super show. Watch them use their tails as rudders and parachutes when jumping over branches; sooner or later they misjudge and fall, but up they'll go again and again. No wonder these active creatures can consume more than 100 pounds of food a year!

While exploring, you can learn what constitutes a "natural community." The wide lawn outside the museum is not an example of "natural" secession because regular mowing has cut back wildflowers that would otherwise normally grow here. There are other ways to hold back the normal process of succession; the American Indians used burning, while plowing and clear-cutting were popular with immigrant farmers.

The natural areas you now see were once used for farming, but grasses and shrubs have been allowed to replace the cornfield since the 1940s. Look closely for a grass called "broomsedge." Colored bright red in the fall, this type of grass was popular for making brooms. Lespedeza, a bush clover, and daisy fleabane also grow here.

Farther along on the trails you'll see the eastern red cedar, one of the first trees to appear on abandoned fields. Browsing deer have cut down many of the trees and cardinals have stripped the bark for nests. If you're here just before sunset, there's a good chance of spotting deer grazing in the fields. A bit farther along deciduous trees and flowering dogwoods come into view, as well as the sassafras, white ash, and shagbark hickory.

By taking the Red Trail to the Yellow loop and walking across the stream, you'll come to a peaceful area where frogs and turtles often hang out. Continue onto the White Trail, which loops around again to the Red Trail, and turn left after the Blue Trail turns off into a delightful shaded area. Along the trail are many rock outcrops consisting of red shale, which is so impermeable to water that the excess runs off, eroding the land, breaking off the fragile rock, or remaining to create marshy areas.

Spring, when many wildflowers are in bloom, is a particularly beautiful time in these woods. The blunt-leafed hepatica, once believed to cure liver problems, is the earliest of woodland flowers to burst open. In colonial times farmers knew that when the hepatica was in bloom they'd soon begin planting again. The attractive umbrella-shaped leaves blanketing the forest floor are mayapples, named because it flowers in May. It is also known as the wild mandrake, hog apple, wild lemon, umbrella leaf, and raccoon berry, and its root is poisonous, although the Indians used the boiled root as a laxative. At one time the plant was used to treat warts, and today it's used as a cathartic and in cancer experiments. If you're superstitious, be wary of moving the mayapple: According to mountain lore, any female who pulls up the root will become pregnant! You'll also see lots of sensitive ferns, named because of the speed with which they collapse as soon as frost appears; smooth sumac, identified by its smooth branches; and the black willow, with tapered leaves that move in the slightest breeze.

On the way back to the parking lot watch for earthworms wiggling their way across the path or working the soil loose. Stop a minute to admire their handiwork. The surrounding woods are lush because these worms have been doing what they do best: fertilizing the soil. Their sole job is to eat the dirt, digest its nutrients, and cast it off, thereby creating fertilizer, while their tunnels allow air to penetrate into the soil. It's estimated that 3 million worms are under a single acre of grassland! If you spot any, bend down and watch how they stretch and shorten their segmented bodies in order to move. In *The Backyard Bestiary* (Knopf, New York, 1982), Ton de Joode and Anthonie Stolk note that "the worm's contractions are independent of its central nervous system, so even if those nerves are severed, the segments continue their contractions." And the authors maintain, although many people have cast doubt on their theory, that earthworms, like magic, "can regenerate lost parts, and even a head can be created anew. If a worm is cut in half it does not die, but grows into two new worms."

No matter when you visit Washington Crossing, there's something special to see or learn.

NOTES: Bring a picnic lunch to enjoy outside the museum, along the river just down the road from the center, or try one of the nearby restaurants along Route 29.

39. Herrontown Woods

LOCATION	Mercer County
	Snowden Lane (off Route 206), Princeton 08540
	(609) 989-6532
SEASON	Year round
HIGHLIGHTS	Woodland, birds, brook
ADMISSION	Free
HOURS	Sunrise–sunset
FACILITIES	None

ONE OF THE STATE'S BEST KEPT SECRETS IS HERRONTOWN WOODS. THIS SHORT, EASY trail, located in the heart of Princeton, is a perfect way to spend about two hours walking, bird watching, or discovering wildflowers.

In spring huge stands of mountain laurel burst open with a show of color that's dazzling. It's fun to identify the multitude of wildflowers that thrive on the forest floor into late summer. Jack-in-the-pulpit is one that's easy to spot. Bring a magnifying glass or telescopic lens to inspect its flower-bearing stalk (known as the "Reverend Jack silently preaching") within its protective hood (which forms the "pulpit"). The pulpit is usually heavily striped, and during summer clusters of red berries appear on the tops of these fleshy stalks, replacing the Reverend Jack.

Another summer favorite is the blue violet, so beautiful that poets have written about it through the centuries. In the wetter areas you may come across the swamp or marsh buttercup, a delicate five-petaled shining yellow "cup" flower normally in bloom April through July. There are dozens more to be found here if you take your time to search them out.

The trail begins at the parking lot behind the trail map. Take the red-blazed trail to the right, walking toward the log cabin. Don't mind the steel fence on your right; although it detracts from the surroundings, you'll pass it in a few minutes. When it ends, go right, and continue on the red-blazed trail until you enter an open area with an old barn and farmhouse. There's a bronze plaque on a rock in this area, thanking Professor and Ms. Oswald Beblen for their gift of land. The woods are now maintained by the Mercer County Park Commission.

Pick up the blue-blazed trail from here, following along to the gas-line right-of-way, marked by yellow posts. The boulders you see are diabase, formed during the Triassic period. Continue on the blue-blazed trail, always watching for another blaze in front of you. Finding them can be a bit tricky

A hiker enjoys a brief rest beside one of the huge boulders found in the woods.

since they're placed on tree trunks, rocks, and sticks in the ground. They are fairly close together, so should you walk more than a few yards without seeing one, turn back immediately, return to the last one, and scout around until another appears in front of you.

Red branches contrast nicely against the snow in winter, while mushrooms poke up from the ground, and a few beech trees still have some stubborn golden leaves that have refused to be shaken free. At this time of year the earth emits a pleasant crackling sound when it's frozen, breaking the silence around you.

Oaks line the top of the ridge, and soon the sweet gums appear. Named sweet gum because of the sticky substance that oozes from cuts in its branches or trunk, it litters the path with one-inch globular seed capsules. In the fall, its star-shaped leaves turn bright crimson and orange.

At the junction of the red-blazed trail, turn right. Huge boulders come into view a bit farther along—a good area to pause for a while, have a drink or lunch, and listen to the birds as they flit from tree to tree. The chickadees are amusing to watch as they perform fascinating acrobatics.

Turn left onto the white-blazed trail. Here tulip trees tower majestically overhead while lush, green Christmas ferns thrive and push up among the fallen leaves. At the yellow-blazed trail bear right, continuing downhill. Soon you'll come to a narrow stream, another nice spot to reflect on your natural surroundings and relax before practicing your balancing act walking over rocks to get to the other side of the water. This spot is fun, especially for kids who like to hop and skip across the rocks, and often "accidentally" fall in.

Turn left onto the green-blazed trail, then right onto the white-blazed trail. Watch for the red-blazed trail again, following it along the fence until you come to a fragrant stand of pines. The parking lot is to the left.

NOTES: Sturdy waterproof shoes are preferable as the boulders can be a little hard on your toes and the trail is often wet. Take along water. Numerous restaurants are located in Princeton and nearby Kingston.

40. Hacklebarney State Park

LOCATION	Morris County Follow signs from Route 24 in Chester to the park in Long Valley 07853 (908) 879-5677
SEASON	Year round
HIGHLIGHTS	Trout fishing in Black River, hemlock and hardwood forest, picnicking, bird watching, hiking
ADMISSION	Free, except for parking fee on weekends and holidays Memorial Day–Labor Day
HOURS	Opens 8 A.M. daily, closing time subject to season; call for hours
FACILITIES	Picnic tables, grills, fireplaces, rest room, snack bar on weekends and holidays during summer

MY FIRST TRIP TO HACKLEBARNEY STATE PARK WAS IN THE DEAD OF WINTER, WHEN the tips of large boulders poked through a blanket of freshly fallen snow. As I shivered in the cold I spotted a deer munching a tender hemlock shoot while birds circled above searching for seeds.

The hemlocks, apart from adding a deep green to the landscape, were particularly valuable to early settlers who made a medicinal tea from the tree's twigs and leaves. A beautiful evergreen, the hemlock has a graceful pyramidal shape; its half-inch needles have dark green tops and glisten with a silvery sheen underneath.

Winter is an excellent season to study the birds that forage in these woods. Using binoculars, it's possible to observe how they fluff their feathers during cold weather to trap warm air close to their bodies. By spring, when the sounds of birds fill the air, it's commonplace to spot cardinals, mockingbirds, finches, and orioles flying between the hemlocks, hickory, and gray birch. Fall, when the crowds are gone, is a rewarding time to enjoy the surroundings in solitude. Only the rustle of a squirrel rummaging through fallen leaves, the sound of a bird's call, or the rubbing of one tree limb against another breaks the silence.

Situated along the Black River in a gorge of unusual beauty, the park, established in 1924 with a 32-acre gift from Adolphe E. Borie, is accessible

Year round, Hacklebarney State Park provides a visual treat as well as a good way to stretch one's legs, catch a fish, or enjoy the sound of the swift-moving water.

only on foot. Covering 574 acres, it lies primarily in a glacial valley through which the Black River flows. The constant flow of water creates an indescribable melody and tranquillity.

According to the park brochure, the park acquired its name from a local iron mine worker who persisted in "heckling" a quick-tempered foreman by the name of Barney Tracey. Over a period of time, "heckle" Barney became "hacklebarney." However, according to Charles A. Philhower, an authority on Indian history, "hackle" is probably a variant of "haki" meaning ground, and "barney" is a variation of "bonihen," to put wood on fire; hence "hackiboni," to put wood on a fire on the ground, which describes the image of a bonfire. Folklore also relates that this park may have got its name from homesick Irish miners who named an early industrial settlement after their village in County Cork.

Although not as large as the boulders found in the Rockies, the rocks here are still impressive, and visitors usually can't resist scampering from one to the other. To get down to the Black River, take the easy one- to two-hour trail from the parking lot. Go beyond the rest rooms and take the deep stone steps leading to the first picnic area and Trout Brook. Here you'll be able to hear the water as it cascades over the boulders lining both sides of the brook. This is a good place to linger before weaving through the rocks and onto the trail.

Farther down on the right you'll be rewarded by a small waterfall, another fine place to relax, meditate, and pay homage to Mother Nature. Except for the water all noise becomes only a vague memory.

During summer months a canopy of green leaves provides shade, while autumn lays a thick carpet of leaves at your feet. Once back on the trail you'll notice tree trunks that seem to spring from bare rock, even though they're firmly anchored in thick earth deposits accumulated over the years. Many of the trees have sprouted in cavities of other fallen trees, now decayed and known as "nurse logs," which provide nutrients and a foundation for the new growth. Hemlocks are particularly suited to this form of growth because they're able to survive in deep shade, sending their roots into the stump or host log.

During spring various shapes and patterns of flowering plants and trees can be observed. Sassafras, highly sought after in colonial times for its medicinal value, produces spicy, aromatic flowers. For centuries its roots have been used to make tea, but if you try the brew, be careful not to drink too much. It can have a narcotic effect.

Jack-in-the-pulpit grows in the moist wooded areas and is identified by the hood that arches over the plant. The upper part is often striped green or purplish brown; it bears bright red berries in the fall. American Indians pounded the root into a pulp, placing the finished product on the forehead to treat headaches. Although the ring-necked pheasant and wild turkey like the plant's leaves and red fruit, it's wise not to taste it yourself; the calcium oxalate crystals in the plant can cause a burning sensation and great distress. Laura Martin writes in *Wildflower Folklore* (Globe Pequot Press, Chester, CT, 1984) that as a joke, country boys would often urge unsuspecting city dwellers to have a nibble. Although the first bite tasted okay, it didn't take too long for them to catch on, and second helpings were rarely requested!

Another interesting plant growing here is the jewelweed, with bright yellow-orange flowers shaped like tiny lanterns. Its fruits shoot out great distances when touched, warranting the plant's nicknames of touch-me-not and snapweed. When dew or raindrops fall, the flowers reflect light and resemble tiny jewels; hence the name "jewelweed."

Spend some time on top of one of the giant boulders along the river to watch the water carry twigs and leaves, creating fascinating moving patterns. From the river the trail goes up a steep hill past a playground, the rest room, and then back to the parking area.

NOTES: Sturdy walking shoes are recommended. Bring a picnic lunch to enjoy near the water, or if you prefer, Larison's Turkey Restaurant is nearby as are some fast-food restaurants.

41. Bass River State Park

LOCATION Ocean County
Exit 52 off the Garden State Parkway, New Gretna
08224
(609) 296-1114

SEASON Year round; excellent in spring and fall

HIGHLIGHTS Camping, boating, fishing, hiking, children's
playground, nature area, picnicking

ADMISSION Fee Memorial Day–Labor Day except Tuesdays;
fee for camping

HOURS For day use, 8 A.M.–8 P.M.

FACILITIES Campsites for trailers and tents, closed lean-tos,
flush toilets, hot showers, dumping station, laundry,
fireplaces, picnic tables, snack bar during summer

CAMPERS AT BASS RIVER STATE PARK RARELY COMPLAIN ABOUT HAVING TO "ROUGH it." In fact, the hot showers, flush toilets, and large wood sites make comfort a large part of this "camping" experience. This is a great place to unwind for both campers and daytime visitors, who can enjoy a couple of hours or several days boating, fishing, hiking, or simply admiring the surrounding 13,645-acre resort.

Chipmunks and squirrels usually hang out around the campsites, where it's easier to get food. The raccoon, recognized by its black mask, may be lurking about as well but does so mostly at night. While this notorious campground bandit eats anything from fruit and nuts to frogs and birds' eggs, it particularly loves to rummage around for leftovers. Since you'll probably be awakened, have a flashlight handy so you can catch it in the act!

The Absegami Trail, located near the park entrance, offers a short, delightful walk. "Absegami," an Algonquin Indian word meaning "the Place of the Swans," is believed to have referred to a broad location including the stretch of bays and inlets from Tuckerton to Atlantic City. The trail loops through the pine barrens and a white cedar bog. The pitch pine, a three-needled cone-bearer, is a dominant tree here; the scrub oak, a common shrub in the park, is found on drier ground. As you inhale the fragrant aroma of pine along the white, sandy trail, you may wonder why this area is part of the "pine barrens." One theory is that because most of this area of the state was once covered with pines, it was a fitting name. However, the expression comes from colonial days when land was judged barren if it

Spring is a wonderful time to visit Bass River, a time when you can discover delicate trillium.

couldn't sustain traditional crops. Although pine barren soil is acid and wasn't good for agricultural purposes, it does support many interesting plant communities.

In May the yellow flowers of false heather appear, and if you look closely, you'll also find pixie-moss. This light-green foliage hugs the ground and has showy white and pink blossoms each spring. Another ground runner is the foxtail clubmoss. Bring along a magnifying glass and search for two extraordinary insect-catching plants common in this area, the sundew and the pitcher plant.

When the sun shines, the sundew's leaves glisten with a sticky substance the plant uses to attract insects. Tiny red hairs on its leaves also help to hold the trapped insects. The pitcher plant is also unusual and amazing to see in action. With its curled leaves forming a cylinder, the "pitcher," it not only curves upward to catch the rain but also traps curious insects who sniff the plant's scent and descend into the pitcher. Once in, they're trapped by a sticky substance and held back by hundreds of hairs at the edges of the leaves. They finally fall into the water and drown and are ultimately digested by the plant.

You'll find a variety of orchids here, too, such as the white-fringed orchid, a beauty during summer when its white flowers are in bloom on a foot-high stalk.

When you leave the roadway, turn right into a totally different environment, the cedar swamp. Huckleberry bushes grow profusely and are loaded with berries in August. In a short distance you'll see stands of swamp magnolia, a sight to behold in late summer when its two-inch pink fruits are visible. Use caution if you come during July and August, for not only does the sweetpepper bush attract honeybees, but that's when the poison ivy springs out from everywhere. You will recognize it by the three smooth leaves growing together from the stem and its reddish leaves during the fall. Remember: "Leaves of three, let it be!"

After crossing the boardwalk you'll see impressive white cedars. Even after having been buried for generations in the swamps, their wood is still sound and usable. The grayish green moss on the swamp floor is sphagnum moss, prized today by nurseries as packing material. Indians found it so absorbent that they collected, dried, and packed it around infants in cradle boards as a natural diaper. During World War I it was used in antiseptic dressings, and it has also been used for insulation. If you were to jump on it, you'd bounce easily; that's because sphagnum can hold 10 times its own weight in water.

The large scarlet oaks you pass on the way back from the swamp turn a brilliant red during fall, and from late August through September you may notice a tiny, red-flecked orange flower growing in masses. If it's raining, or dew has beaded up on its leaves, you'll know why this sparkling flower is commonly known as the "jewelweed." A favorite with bumble bees and hummingbirds for its sweet nectar, it's also used by many people who believe it can cure poison ivy when crushed and rubbed on the skin. I once tried it after having been bitten by a nasty mosquito and it actually stopped the bleeding.

If you feel like swimming after the walk, try the bathing beach on the east shore of Lake Absegami. The bathhouse, first-aid station, refreshment concession, and canoe rental are open from Memorial Day to Labor Day. Lifeguards are on duty until 6 P.M. There's a boat launch area for small electric-powered or nonpowered boats. Bring along a rod; if you're lucky, catfish and pickerel may take the bait.

NOTES: Picnic facilities are available. Nearby Smithville Village has a few snack places and a restaurant. The park is only 25 miles north of Atlantic City and is near historic Batsto Village, Forsythe National Wildlife Refuge, and the Noyes Museum (see chapters 5, 33, and 50).

42. Merrill Creek Reservoir

LOCATION	Warren County
	Off NJ 57 on Montana Road, Washington 07882
	(908) 454-1213
SEASON	Year round
HIGHLIGHTS	Boating, fishing, hiking, cross-country skiing, spring wildflowers, fall migration path for birds of prey, hummingbird and butterfly garden, exhibits in visitor center
ADMISSION	Free
HOURS	Trails: dawn–dusk
	Visitor center: daily except major holidays, 9 A.M.– 5 P.M.
	Call for boating hours
FACILITIES	Rest room, drinking water, binoculars, and telescope inside the visitor center

THE QUOTE, "WATER, WATER, EVERYWHERE, NOR ANY DROP TO DRINK" BEST describes Merrill Creek Reservoir. Although billions of gallons of water are contained within this 650-acre holding area, it's not for drinking purposes but for generating electricity to surrounding towns during times of drought.

Once inside the posh, modern visitor center, I discovered that the reservoir, situated atop Scott's Mountain, is owned by seven electric utility companies spread out along the Delaware River. Excellent displays explain how the water to fill the reservoir is pumped from the Delaware River during times when the river flow is high. Then, it's carried uphill through a 3.5-mile-long pipeline. When the river is low and a drought warning is declared, the water can be released from the reservoir through that same pipe.

Although swimming isn't allowed, and you can't drink a drop of the water, there's lots to do at this beautiful facility. For starters, spend some time inside the visitor center. Not only is the view of the reservoir and some of the surrounding 2,000 acres of forest exquisite, but you can use the supplied binoculars and telescope to spot a few of the many species of birds

Whether you like to fish, hike, boat, or just relax, exquisite views await you at Merrill Creek Reservoir.

that frequent the area. During fall and winter, a roaring fire in the stone fireplace is an added bonus.

Once outside, try your luck fishing; the water is stocked with tasty trout, large- and smallmouth bass, and a variety of game fish. (All state fishing rules and permits apply.) During summer months, the garden behind the visitor center attracts butterflies and hummingbirds.

There's also wonderful hiking through dense woods and huge fields. Trails include the 0.9-mile orange-blazed Creek Trail, which traverses upper Merrill Creek and the northeast arm of the reservoir with some low wet areas through woods; the 0.8-mile green-blazed Orchard Trail, which passes through a managed orchard, an old farm, and an abandoned orchard; the 0.7-mile red-blazed Timber Trail, which passes through pine plantations and hardwood forests in various successional stages; the 0.4-mile yellow-blazed Historic Farmstead Trail, an easy walk on an old farm road through fields and woods; and the 1.5-mile blue-blazed Shoreline Trail, which follows the perimeter of the reservoir and offers scenic vistas.

If you're feeling energetic and want a good leg stretcher, my favorite is the 5-mile hike around the reservoir. The walk is moderate and pleasant with some gentle ups and downs. It's best to wear sturdy shoes on this hike because the small rocks along the trail can be hard on the feet.

For the reservoir trail, walk downhill from the visitor center along the narrow dirt trail heading toward the boat launch, cross the bridge to the parking lot, pass through the gate with a "no unauthorized vehicles" sign, and, walking south and clockwise, prepare for an exciting couple of hours with no traffic or distractions—just wonderful views of the water, fields, and woods. For the first few minutes, open fields provide a clear view of the reservoir and those canoeing, sailing, or fishing. In about 0.5 mile, woods appear. During summer months, an overhead canopy of natural leaves provides welcome shade. At this point, you'll be a few feet above the reservoir.

While crossing over the first dike via a wide, flat, stone-covered path, the square, concrete, 180-foot-high inlet-outlet tower used to control water flow can be seen to the west. Continuing on, the only sounds heard will be those coming from birds, insects, or gravel crunching beneath your feet. Before reaching the next dam, there are more fields, which, in spring, are ablaze with wildflowers. Soon after, the reservoir is on one side a few feet below, while on the other side, there's a slope filled in with stands of pine trees resembling matchsticks. When you reach the end of the dam, beautiful vistas await making the slight climb worthwhile. During fall, the milkweed seeds in this area float like parachutes with each passing breeze.

Turn right into the parking lot at approximately 2.5 miles, and head toward the bulletin board, taking the narrow foot trail next to it into the woods. Continuing straight ahead will take you to an observation point along the water, but if you don't want to leave the main trail, take the first left and continue along the narrow and rocky path beneath lovely beech and birch trees. Water appears in about a mile and, after crossing the dike, you'll have a closer view of the inlet-outlet building. A beautiful panorama of the countryside awaits, plus a wonderful view of the reservoir.

Up ahead, the sight of many species of gulls flying overhead and water slapping against the rocks is a joy, as are the dozens of dead tree "sculptures" standing submerged along the shore. After the reservoir basin was scoured out, the trees were intentionally flooded so that better aquatic life will abound once they're completely decayed. The reflections of the dead trees in the water late in the day are a sight to behold, as are the white-tailed deer found in this area throughout the year. Once in a while you may even see a wood turtle, identified by a bright orange neck and legs and a distinctive shell pattern.

You'll smell the aroma of fresh pines before you walk beneath them; their needles form a smooth carpet along the trail. But no sooner will you be giving thanks that the rocks are gone than they reappear! However, I can guarantee you won't mind, not when the water finally narrows to a little stream and plays its special melody while tumbling down over larger rocks. Listen for a while as you cross the wooden bridge and search for jewelweed, nicknamed "touch-me-not" because seeds will shoot out when the mature fruit is touched.

When you reach the bench, the water disappears once again. Turn left at this point, and at the orange and green blaze, turn right and head uphill through the woods. After concentrating on a mass of rocks and tree roots, it's easy going. Once past the open field, you'll find a spot Tarzan would have loved because there are loads of vines hanging down from huge trees. Turn left at the flat road, a popular place for deer and rabbits, and continue to the main road where a right turn will bring you back to the visitor center.

NOTE: Bring a snack and drink; restaurants are a distance away.

43. The Wetlands Institute

LOCATION Cape May County
1075 Stone Harbor Boulevard, Stone Harbor 08247
(609) 368-1211

SEASON Year round

HIGHLIGHTS Exhibit and lecture hall; Diller Center for Coastal Education and Wetlandia with special displays on the salt marsh and continental shelf, plus local shells, horseshoe crabs, and marsh creatures; touch museum; research labs; saltwater aquaria; library; elevated marsh boardwalk and trail; observation tower; 6,000-acre salt marsh; excellent gift shop

ADMISSION Fee; members free

HOURS 9:30 A.M.–4:30 P.M. Monday–Saturday and 10 A.M.–4 P.M. Sunday, May 15–October 15; 9:30 A.M.–4:30 P.M. Tuesday–Saturday October 15–May 15

FACILITIES Rest room, water, book and gift shop, library, telescopes for viewing the marsh

EVENTS Annual weekend Wings 'N' Water Festival, a major environmental extravaganza the third weekend in September; family beach and salt marsh safaris; birding expeditions; quilt show; evening lecture series; mini-ecology classes for youngsters; family-fun days; call or write for schedule

STONE HARBOR IS TINY. MEASURING SEVEN MILES IN LENGTH AND THREE OR FOUR CITY blocks in width, it's flanked by the Inland Waterway to the west and the Atlantic Ocean on the east. Until 1911, the only way into this scenic municipality was by train, from the north, via a bridge over Townsend's Inlet. When a highway and bridges were finally built, visitors flocked to the scenic town, and with good reason.

One of Stone Harbor's gems, registered as a national natural landscape, is the Stone Harbor Bird Sanctuary where, during nesting season in early April, thousands of birds find refuge among the dense foliage and nearby marshland. For birders, the area is a virtual paradise.

Another gem is The Wetlands Institute. Founded by Herbert Mills in 1969 to further coastal environmental knowledge and appreciation, the private, nonprofit venture, which occupies a 34-acre site, is "dedicated to research and public education concerning wetlands and coastal ecosystems."

The best place to begin the self-guiding tour is inside the institute's handsome cedar shake building, which resembles an old Coast Guard station. Watch the short, interesting film explaining why salt marshes are vital to our well-being and irreplaceable as hunting and wildlife preserves, barriers against storm damage, recreation areas, and nursery grounds for fish and shellfish. You'll also learn how important grass harvesting was during colonial times and how salt marshes such as this distribute their riches through the food chain.

The Diller Education Center for Coastal Education, connected to the main building by decks and a garden walkway, provides an opportunity to explore the world of the marsh via hands-on exhibits filled with preserved specimens, microscopes, quiz boards, and games, as well as live fish, turtles, and mollusks.

By beginning with the concept that life in the salt marsh begins with the sun, an exhibit shows how the basic salt marsh food chains progress from grasses and phytoplankton through microscopic organisms to fish and finally peoples. The realistic 12-foot diorama actually brings the salt marsh indoors, with marsh birds and insects shown along with a cutaway at the front edge revealing fishes in the tidepools and the mud-burrowing creatures in their tunnels beneath the marsh surface. A corner is devoted to the diamondback terrapin, the only turtle that lives in salt marshes. Linger afterward on the huge observation deck atop this building.

Outside, the interpretive Salt Marsh Trail addresses how harsh this environment can be for plants and animals, which must adapt to extremes of temperature and salinity and to alternate flooding and drying conditions. A 150-foot boardwalk allows a closer look at the low marsh area, and a 120-foot pier over Scotch Bonnet Creek overlooks Ring Island, site of the world's largest nesting colony of laughing gulls. A boathouse, utilized as a classroom for summer programs, and the institute's 17-foot research vessel are at the end of the trail. Take along binoculars; they'll come in handy if you'd like to spend time sitting on the pier observing wildlife.

Stop 1 along the trail is a prime example of how "phragmites" or reed grass grows on marsh edges where land has been disturbed. This plant, sporting large, fluffy plumes, is considered a pest because it crowds out more valuable native plants. However, with the sun shining behind, it looks glorious as it waves in the slightest breeze.

Be careful of the poison ivy growing on the right side of the path. Remember, "leaves of three, let it be."

Many ponds dot the surface of the marsh; these shallow bodies of water

The observation deck atop The Wetlands Institute building is a great place from which to spot nesting osprey.

contain small fish, worms, insects, and plants such as widgeon grass and algae. Herons, terns, shorebirds, ducks, and geese usually can be found here waiting for a tasty morsel.

At stop 3, you'll find "bayberry." A dominant shrub of the upland border, the bayberry has aromatic waxy gray berries that have been used for candlemaking since colonial times. Migrating swallows and wintering yellow-rumped warblers love to eat these berries.

You may have an opportunity to see osprey during your visit. Each year they nest on the platform above the marsh close to stop 4, returning to Cape May County in late March to spend the summer raising their young before migrating to Central or South America during fall.

Walking from the road into the marsh, you'll notice a change in plant growth. Only salt marsh cord grass can withstand the daily inundation by salt water. Stop 6 has a bare area of marsh known as a "panne," formed when salt water is trapped in a small depression. With the heavy salt deposits, not even cord grass can survive. Small piles of sand indicate the presence of insects called earwigs.

The small holes you may see in the marsh around stop 9 are the burrows of fiddler crabs. As you return to the institute, you'll probably be able to identify many birds. During summer there are lots of willets and red-wings flitting about.

If you'd like to browse through an interesting collection of science and natural history books, try the Herbert Mills Memorial Library housed within the insititute. It's not only cozy but offers a great view of the marsh.

44. Great Swamp Outdoor Education Center

LOCATION	Morris County
	247 Southern Boulevard, Chatham 07928
	(973) 635-6629
SEASON	Spring, fall, and winter
HIGHLIGHTS	Hands-on museum, wildflowers, marsh, swamp, open fields, pond, nature trails, large variety of plants and wildlife, and observation blind
ADMISSION	Free
HOURS	Trails: dawn–dusk
	Museum: 9 A.M.–4:30 P.M., September–June
FACILITIES	Rest room, library, large parking area, and handicapped-accessible boardwalk trail and observation blind
EVENTS	Lectures, guided walks, maple tapping; call or write for schedule

WHETHER YOU'RE A FIRST-TIME HIKER, HAVE YOUNG CHILDREN, ARE LIMITED IN TIME, or are handicapped, you'll love the short, easy trails at the Great Swamp Outdoor Education Center.

Start inside the education center, where a knowledgeable, friendly naturalist is always on hand to answer questions. By examining the interesting exhibits, you'll learn a lot about the Great Swamp, as well as which critters are on the endangered list; what purpose wetlands serve; and what muskrat and raccoon furs feel like. If you're brave, stick your hand inside a multi-compartment box and, by touch alone, try to figure out what objects lie inside.

Before leaving the building, ask for free self-guiding trail brochures and maps of the trails. Two trails, each 1 mile long, meander over four different habitats, including dry woods, fields, marshes, and swamps. The 200-foot-long handicapped-accessible boardwalk trail, traversing swamp and dry woods, leads to an observation blind. All of the trails are perfect for getting in touch with nature and are bound to leave you feeling invigorated.

Had you been to the Great Swamp 25,000 years ago, hiking would have been impossible even with the best boots. During this period, the Wisconsin Glacier stopped abruptly on its way south and melted. A huge lake formed;

Linger as long as you like at the observation platform overlooking the pond. Turtles can be seen sunning themselves, and sighting a bluebird is a real treat.

when it finally drained, marshes and swamp remained. The marshes and swamps are still here, but thanks to the Morris County Park Commission, with assistance from the Bell Telephone Pioneers of America and local Boy Scout groups, numerous boardwalks have been erected over the wet areas.

If you don't have much time, or if your movement is restricted, you can still savor the beauty and uniqueness of this area by taking the nature trail starting from the handicapped parking area. Bring binoculars along; numerous species of birds have been sighted at the observation blind at the end of the boardwalk.

Numerous gray birch have sprung up in the fields, and in many places along the trail there are beautiful green mats of hair cap moss, so-named for the fringed "hat" that develops atop the female part of the plant.

The small box that's mounted on a wooden post was placed here to encourage increased breeding of bluebirds. Although once abundant in our state, the eastern bluebird has declined rapidly in the past 40 years as the wooden fence posts they loved to build their nests in disappeared as farmland gave way to suburbia. When the center began supplying wooden boxes for nesting, many bluebirds returned, and today the Great Swamp boasts one of the largest bluebird populations in New Jersey.

During late summer, mockingbirds, catbirds, and robins feast on the highbush blueberry bushes along this trail, as well as the thorny multiflora rose, which was originally planted as a natural fence by farmers. These roses, now growing wild, attract not only many species of birds but also bees and other insects to their fragrant blossoms.

Admire but don't touch poison sumac, a tall, stout-branched shrub found in the wet sections. It may look beautiful when it's adorned with clusters of greenish white berries or decorated with bright orange leaves, but touching it can cause a serious skin irritation similar to poison ivy.

Great Swamp Outdoor Education Center   **175**

At the pond you'll find giant phragmites, a common marsh grass that can reach a height of 15 feet. Sedges, which form thick, grassy mounds from which red maple saplings sprout, are also in this area. That lush green carpet over the water is duckweed; it consists of thousands of individual tiny, floating plants. Each plant body is composed of a single leaf or a few small, flat leaves, each with a single trailing root. It reproduces by "budding off," a dividing of the plant into two separate parts.

That light-green, soft-looking low plant you see in the wet areas is called sphagnum moss. The Indians discovered that it made a terrific natural diaper, and plant nurseries use sphagnum moss today as packing material because it can hold 10 times its weight in water.

Peeking through the slots at the observation blind can be very rewarding. Although the woodpeckers are sometimes too fast to be seen, their rat-tat-tat sound can be heard for long distances as they search for insects in dead trees. If you're patient, you may spot a snake or muskrat at the water's edge or perhaps a turtle sunning itself on the floating platform the center erected. Or a wood duck may be using one of the nesting boxes.

If this short, interesting trail has whetted your appetite to see more of Mother Nature's wonders, try one of the longer trails. When you reach the swamp area, pause for a few minutes and examine the surroundings. Only a few feet in elevation makes the difference between dry land and wetland.

The Great Swamp consists of 40 percent wetland, and at the beginning of the trail, at stop 3, you'll find a huge depression thought to be a "kettle" hole. Scientists theorize that this hole was formed thousands of years ago when a large ice chunk broke off from the Wisconsin Glacier as it retreated. After heavy rains, this depression fills with water. It's also home to many creatures, including insects, frogs, and salamanders. During dry weather, it empties, and often these critters have to fend for themselves or die. When winter comes, many animals hibernate under the earth, but when spring arrives, they're quite awake and chatter away endlessly in a delightful chorus.

Where the power-line path comes in, both sides of the trail drop off into wet areas that are filled with cattails, reed grass, and sedges; these provide shelter for waterfowl, nesting places for birds, and food for muskrats.

The boardwalk leads to an observation platform overlooking a small pond that's teaming with frogs, turtles, and snakes, before leading through a woodland area where mountain laurel are ablaze with pink and white flowers each spring.

In 1992, over 300 school groups and 25,000 people visited the Great Swamp Outdoor Education Center. Many were repeat visitors. It's a good bet that you'll be a repeat visitor after walking the well-kept trails, too.

NOTES: The Great Swamp Outdoor Education Center borders the 7,500-acre Great Swamp National Wildlife Refuge. Picnicking isn't allowed, but there are many restaurants close by.

SPECIAL INTERESTS

45. Pequest Trout Hatchery and Natural Resource Education Center

LOCATION	Warren County
	Off Route 46, east of the Route 31 junction,
	Pequest 07863
	(908) 637-4125
SEASON	Year round
HIGHLIGHTS	Self-guiding tour of trout hatchery, exhibit hall, nature trails, educational courses
ADMISSION	Free
HOURS	Daily except holidays 10 A.M.–4 P.M.
FACILITIES	Rest room, drinking water, picnic tables
EVENTS	Special weekend nature programs; fishing lessons April–October

WHETHER YOU ALREADY LOVE FISHING, WANT TO TRY IT FOR THE FIRST TIME, OR ARE simply curious about where the trout for New Jersey's stocked waters come from, the Pequest Trout Hatchery and Natural Resource Education Center is the place to visit. This is where the approximately 600,000 brown, rainbow, and brook trout are raised each year to stock over 200 lakes, streams, reservoirs, and rivers.

The center, located in the northeast quadrant of the Pequest Wildlife Management Area, occupies a lovely 1,600-acre site covering part of the Pequest River watershed. The area offers lovely scenery year round, especially in the fall, when the thickly forested rolling hills are transformed into a colorful kaleidoscope.

Opened in 1982, the hatchery, according to naturalist Paul Tarlowe, "provides ideal growing conditions for raising trout and supplies more than 250,000 licensed fishermen with healthy trout each year." He encourages visitors to "come and learn what makes this facility one of the most modern in the nation." The center's goal is to provide a better understanding of the importance of natural resources to people, as well as the importance of protecting wildlife habitats.

After viewing "Hooked on Nature," a 16-minute video describing how

The visitor center has interesting exhibits as well as hands-on displays.

eggs are taken from the hatchery's own brood stock and how the brooks and streams are stocked with fish raised here, visitors follow a self-guiding tour of the grounds. At the first overlook you'll see 3,000–7,000 gallons of water a minute flow through raceways. Next is the nursery building where eggs are transferred to be incubated in the fall. Peek inside the windows to see how the trays, each filled with about 20,000 eggs, are stored. The eggs take about 28–35 days to hatch into inch-long fry before they are transferred to tanks and fed by automatic machines until they're big enough to be moved outside to the raceways.

From the Observation Deck you'll see one mile of concrete raceways used to keep trout until they're large enough to be released. When the fish are 18 months old, they're transferred by special trucks to lakes and streams throughout the state. Recent counts show there are over 4,100 significant freshwater lakes, ponds, impoundments, and reservoirs in New Jersey. There are also 8,600 miles of freshwater streams in the state, proving that the trout don't suffer from a shortage of space in which to swim and grow. From here you can also see the Broodstock Building, where 2,000–3,000 two- and three-year-old broodfish produce the hatchery's entire supply of eggs.

Inside the exhibit hall are many hands-on displays for young and old alike. "The Pequest Story" describes how geologists discovered the huge aquifer located in the Pequest Valley. By operating a hand pump, you'll learn how water percolates through the underlying glacial till. There's also a small computer center for testing your skills as a "wildlife manager," and you can design a plan for watershed development.

"The Department of Environmental Protection and Energy (DEPE) at a Glance" exhibit is synchronized with a series of telephones; when visitors lift a phone, they receive a 20-second message about the activities in the various divisions of the DEPE, such as the Division of Parks and Forestry and the Division of Fish, Game, and Wildlife. In the "Habitat Match" exhibit there are 24 organisms keyed into a computer and panel. The panel presents clues on where the organism lives. And if you guess the right habitat—a pond, stream, or estuary—the panel lights up.

Spend some time at the new backyard wildlife habitat, an example of what homeowners can construct on their own properties. Also try one of the three easy hiking trails. The longest, the Natural Resource Trail, is a 1.5-mile loop meandering through woodlands and fields, with numbered stops at points of interest. A kiln that was used by farmers in the early 1800s to correct a soil problem resulting from intensive grain farming sits at stop 2. By firing limestone in kilns and spreading it on their fields, farmers could restore fertility by balancing the acidity of the soil. Even though the honeybees are gone, their former nest shows their fondness for the black walnut tree at stop 3, while the rusty patches on the rocks near stop 4 indicate iron content.

One of the prettiest fishing spots in the area is just outside the hatchery along a one-mile conservation stretch of the Pequest River. It extends from the county bridge on Pequest Furnace Road upstream to the old railroad bridge over the river. Between late May and mid-March no live bait of any kind may be used; only artificial lures and flies are permitted. If you've never gone fishing, take advantage of the annual "Free Fishing Days" offered in June. During this special time, in celebration of National Fishing Week, a license is not required for fishing in public waters within the state.

NOTES: Write for a free copy of the "Budding Naturalist," a schedule of upcoming events (Pequest Trout Hatchery, RR #1, Box 389, Oxford 07863). All programs are free, but reservations are necessary on a first-call, first-served basis. Bring along a picnic lunch, or try one of the restaurants along Route 46.

46. Volendam Windmill Museum

LOCATION	Hunterdon County
	Adamic Hill Road off Route 519 west on Anderson Road, Milford 08848
	(908) 995-4365
SEASON	Summer
HIGHLIGHTS	Engineering and architectural wonder, beautiful scenery
ADMISSION	Fee
HOURS	May 1–September 30, Saturday and Sunday, noon–4:30 P.M.; other dates and times by appointment; call for schedule
FACILITIES	Picnic tables, rest room, gift shop

THERE'S NO NEED TO FLY ALL THE WAY TO HOLLAND TO SEE DUTCH WINDMILLS—NOT when, for less than the cost of a tankful of gas, you can visit an exact replica of a Dutch windmill right here in New Jersey. Thanks to Poul and May Jorgenson, visitors to the picturesque Volendam Windmill Museum, located in the gentle, rolling hills of Hunterdon County, have an opportunity to examine this lovely windmill and to learn how it works.

The concept of windmills dates back to at least 400 A.D., when the Persians harnessed winds for power in order to grind grain into flour. During the 19th century, thousands of windmills were built in Europe; these too were used for grinding grain and pumping water. Less than a century ago over one million windmills were in operation in the United States, but by the 1930s, when electricity provided by power companies proved to be a less expensive and more dependable system, most windmills were put out of commission.

Building the Volendam Windmill was a dream-come-true for Poul Jorgenson, who unfortunately died shortly after its completion. Jorgenson never forgot how scarce food was while he was growing up in Denmark during World War I, and he remained grateful to a miller who had allowed neighborhood children to sweep the floors of his windmill for any remaining flour that their mothers could turn into bread. Jorgenson associated windmills with a feeling of well-being and wanted to share what

The picturesque Volendam Windmill Museum located in the gentle green hills of Hunterdon County is a living museum of the windmills in Volendam, Holland.

he had experienced with others by building a working windmill so that visitors could learn about the milling industry.

Having joined the Royal Navy at the age of 14, Jorgenson mastered seven languages, became an engineer, and, after receiving United States citizenship, worked as a toolmaker. He bought land in Hunterdon County and, after retiring in 1963, decided to build an authentic working model of a centuries-old wind-driven mill used for grinding raw grain into flour, similar to those he had seen on a vacation in Volendam, Holland.

Traveling through many countries, measuring, sketching, and photographing mills and components, Jorgenson laid out the plans for the windmill of his dreams, incorporating the best features of those he had studied.

When ground was broken in 1965, Jorgenson not only carried fieldstone to fill the 13-foot foundation and laid the masonry work on the mill floor, he also installed the one-ton center grindstone in the proper location. Steel workers erected the frame and masons laid brick, but the remainder of the work was done by Jorgenson and his wife, May. Both were in their mid-60s at the time, and the job was extremely difficult. May had to carry 2-by-12-by-20-foot planks up three flights of stairs, while similar-sized boards were carried up six flights to create the floors.

Upon entering the first floor, you'll see two sets of doors. During times of operation, doors were open on both sides of the mill to enable a farmer driving down the road to enter the mill from the uphill side. Once inside, the miller would lower a hook for the farmer to hang his bags of grain on, and these would then be pulled up to the bins located above the stone floor.

On display in this museum you'll also see a "dog treadle," once commonly used on Pennsylvania Dutch farms. As a dog trotted uphill on the treadle, a shaft moved up and down in a keg that, in turn, churned butter.

On the second floor is an old farm tool, dating to the 1700s, which was used to winnow grain after it had been threshed. There are also unusual handmade, homespun linen flour sacks, woven in a circular manner, thereby eliminating side seams that could allow flour to seep out.

As you enter the third floor you'll see the heart of the windmill. Standing at the front door and looking back into the room, you'll be standing between two stones. On the right are composites of many pieces of stone cut by a mason and held together with an iron band riveted on by a blacksmith. Shrinking as it cooled, the band has held these stones together for hundreds of years. The top stone "floats" on the shaft, while the bottom stone is stationary.

Looking up through the trap door, you'll see a gray vertical shaft used for transferring power from the sails to the stone gears through the main gear above you. The gear has 89 large hickory teeth along with four 12-by-

14-inch oak cross beams and two 2-by-6-inch oak curves above and below the teeth to give the gear form, while the main gear is held in place on the shaft by oak wedges only. There aren't any bolts, nails, or wooden pegs to help hold it together.

If you aren't afraid of heights or narrow decks, walk outside around the bridge of the windmill. Here you'll find the tail used to turn the cap and the sails. From a height of 60 feet are sail arms measuring 68 feet tip to tip. They are capable of turning at eight revolutions per minute, producing about 40 horsepower; this is sufficient to turn the one-ton millstone at about 30 revolutions per minute.

In addition to seeing a windmill close up, you'll have an unforgettable view of the beautiful countryside. Unfortunately the Board of Health no longer allows the sale of the mill's flour, but if you're lucky, you may come during a demonstration. May died in 1993, but one of her relatives will be on hand to answer any questions about how she and her husband built his dream windmill.

NOTES: Bring a picnic lunch and enjoy it in the picnic grove; there aren't any restaurants in the immediate vicinity. The gift shop carries interesting Dutch items.

47. Franklin Mineral Museum and Mine Replica

LOCATION Sussex County
Evans Street between Main Street and Buckwheat
Road, off Route 23, Franklin 07416
(973) 827-3481

SEASON Spring, summer, and fall

HIGHLIGHTS Display of over 300 minerals from the Franklin-
Ogdensburg area, the world's largest fluorescent
display, a replica mine, and a mineral dump to
collect specimens

ADMISSION Fee; separate admission for mineral dump

HOURS Monday–Saturday 10 A.M.–4 P.M.; Sunday 12:30–
4:30 P.M. March 1–December 1; closed Easter,
Thanksgiving

FACILITIES Rest room, picnic area, soda machine, gift shop

SCIENTISTS HAVE SUCCEEDED IN DIGGING 5.5 MILES INTO THE EARTH, BUT TO REACH the center of our planet, which weighs about 6,600,000,000,000,000,000,000,000 tons, they'd probably have to go 4,000 miles deeper. Fortunately, when 17th-century French chemist P. Berthier investigated a new mineral, he didn't have to dig that far. Berthier discovered a mineral rich in zinc and manganese, which he named franklinite, after Franklin, the town in New Jersey where it was found. Since that time, deposits from the Franklin Mine have yielded over 300 different minerals, including many fluorescent ones and 30 that have never been found anywhere else in the world.

A tour guide leads visitors on a tour of the Franklin Mineral Museum and the adjacent replica of the Franklin Mine, one of the most productive zinc-mining operations in the nation from 1838 to 1954. Afterward you can try your luck digging for an unusual specimen in the slag, or leftover rock piles, heaped in the Buckwheat Dump.

The Fluorescent Room, reputed to contain the world's largest fluorescent display, is one of the highlights of the one-hour guided tour. Although resembling ordinary rocks under regular light, dozens of various ores and minerals glow in brilliant shades of green, red, blue, and yellow under ultraviolet light, the fluorescence caused by manganese in the rocks.

Steve Sanford, a former Franklin Mine worker, points out the powerful air shovel, which was once used to load coal and which, when operating, sounds like "killer bees."

There are two stories on how the fluorescence was discovered in the 1880s. One story relates how a worker noticed a color change in the rocks when a spark went off atop a trolley. Another version tells how workers leaving for the day turned out the lights in a sorting room and noticed the glow. No matter what happened, once word got out about the "glowing" rocks, people came from miles around to view them.

New Jersey's mines have always yielded important minerals. During the revolutionary war, copper was mined in Somerville for the making of cannons, one of which was used in the siege of Yorktown. Allaire and Batsto were also important sources; their bog iron deposits were used in the production of cannonballs. Most mines stayed in operation through the 19th century, but the Franklin Mine remained in full swing until 1954, when its zinc deposit was depleted.

Physician and congressman Samuel Fowler began mine operations here in 1836, on the same day that Congress passed a law requiring that every customs house in the United States use brass weights and measures. This wasn't a coincidence: Fowler, who in 1830 had invented the first zinc-based paint, knew he held land with huge quantities of franklinite, willemite, and zincite—all rich in zinc. And, knowing that brass is an alloy of copper and zinc, he sold Congress on its importance. He even convinced them to call it "New Jersey Red Oxide Zinc," confident that working the mine for its zinc deposits would eventually make him a richer man. Today most zinc is imported from abroad, but it's still important for making paint, linoleum, galvanized garbage cans, paper, printing inks, cosmetics, and human and animal food supplements.

The replica mine housed next to the museum was built with the timber, rails, ore carts, drilling equipment, and ore scoops once used here. On the way through the mine you'll pass a display showing mules carting ore from the first shaft in the northern part of the mine. Dug in 1890, this section of the mine was operated for 20 years and became famous for the variety of minerals that appeared. Every scrap of ore in the mine was blasted. Explosives were used to break the rock, which was then sent down a crib to a chute. By opening and closing boards, the chute allowed the ore to flow down into the mule carts, which carried 1.5 tons each. Also on exhibit are the shoes miners wore; to prevent them from wearing out, miners hammered short nails into the bottoms, giving them the name "hobnail" boots. You'll also see a typical miner's lunch bucket as well as the safety masks the miners used if dust got too thick or if carbon monoxide was present.

In 1912, miners, who usually came from eastern European countries, earned $20 every two weeks. Life underground was dangerous, yet the Franklin Mine was considered one of the safest. As each area was blasted, the ceiling was reinforced with beams and a floor was put down. After the ore was brought to the surface, it was crushed several times to isolate the valuable zinc.

The gift shop is loaded with minerals at truly rock-bottom prices, as well as ultraviolet mineral lamps, mining tools, and books. Retired Franklin Mine miners are also available to answer any questions.

NOTES: If you want to dig in the dump, wear sturdy shoes, gloves, and old clothes. Drinks can be purchased inside the museum, and restaurants are nearby.

48. Golf House

LOCATION Somerset County
Liberty Corner Road (Route 512), off Route 287, Far
Hills 07931
(908) 234-2300

SEASON Year round

HIGHLIGHTS United States Golf Association (USGA) Research
and Test Center with visitor observation deck;
museum on origins of the USGA and the game's
evolution, paintings of golfers, sculpture, ceramics,
silver, videos, and games on golf; and extensive
golf library

ADMISSION Free

HOURS Monday–Friday 9 A.M.–5 P.M., Saturday and Sunday
10 A.M.–4 P.M., closed Christmas, New Year's,
Thanksgiving, and Easter. The library is open on
weekdays only.

FACILITIES Rest room, library

YOU DON'T HAVE TO LOVE GOLF TO ENJOY A VISIT TO THE GOLF HOUSE MUSEUM IN Far Hills. But be forewarned: Once you visit, you may want to play a few rounds. Even if you don't, you'll learn amazing facts. And you'll definitely heed the warning when someone shouts "fore" on a golf course after learning that the initial velocity of a golf ball is 174 miles per hour!

Golf has grown tremendously since the game was developed in Scotland by the 15th century, and today over 500 million rounds of golf are played in America each year. Although the 1900s golf courses had only tee boxes, Dr. William Lowell—a New Jersey dentist—changed this in 1920 after deciding he didn't like the messy job of taking sand from a tee box and mixing it with water to make a tee. So he patented a wooden one and named it the "Reddy Tee." The public wasn't too impressed by this innovative device until Walter Hagen won the British Open in 1922 using one of Dr. Lowell's tees.

At the Golf House—the largest museum of its kind in the country—you'll learn not only about tees but also about the history of the game from its beginnings to the present time. Exhibits are housed in an impressive red-brick Georgian mansion designed by John Russell Pope in 1919. (Pope also

At the Golf House, visitors can see early clubs and memorabilia from a game that dates back as early as the 15th century.

designed the National Archives Building and the Jefferson Memorial.) The house is located on 62 acres of rolling land graced by spruce, pine, maple, magnolia, oak, Chinese elm, dogwood, and a small apple orchard. It was acquired by the United States Golf Association (USGA) in 1972 for its national headquarters, testing laboratories, and library.

Exhibits include a collection of clubs and balls signifying three distinct eras in the evolution of golf. The first period covers the game as it developed in Scotland and England from the 17th to the 19th centuries. At that time balls were made of two pieces of leather cut from sheepskin and stuffed with goose feathers, a costly and tedious process. Wooden clubs were also used, adding to the cost.

The year 1848 marked the introduction of the molded gutta percha balls, made with a rubber-like substance from Malaysian Sapodilla trees, along with steel club heads. With the creation of a rubber golf ball, the game literally took off. Made by winding rubber thread under tension around a solid rubber core, the new ball proved livelier, and because it could be mass produced, it cost much less. In turn, lowering the price of playing golf added to the game's popularity.

Plan to spend an entire morning or afternoon at this fascinating museum. The magnificent hanging staircase near the entrance is one of the outstanding architectural features of the house. On the first floor you can trace the history of golf through paintings, prints, clubs, and balls. You'll learn how golf was played by kings and "commoners" in Scotland and England and how the design of the courses developed.

Today over 70 percent of all golfers are men, but women are quickly catching up. One display is devoted to women golfers and the role they have played in the establishment of golf in this country. Don't miss the exhibit showing the typical golfing attire of the 1900s or the display of golf motifs used in decorative objects such as pitchers, steins, buckles, hat pins, and bottle openers.

The second floor depicts the golf age from 1945 to the present. The golf club astronaut Alan B. Shepard, Jr. used to hit a golf ball in space is on view here, along with clubs and photographs of champion golfers. Watch the latest golf videos, known as Compact Disk Interactive (CD-I) videos; take the quizzes, play the "mysterious" 18th hole, view a short series on the history of the game, or try the time cart for a look at yesteryear. On this floor you can also study the history of the rules of golf and learn about golf course architecture and turf maintenance.

You're welcome to use the library, which contains the world's largest collection of books on the sport of golf. In addition to browsing through the extensive collection of memorabilia and paintings of golf greats, plan on visiting the new 1,000-square-foot exhibition space within the Research and Test Center located next to the museum. From the observation deck you can view both indoor and outdoor test activities while a videotape describes what's happening.

In the Initial Velocity Laboratory golf balls kept at a constant temperature of 23 degrees Celsius are automatically placed on a tee and hit with a metal striker. As the ball travels through an enclosed tunnel six feet long, its speed is recorded by a photoelectric device.

The Wind Tunnel Laboratory shows how a golf ball is able to travel great distances. The dimples on the ball's surface help to create an air-flow pattern that results in a lift force. This is measured by mounting a ball in the test section of the wind tunnel, sending it through at high speed, and measuring what happens. The outdoor test range, part of the Main Test Laboratory, measures the ball's distance by using an air gun to launch the balls and then hitting them with an automatic club.

Did you realize that the spin rate of a ball when hit by a driver is approximately 3,600 revolutions per minute? Or that the maximum ball weight is 1.62 ounces, with no minimum requirement? Even if you're not inspired to play golf after visiting the Golf House, you'll probably leave knowing much more about the game.

NOTE: Buck Garden (see chapter 19) and restaurants are nearby.

49. Renault Winery

LOCATION	Atlantic County
	Off Route 30 on Bremen Avenue, Egg Harbor City
	08215
	(609) 965-2111
SEASON	Year round
HIGHLIGHTS	Wine tasting, winery tour, glass museum
ADMISSION	Fee
HOURS	Monday–Saturday 10 A.M.–4:15 P.M.; Sunday
	noon–4:15 P.M.
FACILITIES	Picnicking, rest room, restaurant, snack bar
EVENTS	Spring Wine Festival, Fall Harvest Festival, and craft
	shows

THE EXPRESSION "TO DRINK A TOAST" ORIGINATED IN ELIZABETHAN ENGLAND, WHEN IT was customary to put a small piece of toast in a glass of wine to improve its flavor. According to legend, a noted beauty was enjoying a public bath and an admirer drank to her health, while another admirer commented that he didn't like the wine but he wanted the toast. For a time thereafter ladies were called "toasts," and at dinner it became fashionable to drink to their health, a custom that eventually became known as "toasting."

In Aesop's fable "The Fox and the Grapes" another expression was started that we use frequently today. In this tale a fox hungers after a bunch of grapes hanging just out of his reach. Finally he quits trying, thinking that he was probably lucky because the grapes looked sour anyway! How many times do we use the fox's "sour grapes" rationalization when things seem beyond our reach today?

At the Renault Winery you'll have an opportunity to "drink a toast" while sampling a variety of wines that definitely aren't made from "sour grapes." The winery, the oldest continuously operated vineyard in the United States, was founded by master winemaker Louis Nicholas Renault, who came to California in 1855 representing the well-known champagne house of the Duke of Montebello at Rheims, France. Renault tried to establish a vineyard on the West Coast free of the phylloxera aphid, which was destroying the grapevines of western Europe.

Renault's attempt to establish grapes in California failed, but after learning that there was an East Coast Native American grape known as the

At the oldest continuously operated vineyard in the United States you can enjoy a tour to learn the winemaking process, taste the finished product, and participate in weekend celebrations like this.

Labrusca, which was resistant to pests and disease, he decided to investigate. Finding the soil of southern New Jersey similar to that of certain vineyards in France, he settled on 1,100 acres in Egg Harbor. By 1870 Renault had become the largest distributor of champagne in the nation, winning prizes at the Centennial Exposition at Philadelphia in 1876.

When Renault died in 1913 at the age of 91, his son, Felix, continued the business until 1919 when it was sold to the John D'Agostino family. The D'Agostinos ran it successfully through the Prohibition years, even though this era spelled the end for other wineries.

The reason for Renault's continued success was a brilliant marketing ploy. The company began shipping a new product, Renault Wine Tonic, to drugstores nationwide. The demand for this elixir, advertised as a youth potion and backache remedy, was terrific. And no wonder, for it had an alcohol content of 22 percent! Although it was really wine in disguise,

Renault didn't advertise it as such, nor did the company use the word "wine" anywhere in the front label. However, the back label bore a simple message that read "Caution: Do not refrigerate this tonic as it will turn into wine." A brilliant approach, guaranteed to get around the regulations and to send people rushing out to buy this "medicine."

After repeal, D'Agostino purchased two additional wineries in California, bringing these wines back to New Jersey for blending and bottling. Eventually they were sold throughout the country, and giant reproductions of Renault bottles advertising the product lined highway roadsides in New Jersey, Massachusetts, Florida, and California.

When D'Agostino died in 1948, his sister created a showplace of the old winery by building a chateau-style hospitality house and added a museum to display her wine glass collection.

The Milza family purchased the vineyard in 1978, opening it to the public for banquets, special seasonal events, and daily tours. Joseph P. Milza, a former newspaper owner and publisher, added French hybrids to the vineyards, made improvements in the table wines and Charmat process champagnes, and held several festivals throughout the year.

Tours begin in the Glass Museum, where over 300 champagne glasses are beautifully displayed, including a lovely Venetian wine goblet from the 13th century and a delicate bohemian glass of clear crystal on which grape clusters have been etched in gold. Old wine presses and antique bottling machinery are on display just past a lovely enclosed Italianate-Spanish–style courtyard. The next stop includes a look at the warehouse area, where 300,000 gallons of wine rest in huge oak barrels awaiting further processing: The youngest wooden barrel is 60 years old, and many are as much as 100 years old.

Today the winery produces a large variety of wines, such as champagne, cabernet sauvignon, Riesling, blueberry champagne, chardonnay, May wine, and Chablis. All are sold at the retail store located on the premises and by mail order.

Milza points out that Renault is a "completely self-sufficient facility. We grow the grapes, make the wine, bottle it, wholesale it to other retail facilities, retail it on the premises, and offer tasting at the end of each tour." Sixty people work in the family-run winery and 80-acre vineyard, which produces over 200,000 gallons of wine annually.

Grapes are harvested during September and October, the most active time for the winery; visitors are invited on consecutive Sundays beginning with Labor Day weekend to join in on the fall festival, complete with grape contests, hayrides into the vineyards, entertainment, and, of course, wine tasting.

NOTES: Where to eat isn't a problem; a café, located on the grounds, is open for lunch Monday through Saturday 11:30 A.M.–2:30 P.M., with an award-winning brunch served Sunday 10:30 A.M.–2 P.M. For an unusual experience, try dinner at Restaurant Renault, open Friday, Saturday, and Sunday evenings. Reservations are necessary. An excellent six-course dinner is served, including various wines, in beautiful surroundings. Entrance to the restaurant—an experience in itself—is through three authentic 80-year-old redwood wine casks. And if that's not enough, you'll be seated in booths made of 100-year-old oak wine casks. Plan on taking a full day so you can also visit the nearby Brigantine Division of the Edwin B. Forsythe National Wildlife Refuge, located off Route 9 south in Oceanville (see chapter 33). See chapter 51 for a description of Cream Ridge Winery and chapter 58 for the Four Sisters Winery. For updates on wine festivals, special events, and additional wineries throughout the state, call 1-800-524-0043, or contact the New Jersey Wine Industry Advisory Council at the New Jersey Department of Agriculture, CN330, Trenton, NJ 08625, (609) 292-8853.

50. Noyes Museum

LOCATION	Atlantic County
	Lily Lake Road (off Route 9), Oceanville 08231
	(609) 652-8848
SEASON	Year round
HIGHLIGHTS	American Folk Art and American fine arts and crafts from the mid-Atlantic region; bird decoys; unusual architecture; lovely view
ADMISSION	Fee
HOURS	Wednesday–Sunday 11 A.M.–4 P.M.
FACILITIES	Rest room, drinking water, restaurant, museum shop
EVENTS	Rotating exhibits, Meet-the-Artist Day, concerts; craft marketplace in November; for free schedule of events, write Noyes Museum, Lily Lake Road, Oceanville 08231

THE NOYES MUSEUM IS ONE OF SOUTHERN NEW JERSEY'S HIDDEN GEMS. LOCATED IN A beautiful building set in natural surroundings, it offers changing exhibitions of American folk art and American fine art and crafts, with a special emphasis on objects made by New Jersey artists or relating to New Jersey culture.

Financed by Ethel and Fred Noyes, the museum opened in 1983. Their goal was to increase public appreciation of arts and crafts through exhibitions and educational programs. Although Mrs. Noyes died in 1979, her love for the outdoors was not forgotten: Lily Lake, in Oceanville, was chosen as the ideal setting for the museum. Besides its scenic beauty, it incorporated her historical and cultural interests and the outdoor beauty of Galloway Township, where the couple lived most of their adult years.

According to the architect, Paul Cope, the location and museum design represented the eclectic personalities of Ethel and Fred Noyes, both of whom spent a great deal of time outdoors. Most visitors are surprised the moment they drive up to the building to see that its form, scale, materials, and detailing include features of regional frame structures from the 18th and 19th centuries. The contemporary exterior, sprinkled with early rural architecture, sports native white cedar horizontal siding stained a weathered gray, while the steeply sloped roofs are sheathed in wood shingles. Heavy wood framing timbers are exposed to recall barn construction.

The permanent sculpture collection in the Noyes Museum is housed in an interior of architectural beauty.

Another surprise awaits when you open the door and enter the museum. The four gallery wings and central circulation gallery are striking; natural light streams in from skylights, making the outside even more obvious through high, clear-glass windows. Attractive interior wood trim, cabinet work of natural finished yellow pine, and floors of end grain woodblock add to the beauty.

From inside you can view the lake through the glass end wall of the central gallery, where the four gallery wings are arranged at different descending levels. What will probably catch your eye first is a newly installed six-foot-high, 500-pound "purple martin palace" featuring 112 bird apartments. Built by New Jersey Pine Barrens native Leslie Christofferson, the unusual 14-sided wooden birdhouse—capped with a bright red tin roof—is probably one of the largest of its kind ever built. According to Robert J. Koenig, museum director, this piece "signals the first major purchase to develop the museum's folk art collection and is the beginning of a new era for the museum as an important regional center for folk art."

You won't be disappointed in the hand-carved American decoys on exhibit, for when Fred Noyes died in 1987, he had amassed nearly 4,000 decoys. About 250 remain in the museum's permanent collection.

Another permanent collection, focusing on American painting and sculpture, is rotated whenever a gallery is free. Richard Anuszkiewicz's acrylic on canvas entitled *Rainbow Squared Red Ocher* is a good example of Op Art, which was important in the 1960s when paintings were based on optical illusion, perception, and their psychological and physical effects. A ceramic by Coco Schoenberg entitled *Raspberry Godot* reflects her interest in form as well as the space in and around an object. Her vessels are constructed with clay bands that often result in irregular and organic final products.

Two additional selections from the permanent collection include Lucy Glick's *Marine Drama*, a watercolor that is primarily abstract, alluding to familiar images of figures and landscapes; and Clarence Holbrook Carter's *A-Round*, an acrylic on paper, which is an abstract exploration of the egg shape. The egg, a symbol of life, is surrounded by circles representing infinity and the universe. The yellows and grays used in this piece create illusions of vibration, and the effect is hypnotic, inviting contemplation of the egg as symbol.

NOTES: Plan on making this a full day's outing. Eat at the museum or pack a picnic lunch, bring along binoculars, and walk or drive through the Brigantine Division of the Forsythe National Wildlife Refuge next door (see chapter 33). A bird book will be helpful for identification; if you come during summer, insect repellent and a hat are recommended.

51. Cream Ridge Winery

LOCATION Monmouth County
Route 539, south of Allentown, Cream Ridge 08514
(609) 259-9797

SEASON Year round

HIGHLIGHTS Wine tasting, guided tours of winery

ADMISSION Free

HOURS 11 A.M.–6 P.M. weekdays; noon–5 P.M. Sundays

FACILITIES Rest room, salesroom

EVENTS Festivals and introductions of new wines throughout the year; call for schedule

FOR AN ART ASSIGNMENT IN HIS FIRST YEAR OF HIGH SCHOOL, TOM AMABILE PAINTED A watercolor showing a barn-like structure surrounded by flat, open land. That was in 1941.

The painting was forgotten until 47 years later, when it was found in Tom's cellar by his son Jerry. "I almost fainted when I saw it," recalls Tom, "because it was identical to the winery my wife, Joan, and I opened here on April 16, 1988. Even the barrels in front of our building are in the same place as those I painted in the picture." Tom doesn't believe anyone can predict the future, but he feels that "subconsciously, this painting remained in my memory all those years and surfaced when I was designing Cream Ridge Winery." The only connection Tom can see between his full-time employment as a network analyst specialist for Public Service Gas and Electric Company in Newark and his part-time job as wine master at Cream Ridge is that "the flow of gas is similar to the flow of wine, as is understanding the pressure of each."

Except for an unusual fence made of wine barrels around the vast front lawn, the outside of the new winery looks quite plain. However, visitors are pleasantly surprised once they step inside. Not only is the decor attractive and cozy, but the warmth extended by the Amabile family is contagious. Jerry, Tom and Joan's son, quit his position as a social worker to serve full-time as manager, while his wife, Diane, handles sales. When listening to what led to opening the winery, it's obvious that this family business is a labor of love.

Tom first became interested in winemaking as a hobby in the late 1960s, after a coworker at Public Service gave him a recipe calling for four of everything: four pounds of sugar, four pounds of fruit, four gallons of water,

Jerry Amabile describes the winemaking process to visitors, who stand in the balcony so they can overlook the entire operation.

four orange slices, four lemon slices, and one-fourth pound of yeast. All the ingredients were supposed to be fermented for—you guessed it—four days. Tom picked cherries for this wine from a neighbor's tree and it turned out to be not only sweet and delicious but the start of his winemaking days.

Reading all he could about making wine, Tom began experimenting with every fruit he could lay his hands on. He also began visiting wineries and talking with growers to learn about French hybrids and other grape varieties that would grow on the East Coast. Next, he enrolled in a wine-making course taught by Frank Gadek at Allentown College in Pennsylvania. By the mid-1970s Tom was so well versed in the subject that he was asked to teach classes and lecture on wine appreciation. When one of his hobby wines received top honors in a tasting that included California commercial wines, Tom realized it was time to become a professional wine maker.

Tom's first experience as a wine maker was working for a friend in Pennsylvania, which required him to commute 3½ hours from New Jersey on weekends. Marketing, however, proved to be a problem, and the winery kept losing money until Tom decided to experiment with fruit wines. Not only did sales pick up, but his wines won medals. When New Jersey broadened its winery laws, Tom decided to open one of his own in the Garden State, and he purchased six acres of open land in 1984, with an option to buy the adjoining six acres later. Cream Ridge finally became a reality in 1988.

Cream Ridge is different from most wineries because of the wide variety of fruit wines, which are made from locally grown fruit. Although a newcomer in the field, Cream Ridge has already produced dry cherry, sweet Morello cherry, pear, peach, blueberry, and strawberry wines in addition to about a dozen white, red, and rosé wines made from grapes grown on the two-acre vineyard and from vineyards in surrounding states.

Delightful, informative tours are offered on demand. While standing on a balcony overlooking the entire operation, visitors are treated to an excellent 25-minute talk on the winemaking process. You'll learn how the fruits are crushed, destemmed, and fermented, as well as discover how the wine maker judges the correct amount of sugar to add. On production days you'll see the final product being bottled, labeled, and corked, and you'll receive tips on how to store your own wine at home. State-of-the-art equipment is used in this tiny winery, and when things are in full swing, the procedure is amazing to watch.

During its first year in operation Cream Ridge Winery sold 40,000 bottles of wine. When I visited, Jerry predicted that raspberry would be the winning wine that year, but I preferred the pear flavor. The only way to decide on your favorite is to stop in, savor the blueberry and other fruit wines, and enjoy a taste of the burgundy and pink catawba among a variety of wines available when you visit. Jerry will pour as many as you'd like to try, and even if you don't buy anything, it's an educational and fun experience.

NOTES: Six Flags Great Adventure Safari Park (see the following chapter) is only a few minutes away. See chapter 49 for a description of the Renault Winery and chapter 58 for the Four Sisters Winery. For updates on wine festivals, special events, and additional wineries throughout the state, call 1-800-524-0043 or contact the New Jersey Wine Industry Advisory Council at the New Jersey Department of Agriculture, CN330, Trenton, NJ 08625, (609) 292-8853.

52. Six Flags Great Adventure Safari Park

LOCATION	Ocean County
	Exit 7A off the New Jersey Turnpike at Jackson
	08527
	(908) 928-2000
SEASON	Late spring–early fall
HIGHLIGHTS	Free-roaming animals from Asia, Africa, Australia, Europe, North and South America, plus a variety of swans, geese, wood ducks, hawks, beavers, and otters
ADMISSION	Fee; children three and under free, children under 54 inches pay less
HOURS	Park: open weekends only late March–end April, daily thereafter through early September; hours seasonal, call before going
FACILITIES	Picnic tables, restaurants, food stands, and rest room

SIX FLAGS GREAT ADVENTURE SAFARI PARK ISN'T AFRICA, BUT IT MAY BE THE NEXT best place for viewing exotic creatures in a natural setting. As you drive your own vehicle through a smooth, winding four-mile roadway at your own pace, anything is possible. An ostrich may size you up as a frisky monkey relaxes on top of your car hood; these are only a few of the 1,500 exotic animals representing 50 different species found in the park.

Reputed to be the largest game preserve of its kind outside Africa, Safari Park provides an opportunity to observe and photograph animals from Asia, Africa, Australia, Europe, and the Americas. Whether you choose to watch the antics of pecking ostriches, jumping kangaroos, mischievous monkeys, rare Siberian tigers, or other animals, it's much more exciting to study the animals in this open environment—with a few unobtrusive fences—than to view them behind bars at the zoo. And don't worry: There isn't any danger of the animals stalking one another or you—they're well fed.

Divided into 11 sections, the park is arranged to allow visitors to drive from one area to the next, starting at the American section where bison, elk, fallow deer, llama, rhea, and white-tailed deer are found. The American

The Watusi cattle found at Great Adventure Safari Park protect their young by threatening enemies with their sharp horns. These cattle are considered sacred by tribespeople in Africa.

black bear is close by. Considered the smallest of all bears found in the wooded areas of North America, this creature can attain a height of 5 feet and weigh 200–500 pounds.

Huge African elephants, weighing as much as 14,000 pounds, reside in the African Plains sections along with white rhino, Greater Kudu addax, giraffe, peacock, red ankoli, sable antelope, zebra, horned oryx, white-bearded and white-tailed gnu, yellow-billed stork, and guinea fowl. The lion section is an ideal place to observe the habits of these great cats. As a sign of friendship the golden lions frequently rub against one another, but most of the time they're content to just sit around grooming themselves or stretch out to bask in the sun.

Swans, geese, wood ducks, mallards, blue heron, hawks, beavers, and otters are fun to observe in the pond areas, but watching the male ostrich display his feathers as he performs the mating ritual is riveting. The kangaroos are equally enjoyable. Butch Dring, director of Safari, suggests taking a close look at the kangaroos' pouches where any movement from within is caused by a baby kangaroo, known as a "joey." Born the size of a lima bean, the baby crawls into the mother's pouch and stays there several months while feeding and continuing to grow.

The Siberian tiger, now on the endangered species list and usually found in the cold and snowy forests of northern Manchuria and southeast Siberia, can also be seen here. The largest of all the big cats, it can reach a length of 14 feet and weigh 650 pounds. It's easily identified by its beautiful orange coat and black stripes.

You'll probably come across the one-humped dromedary camel; the aoudad, commonly called Barbary sheep, recognized by thick, long horns; the Markhor, largest of all wild goats; and the Rhesus monkey, an amusing animal until it jumps on your car, stares in through the windshield, and proceeds to scratch the paint or vinyl roof. Old-timers will probably remember this type of monkey from organ-grinder days. In many parts of India this monkey is thought to be sacred and is protected.

All the animals are exciting to see, but the giraffes and unusual Watusi cattle are extraordinary. Watusi cattle stick together at all times and at a moment's notice can form a protective circle and use their huge horns as weapons. They also sleep in a circle formation, placing their young calves in the center for protection.

According to Dring, Watusi cattle have existed for thousands of years and are descendants of the aurochs, the prehistoric wild ox mentioned in the Bible. Watusi is the most common of a number of names given to several lines of similar cattle raised in eastern Africa. Their horns often measure 5 feet in length, 6 feet tip to tip, and 16–18 inches in circumference. These cattle are also considered sacred to the tribesmen.

As many as 80 animals are born here each summer. Apparently the daily allowance of 2.7 tons of hay, along with the normal diet of their species supplemented with vitamins and minerals, agrees with them. During winter months, when the park closes, animals unaccustomed to cold weather are boarded inside heated buildings.

It's wonderful to see so many animals roaming freely here in the Garden State, and a visit to the park is a lot less expensive than flying to Africa.

NOTES: Visitors must keep car windows closed at all times. If you don't want the monkeys climbing on your car, take the bypass road; or, for a small fee, an air-conditioned bus is available to take you through the park. Bring a picnic lunch to enjoy in the grove or try the restaurant.

53. New Jersey State Museum

LOCATION Mercer County
205 West State Street, Trenton 08601
(609) 292-6464, (609) 292-6308

SEASON Year round

HIGHLIGHTS Decorative and Fine Arts collections; Hall of Natural Sciences; Sisler Collection of North American Mammals; New Jersey's Native Americans: The Archaeological Record; astronomy exhibits; planetarium

ADMISSION Free; fee for Planetarium

HOURS Tuesday–Saturday 9 A.M.–4:45 P.M., Sunday noon–5 P.M., closed Mondays and major holidays

FACILITIES Rest room; parking; handicapped accessible, wheelchairs available free; for reservations call (609) 292-6341

EVENTS Year-round lectures, films, demonstrations, plays, and planetarium shows

TRENTON WAS A THRIVING SHIPPING CENTER IN THE 1700s. IT WAS HERE, ON December 26, 1776 and again on January 2, 1777, that American forces defeated the British. When it was named the state capital in 1790, it was just the beginning, for the city continued to prosper during the 19th century as a manufacturing center for steel and pottery.

Lenox, the first American company to make china for the White House, has been based here since 1889, when it was known as the Ceramic Art Company. Begun by Walter Scott Lenox and Jonathan Coxen, the company's first few years were shaky due to America's preference for imported china. When Tiffany & Company ordered Lenox china for its New York store at the turn of the century, attitudes changed. Not only did wealthy families buy it for status, but in 1918 President Woodrow Wilson replaced the White House Wedgwood with a 1,700-piece set of Lenox china. Trenton also gained a reputation for fine ceramics by producing the first American-made porcelain bathtubs in 1873.

After World War II Trenton fell into a slump. Although many of its

Relics of the past tower over visitors to the New Jersey State Museum.

neighbors are still struggling to survive, the city has much to offer visitors. Old Barracks (Barrack Street, 609-396-1776) is the only remaining French and Indian War–era barracks in North America. Built in 1758 for the army of King George II, it housed Hessian troops at the time of Washington's famous Christmas night crossing of the Delaware in 1766 and was later used as a hospital by his army. It has been a museum since 1902, exhibiting a restored soldiers' squad room, 18th-century period rooms, decorative arts, firearms, and revolutionary war and Americana collections. A donation is requested; hours vary.

William Trent House (15 Market Street, 609-989-3027), one of the oldest buildings, was built in 1719 by Scots merchant William Trent for whom the city is named. Trent served as New Jersey's first chief justice until his death on Christmas Day, 1724. The elegantly restored home was furnished according to an original inventory and has been called "the finest Queen Anne house in America." There is an admission charge; call for hours. The Meredith Havens Fire Museum (244 Perry Street, 609-989-4038) houses a collection of photographs, fire-fighting tools and equipment, uniforms, and items related to the 1747–1892 history of Trenton's volunteer companies. It's free; call for hours.

One of Trenton's gems is the New Jersey State Museum, which began in 1830 with an exhibit of only a few rocks. These weren't foundation rocks but the prized minerals rock hounds stored in the attic of the old State House in Trenton. Recognizing the need to "preserve and celebrate the artistic, cultural, historical, and scientific resources of New Jersey," the State Legislature passed a law in 1895 designating it as the official state museum, and they relocated it to the State House Annex.

In its present location since 1965, the museum occupies a four-story building with an adjoining 150-seat planetarium and a 416-seat auditorium.

Acclaimed for its outstanding collection of New Jersey furniture, ceramics, silver, quilts, and folk art, it also contains a wealth of American paintings, sculpture, prints, drawings, and photographs.

In addition to the outstanding exhibits and the planetarium, there are regularly scheduled films, dance programs, lectures, and children's theater, so you can easily occupy an entire day. From the parking lot entrance you'll first approach the Sisler Collection of North American Mammals. These specimens, including a brown bear, black jaguar, wolf, and bobcat, are impressively set up in realistic dioramas representing their native habitats.

Explore the culture of the Delaware Indians in the New Jersey Room. There are interesting models describing how this tribe manufactured wampum for the European colonists. Purple wampum was more valuable than white wampum simply because the purple lining of the hard-shell clam yielded only a few beads while a great many white beads could be made from a single whelk. In this section you'll also learn how the Indians used burning coals to make their canoes.

The Hall of Natural Sciences, a treat for all ages, dramatically explores the origin of the universe and the solar system. The structure of igneous, sedimentary, and metamorphic rock is also explained, while one of the favorites in this hall is a simulated mine, where 66 fluorescent minerals appear in brilliant, shining colors.

Children are usually reluctant to budge from the dinosaur area, especially when they see the Haddonfield dinosaur, discovered in Haddonfield, New Jersey, in 1958. Nearby is another wonder, a giant "Mammuthus." Mammoths like this once roamed through the state, and dozens of this species have been recovered from the Continental Shelf off the New Jersey coast, indicating that the sea level was much lower during the Ice Age than it is today. Giant mastodons, which became extinct as early as 5,000 years ago, are demonstrated in drawings, but visitors are free to touch a sample mastodon bone. This giant, resembling a huge elephant, preferred woodland areas and browsed on leaves and evergreen twigs.

If you can pull yourself away from the exhibits and are here on a weekend, head to the planetarium for a relaxing first-class guided trip through the universe.

NOTES: It's best to buy tickets for the planetarium show—scheduled on the hour during afternoons—as soon as you arrive. Children must be at least four years of age to be admitted to the planetarium. Additional programs are scheduled weekdays during school recesses and in July and August. Unlimited free parking is available on weekends adjacent to the museum; on weekdays it's limited, but paid parking is available in nearby city lots. Don't miss the Museum Shop on the first floor; it features handicrafts from around the world, books, and inexpensive gift items. It is open Tuesday–Saturday 10 A.M.–4:15 P.M., Sunday noon–4:30 P.M.

54. Toms River

LOCATION	Ocean County, see text for starting points
SEASON	Best after heavy rains, spring, and fall
HIGHLIGHTS	Beautiful scenery, abundant wildlife, fishing, wildflowers, swimming
ADMISSION	Free, excluding canoe rental
HOURS	Sunrise–sunset
FACILITIES	Sandy areas, swimming

ONCE KNOWN AS GOOSE CREEK, TOMS RIVER IS SUPPOSEDLY NAMED FOR THOMAS Luker, who settled among the Indians around 1700. Rumors still abound about the privateering that took place in the town of Toms River, but so far not one canoeist has found any treasure. And although a windmill once stood in the center of the river close to town, today the river provides a pleasant refuge for boating enthusiasts. The upper part of the river is very narrow and ideal for canoeing.

Canoeists have a variety of places to launch their canoes. The river runs over 30 miles from Bowman's Mill Bridge at Route 528 to Barnegat Bay. A normal day trip may run from Route 528 to Bowman Road, from Bowman to Whitesville, or from Whitesville to Route 571. For additional paddling time you can put in at Coventry Road and go past Bowman Road to Whitesville. If you're alone, take Bowman Road to Whitesville. It's a long day trip, with a car shuttle distance of only three miles, but it's within an hour's walk from where you've parked your car. Takeout points are on Route 70, Route 37, and the second crossing at Route 527. Other points have too much traffic and are too dangerous.

The upper section of the river has a width of one canoe length with sharp turns. In addition to holly trees, deciduous bushes cover the low banks. Be prepared to carry the canoe over several large logs, but remember that this is part of the challenge and fun. Sneakers are a good idea to protect your feet. After the wide open area there's a good resting stop at a dry, sandy bank.

Soon the river turns into a wooded area, passing under the Coventry Road bridge. Sharp turns will keep you alert for a while; these lessen around the tributary along the left, another good spot to rest. From here a clearer section enters, with a housing development popping up on the left before the river crosses under a sand road, continuing until Bowman Hill Bridge. Ten minutes away is a low clearing to the left; here a wide trail leads to the pines. Relax a bit. Up ahead the river has fewer turns for a while, then goes through grassy fields and swampy areas.

Soon woods appear again and the foliage becomes dense. Bypass the bulldozed canal straight ahead, staying on course by following the river sharply to the left. Keep paddling until the steep laurel-covered bank appears on the right side, and watch for pines and scrub oaks. This is a good place to splash around in the dark, tannin-colored water and enjoy a breather from your paddling.

When you're ready to start again, stay in the channel and head through another swampy area to the Whitesville bridge. In 10 minutes you'll come to another good spot along the left bank to stretch your legs by walking the sandy trail. Large shade trees appear, a pleasure during hot weather. Be wary, however: They might be covered with pretty mosses and lichens, but they're also loaded with poison ivy. Because poison ivy is prevalent all along the river, it's a good idea to keep a sharp lookout for it if you're allergic.

Once back in the canoe you'll paddle past more pines, laurel, and holly. There's a good ramp to stop at a bit farther ahead. Route 70 is five minutes farther. Past the mobile home development the river widens until reaching Riverwood Park campsite. Route 571 is overhead, and again the river widens at Union Branch. A chemical plant spoils the scenery for a short time, but once past this point the river widens, passing under Route 527.

Route 527 appears shortly; continue along until leaving the woods. Turn left, paddling under the Garden State Parkway, and stay close to the left bank before swinging into the channel heading toward an island. Make a right turn at the lumberyard until you reach the takeout ramp at the Toms River bus stop.

NOTES: Canoes may be rented from Albocondo Campgrounds, (732) 349-4079, and Pineland Canoes, Inc., (732) 364-0389 or (800) 281-0383. Call first for reservations and river conditions. Bring along a picnic lunch with adequate drinks, a change of clothing, and bird identification books if you want help identifying the birds you may see along the route.

55. Oswego River

LOCATION	Burlington County
	Off Route 563; put-in point down the next paved road to the left just past the Pine Barrens; canoe rentals in Chatsworth (see Notes)
SEASON	Best after heavy rains, spring, and fall
HIGHLIGHTS	Magnificent scenery, abundant wildlife, wildflowers, swimming, fishing, historic sites
ADMISSION	Free, excluding canoe rental
HOURS	Sunrise–sunset
FACILITIES	Sandy areas, swimming

O<small>N MY LAST VOYAGE DOWN THE</small> O<small>SWEGO,</small> I <small>EXPERIENCED A FEELING OF SERENITY AS</small> I looked out upon a landscape of wildflowers and spotted an abundance of wildlife. It was indeed difficult to believe that my partner and I were so close to civilization. The New Jersey Pine Barrens, a 2,000-square-mile wilderness in the southeast portion of the state, is truly another world. Far from "barren," it's actually filled with a wealth of trees, plants, flowers, and creatures but was named the Pine Barrens because the land wasn't suitable for farming.

Here, in the heart of the Pine Barrens, you can enjoy this natural environment as you lazily paddle down the Oswego River, serenaded by mockingbirds. Clumps of blue flag iris along the banks are as dazzling as the sweet fragrance of honeysuckle is intoxicating.

Running 8 miles from Oswego Lake in the north to Harrisville Lake in the south, the four- to five-hour trip starts below the dam at Oswego Lake, where the river is quite narrow. At this point the water is very shallow and its amber color is caused by dissolved tannins from the cedar trees and natural iron deposits.

Gliding along the meandering river, you'll discover what makes the Pine Barrens unique as white cedars, pines, and maples stretch overhead. Paddling gently, let the current carry you while keeping a watchful eye for ripples on the water's surface that indicate shallow areas.

When we were there we saw a couple of canoeists in front of us negotiating the frequent sharp turns beautifully. Totally relaxed, it was easy to turn our full attention to the tall cedars that came into view. Every so often we'd pass an overturned canoe and say hello to a novice standing off to the side wringing out clothing. Some paddlers overturned their canoes

Paddling down the meandering Pine Barrens river is glorious.

deliberately to cool off and splash. Luckily most of the Oswego is so shallow that a spill isn't too serious.

As the river widens, lily pads seem to gently float by. At about 1½ hours from the put-in point, you may wish to stop for a rest at the sandy beach along the right bank. This area leads to an open field of pines and low bushes, a fine place to swim and picnic before going on to the next section, which has a lot of sharp turns.

Soon you'll come to another good bank that's ideal for taking a break. Here we got into a discussion with another couple on how the river was named. Rumor has it that "oswego" is an Indian word meaning "where the valley widens" or "flowing out." Another version is that the name came from the Swago Saw Mill, built around 1741, at the town of Martha near present-day Jenkins.

Shortly after starting out again you'll come to a gravel beach; a cinder-block building is on the right along with a sign indicating you've entered Wharton State Forest. In this area the river becomes deeper, with more turns to negotiate.

After a few minutes the river widens as it enters Martha Pond, an open area covered with many cedar and shrub islands. This area is extremely shallow, and underwater grasses constantly swish against the bottom of the canoe. It's a good idea to hunt for clear areas so that the canoe glides more easily. Continue around the island, hugging either bank to stay on course.

Paddling past more islands, the pond alternately narrows and broadens before finally opening wide as the islands turn into grass-covered sandbars. Upon completing the outside bend of a sharp right turn you can see a cleared area leading up to a sand staircase known as Calico Ridge, another good rest stop. Bearing left from here, you'll probably see some of the muskrats and water birds that populate this area. During spring there are countless pitcher plants or even a rare orchid on the left bank. The pond ends a short distance ahead as the river turns sharply right and then left, once again facing another lovely sandy beach.

Soon you'll pass under the old Martha Bridge near the site of an abandoned ironworks that once used the pond as a source of energy. If you get out of the canoe and walk along the sand road leading into town, you'll be able to see the furnace ruins. Many people use this area of the river as their special swimming hole because the water is extremely deep. You can even play Tarzan, if you like, using the rope someone hung from one of the tree limbs.

After passing the bridge, the channel narrows to one canoe length and then the river runs straight. The mountain laurel is outstanding here in the spring. Harrisville Lake appears suddenly; if you're tired, you may wish to stop along the left bank.

Plan on starting this trip as early in the day as possible so you can swim, relax, and cruise leisurely on this very special New Jersey river.

NOTES: Canoes may be rented from Mick's, (609) 726-1380, and Pine Barrens Canoe Rental, (609) 726-1515, both Chatsworth 08019. Call first to reserve and check on the water level. The rental place will drive you to the put-in point, pick you up at Harrisville Lake, and transport you back to your car for a minimal fee. If you have your own canoe, go with another couple and leave one car at each end to make a one-way trip.

56. Zimmerli Art Museum

LOCATION Middlesex County
George and Hamilton streets, New Brunswick
08903
(908) 932-7237

SEASON Year round

HIGHLIGHTS Major focus: French, American, Russian art; graphic arts; major exhibitions of national or international significance; lectures; art demonstrations; children's programs

ADMISSION Free, donation optional

HOURS Tuesday–Friday 10 A.M.–4:30 P.M., Saturday and Sunday noon–5 P.M; call before going, hours subject to change

FACILITIES Rest room, cafe, museum shop, drinking water, classrooms, print and drawing room for viewing and research

EVENTS Regularly scheduled exhibitions, lectures, films, crafts; for free schedule write Zimmerli Art Museum, George and Hamilton streets, New Brunswick 08903

SINCE ITS EXPANSION IN 1983, THE JANE VOORHEES ZIMMERLI ART MUSEUM AT Rutgers University has earned an international reputation. The museum building, originally constructed as a library, incorporates the elegant domed and vaulted space of the handsome turn-of-the-century Voorhees Hall. Known as the University Art Gallery when it was established in 1966, the facilities were expanded in 1983 to include 5,000 square feet of special exhibition galleries and 15,000 square feet of display space for the university's collection. It also features a community education room, administrative offices, and workshops where visitors can gain hands-on experience under the guidance of a visiting artist.

In 1983 it was renamed in honor of Jane Voorhees Zimmerli, an active participant in the New Brunswick community and mother of Alan Voorhees, the major benefactor of the new construction. The museum, which houses around 45,000 objects of art, is divided into the David Lloyd and Carmen Kreeger Special Exhibition Gallery for the graphic arts collections; the newly

The modern interior of the Zimmerli Art Museum makes it worth visiting. Changing exhibits make it worth revisiting.

opened Hall of Russian Art for the George Riabov collection of Russian art; the Anna A. Greenwall Education Room for community projects; the David and Mildred Morse Print and Drawing Room for public viewing and basic research; the Lillian Lilien Room for Friends of the Museum for membership offices and hospitality; and the Gallery of '37 (Rutgers College Class of 1937) for special exhibitions.

Permanent holdings include a collection of Western paintings from the 15th century to the present, with concentrations of 19th-century American art and American surrealism of the 1930s and 1940s. Over 60 works representing 3,000 years of Peruvian culture and a group of Greco-Roman sculptures can also be seen.

The major focus of this museum is on the graphic arts. The Graphic Arts and Works on Paper exhibition presents a survey of the history of printmaking, beginning with prints by German artists at the end of the 15th century and continuing with Rembrandt and other 17th-century Dutch artists. Included are 150 etchings by 18th-century Italian artist Giovanni Battista Piranesi and Western prints from 1800 to the present.

A number of sculptures are on permanent display. Herbert Ferber's *Sculpture to Create an Environment*, completed in 1961, is a room-sized piece consisting of numerous fiberglass elements. Hundreds of original *New Yorker* illustrations by Julien de Miskey are here, along with his Art Deco etchings, paintings, and later constructions.

George Overbury "Pop" Hart, a late 19th- and early 20th-century American watercolorist, printmaker, and painter, traveled around the world recording his impressions of people and places. Thanks to his niece, Jeanne Overbury Hart, the museum owns over 3,000 of his works.

Plan on spending a couple of hours strolling through historic New Brunswick, home to Rutgers, the State University. New Brunswick, settled in 1680 and named in honor of the English royal house of Brunswick, thrived for many years as a shipping center because of its location on the Raritan River. It became known as the "Hub City" in the 1900s when the railroad and highways improved transportation through the area.

The bell tower and clock on the First Reformed Church, Neilson and Bayard streets, marked the passing hours for the tradesmen at the Hiram Market, a center for religious, educational, financial, and commercial activities in the early 1800s. Surrounding the church is a pre revolutionary war–era cemetery with cast-iron fencing. Nearby—Church and Neilson streets—is Christ Episcopal Church, built in the Gothic Revival style in the 1740s. Its octagonal wood steeple topped by a copper spire is original, but in 1852 the church was rebuilt using the original brownstones in order to enlarge the nave. The tree standing in the southeast corner of the churchyard was planted by Joyce Kilmer's father in the 1930s in memory of his son.

Joyce Kilmer, author of *Trees*, was born in the Greek Revival house at 17 Joyce Kilmer Avenue in 1886. Kilmer spent his early childhood here, attended Rutgers College, and was killed in action during World War I in France at the age of 32. The house is open weekdays 9 A.M.–5 P.M. Guided tours are available by appointment; call (908) 745-5117.

At 17 Seminary Place you'll find the original library of the New Brunswick Theological Seminary, the oldest seminary in the country. Known as the Gardner A. Sage Library, it houses special collections, including Bibles from every country in the world, written in every language. There is also a room devoted to books of religious art. Its round-arched design is Romanesque, basilica-style, with clerestory windows illuminating the interior hall. It's open Monday, Tuesday, and Thursday 9 A.M.–10 P.M.; Wednesday and Friday 9 A.M.–5 P.M.; call (908) 247-5243 for further information.

Old Queens, now housing the administrative offices of Rutgers, was originally Queens College, founded in 1766 by the Dutch Reformed Church of America. Constructed of brownstone and cited as one of the finest examples of Federal architecture in the nation, its facade includes Doric pilasters, a cupola housing the Old Queens Bell, and handmade glass windowpanes. On State and National Registers of Historic Places, it's open weekdays 8:30 A.M.–4:30 P.M.; (908) 932-7823.

On your walk you'll pass by Johnson & Johnson headquarters, designed by I. M. Pei, and many unique shops along George Street.

NOTES: Parking is available around the corner from the museum on George Street. Snack shops and restaurants abound in the area.

57. New Jersey State Aquarium

LOCATION Camden County
On the Delaware River opposite Penn's Landing,
Ulysses S. Wiggins Waterfront Park, 1 Riverside
Drive, Camden 08103
(856) 365-3300

SEASON Year round

HIGHLIGHTS Shark petting; open ocean tank; Atlantic fish;
aquatic nursery; hands-on exhibits; rocky tide pool;
wet lab; seal show; movie presentations

ADMISSION Fee for aquarium and for parking

HOURS 10 A.M.–5 P.M., November 1–March 1; 9:30 A.M.–
5:30 P.M. daily the rest of the year; 9:30 A.M.–
8:30 P.M. Sundays from Easter through August; and
closed New Year's, Thanksgiving, and Christmas.
Call to check schedule before going.

FACILITIES Rest room, café with panorama of Delaware River,
gift shop, infant changing facilities, free backpacks
(strollers are not allowed), wheelchair accessible

EVENTS Seal shows; open ocean presentations; and
multimedia presentations at various times; daily
puppet theater performances; scuba diving
demonstrations. Write or call for schedule.

THERE'S SOMETHING WONDERFULLY FISHY GOING ON AT THE NEW JERSEY STATE Aquarium. For starters, the 120,000-square-foot building, which opened in 1992 and sits on a 4.5-acre site on the Delaware River, is magnificent.

The outdoor exhibits, replicas of two different New Jersey habitats, include a rushing mountain trout stream stocked with native species including brook trout, catfish, sunfish, and pickerel; and Seal Shores, a 170,000-gallon pool with above-water and underwater viewing, which was built to resemble a sandy shoreline where harbor seals and gray seals are usually found. The best news is that the seals are always here and ready to perform for the crowds. Don't miss the show; it's really fun and informative watching these creatures ride the waves, roll over, and dive to the bottom.

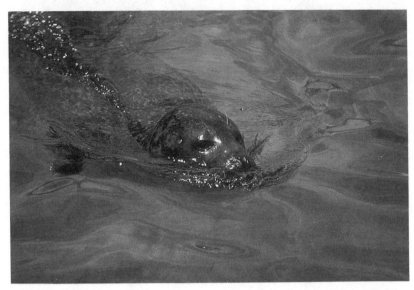

You can't fish at the New Jersey State Aquarium, but you *can* catch a great seal show!

Once inside, head over to the shallow pool area and, if you dare, touch a shark! If not, stand back and watch others dip their hands into the water to pet sharks, skates, and rays. Or head over to the nation's second largest open ocean tank. Filled with 760,000 gallons of water, it contains sharks and hundreds of other specimens native to the North Atlantic. These tiny animals hanging onto the sharks aren't baby sharks but remoras—better known as "sharksuckers." They have an oval disc on their heads that enables them to attach onto another animal. In hitching these rides, they save energy and get a free meal from scraps of food left by their hosts.

Exhibit areas within or around this tank include the Ocean Realm, a giant window showcasing the largest and most active open-water fishes and sharks as they cruise in and out of view; SeaProbe, where a hatch-like entrance leads into a replica of an underwater exploratory station with true-to-life scientific equipment; the Edge of the Abyss, a two-story window offering a view of the edge of the continental shelf with scores of game fish and more sharks; and a long, horizontal window looking into the hull of a shipwreck encrusted with algae and invertebrates.

Many more exhibits are found within the first level. These include an open, skylit area with shorebirds chasing waves lapping against a barrier beach shore; a Pine Barrens stream where water meets land where a stream exits from a cedar-fringed, sphagnum-bearded pond; and exhibits focusing on and exploring the Delaware River's history, its current role, and its future.

The second level, a cheery, open space with excellent views of the Delaware River and Philadelphia's skyline, is designed to amaze, entertain, and inform. Here you'll find a Water Babies display, showing developing trout eggs, larval lobsters and blue crabs, and mated pairs of freshwater fish with their nests and young. The role color plays is demonstrated at the octopus tank; the octopus changes its color according to mood and environment. You'll also learn how fish talk, as you see yourself transformed into an actual fish at the Sea Senses exhibition.

There's usually a crowd around the staffed area and hands-on learning lab. This section combines elements of a wet lab with an eclectic collection of marine-related objects common to New Jersey and is complete with a wet table displaying recently collected items from local habitats. Peering through the microscopes makes it quite a learning experience.

As you wander through the building, you may wonder how much the food bill is for all the hungry mouths. Annually, about $100,000 is spent to feed about 2,700 fish and other aquatic animals. The pickiest eaters are the seahorses; these thrive on small live shrimp and zooplankton. On the other hand, blue crabs will eat anything that smells like it was once alive! Seals eat the most, swallow fish whole, and consume up to 11 pounds a day, while the corals eat the least. They use sunlight and algae living within their tissues to generate food. Feeding the sharks is not only exciting but potentially dangerous. With fish stuck on the end of a pole, the keepers can keep track that each one is eating well. This also discourages the sharks from using other fish in the tank as a snack between meals!

NOTES: There is plenty of parking here with patrolling security guards. Because of the high attendance, officials advise the best time for weekend visits is on Sunday mornings. Tickets may be purchased at the aquarium a half hour before opening until one hour before closing, or ordered by calling (800) 922-6572 and charging to a credit card. Admission is on a timed-ticket basis. Plan on spending half a day at the aquarium, and continue your adventure by visiting the Philadelphia Zoo, just across the river. A Riverbus operates 12 hours a day, with four trips per hour during summer months and less frequently in winter. For more information on fees and hours, call (800) 634-4027. Café prices are reasonable; if you're tired, linger over a cup of coffee or tea and enjoy the view.

58. Four Sisters Winery, Home of Matarazzo Farms

LOCATION Warren County
Route 519, Belvidere 07823
(908) 475-3872

SEASON Year round; fall is best.

HIGHLIGHTS Pick-your-own fruits and vegetables or fresh ready-picked produce, wine tasting, winery tour, barefoot grape stomping, magnificent scenery, farm animals, hayrides

ADMISSION Free

HOURS Winery: 9 A.M.–6 P.M., seven days a week year round
Farm store: 9 A.M.–6 P.M., seven days a week from mid-April to December 24

FACILITIES Rest room, produce stand and store, winery, salesroom, picnic tables

EVENTS Year-round events and activities, including a Native American Powwow; Bluegrass, Strawberry, Peach, and Harvest festivals; free wine tasting daily; free wine cellar tours every weekend; private parties by reservation; grape-stomping parties; hiking in the hills followed by a buffet dinner during winter; and more. Call or write for complete schedule.

WILLIAM TELL BECAME FAMOUS AFTER SHOOTING AN APPLE OFF HIS SON'S HEAD. Robert "Matty" Matarazzo has lots of apples but doesn't choose to repeat Tell's crazy stunt. As a third-generation farmer, he prefers raising apples. Besides, he has four daughters!

Matty's grandparents began farming in North Caldwell in 1921. "Before I got into the picture," says Matty, "they sold only wholesale. As more and more people moved nearer to their farm and begged to buy their produce, my grandfather realized it was a good idea and began selling wholesale and retail."

Matty learned about farming and selling retail from working with his father. "When he took a break for lunch, he'd leave me in charge. I was only nine years old but wanted to impress him. I did new things, put up

Matty Matarazzo doesn't mind carrying heavy crates of grapes—not when they bring so much joy to those who come to crush them the old-fashioned way.

new displays, and anything I thought he'd think was great. As the years went by, the business grew and grew, and we had to expand. My wife, Laurie, and I moved to Warren County, bought 120 acres, and thought we'd work on expanding production-wise. However, after about five years in the production end of farming, I realized I wasn't cut out to be only a truck farmer. I needed to be out there more with people."

Today Matty's farming operation has expanded to 392 acres. Not only does he raise 14 varieties of tasty apples, but 7 varieties of fruit and 75 varieties of vegetables, with everything from pumpkins and strawberries to specialty items such as squash blossoms, flowering kale, and popcorn.

The farm, now one of the largest and most diversified fruit and vegetable farms in northern New Jersey, attracts over 250,000 visitors a year who come for many reasons. Some like the thrill of going into the fields to handpick fruits or vegetables and into the orchards for red delicious apples. Others like to take a drive into the country to purchase fruits and vegetables picked by the employees and handsomely displayed inside a rustic red farm store previously used as a dairy barn. In addition, dried herbs, gourds, all kinds of peppers—frying, chili, Hungarian, and long hots—are available, as is pure honey, turnips, and parsley.

Customers return time and time again for the fresh apple cider crushed on the premises in the cider mill or to relax on the large deck overlooking a beautiful panorama of rolling hills and fields of lush strawberries, grapes, sweet corn, raspberries, and other goodies, depending on the season. Fall is a particularly wonderful season to visit; that's when the trees in the distance are ablaze in every color of the rainbow and when visitors are offered free hayrides into the fields where they can handpick a pumpkin of their choice or tour the farm. The Matarazzo family believes in the personal touch, and frequently, when one of the daughters leads the ride, she'll discuss the problems and challenges of farming and what everyone can do to help assure the future of farming in the area.

No matter when you call, you'll find there's something exciting happening here. There are Mystery Whodunit parties; winter Singles Nights; various festivals, including the Peach, Bluegrass, Harvest, Strawberry, and High Flying Festivals, and a huge Powwow when Native Americans from all over the country get together and provide a spectacular show looking back into a time when Native Americans occupied these lands. The list goes on and on; a schedule of events can be obtained by calling or writing.

There's another reason to head out to Matarazzo Farms—the Four Sisters Winery, adjacent to the farm store, which Matty and his wife, Laurie, opened in 1984. Go on a weekend for a free wine-cellar and vineyard tour with wine tasting, or go on weekdays for wine tasting alone. Tours, led either by a friendly employee or Matty, are not only enjoyable but also educational.

On the one-hour tour, which begins in the 17-acre vineyard, you'll learn why it's so vital to nurture the grapes while they're still on the vine, as well as how the eight varieties of grapes are pruned, why the chill tanks are outdoors and how they're used for stabilization, and the steps necessary before the grapes are washed and dumped into the screw press. The bottling procedure here is simple, especially when everyone on the staff participates in the crushing, corking, or labeling. The four bonnets on each label are a symbol of the four daughters.

After the tour, visitors are invited to taste a number of the award-winning wines, which include the winery's first wine, Papa's Red, a dry red wine with robust aroma and an abundance of complex fruit character which was named to honor Matty's dad. Over 23 wines are produced at Four Sisters Winery. In addition to the various red, white, and rosé wines, there are four delicious fruit wines. These are named for and signed by the four sisters and include Sadie's Apple, Cherry Melissa, Robin's Raspberry, and, my favorite, Strawberry Serena.

If you're looking for a great stress reliever, plan to take your shoes and socks off, jump into a barrel, and crush grapes the old-fashioned way during a regularly scheduled stomping party that's held here on weekends. You'll be guaranteed a rip-roaring time that's followed by a romantic moonlit hayride and delicious buffet complete with wine tasting.

Fun is the key word at Matarazzo Farm and the Four Sisters Winery, where the customer definitely comes first. Go, look around, have a good time, buy some great produce or wine. No doubt you'll return time and time again for a festival, grape stomping, hayride, or one of the many fun-filled activities.

NOTES: For the pick-your-own experience, wear comfortable clothing and shoes, take sunscreen, and call before going to see what's available. The farm and winery is very close to Well-Sweep Herb Farm (see chapter 23); Pequest Trout Hatchery (see chapter 45); and Spruce Run Reservoir, Route 31. See chapter 49 for a description of the Renault Winery and chapter 51 for the Cream Ridge Winery. For updates on wine festivals, special events, and additional wineries throughout the state, call (800) 524-0043, or contact the New Jersey Wine Industry Advisory Council at the New Jersey Department of Agriculture, CN330, Trenton, NJ 08625, (609) 292-8853.

59. Liberty Science Center

LOCATION Hudson County
Liberty State Park, 251 Phillip Street, Jersey City
07305
(201) 200-1000

SEASON Year round

HIGHLIGHTS Over 250 hands-on exhibits, demonstration theater, 170-foot observation tower; 100-foot-long Touch Tunnel; a 700-pound expandable geodesic globe; dazzling laser light display throughout the four-story atrium; "Tools and Toys"™ science specialty store; Kodak Omni Theater; and magnificent views of Manhattan's skyline

ADMISSION Separate entrance fees for science center and for the Omni Theater; reduced admission combination tickets available. Admission to exhibit areas of science center is on a "pay-as-you-wish" basis the first Wednesday of each month from 1 P.M. to closing. Members enter free. Fee for parking until 4:30 P.M.

HOURS 9:30 A.M.–5:30 P.M., seven days a week; hours subject to change during summer months; call to check schedule before going

FACILITIES Rest room, water fountains, gift shop, coat room, lockers, full handicapped access, lunchroom for school groups, snack area with vending machines, Laser Lights Café, limited number of free strollers, and facility rentals for groups and group events

EVENTS Films at the Kodak Omni Theater change every six months; displays are changed regularly; various themed events and traveling exhibitions held year round; call or write for a schedule

OFFICIALS REFER TO THE LIBERTY SCIENCE CENTER AS A PLACE "WHERE SCIENCE = Fun." After spending an afternoon browsing and touching dozens of "hands-on" exhibits, I agree: The Center *is* fun, *and* absolutely "A-OK" for all ages.

Opened in January 1993, the dramatically styled exterior of the huge

**There's something for everyone at the Liberty Science Center; the salt marsh display is
a real attention grabber.**

white building sports a 170-foot observation tower and an impressive 11-ton geodesic dome housing the world's largest Omnimax theater.

Plan on spending an entire day here. If you have time after having explored the exhibits and participated in the activities and demonstrations inside the 170,000-square-foot center, you'll no doubt want to stroll along the easy nature trails within Liberty State Park. Or, depending on the season, you might want to fish, crab, swim, play tennis, launch a boat, bird watch, take a ferry to the Statue of Liberty and Ellis Island, or simply stay until sunset to absorb the fantastic view of Lady Liberty, Ellis Island, and lower Manhattan.

Wear comfortable shoes because there's so much to do, see, feel, and explore in gaining more knowledge of the world through the interactive exhibits in the center. Planned scientific demonstrations throughout various sections of the building enhance the regularly scheduled films and talks. For example, the "Bug Lady" might walk by with a giant live millipede or tarantula or even a giant Madagascar cockroach!

Entry to the $68 million center is through a 90-foot-high atrium that offers clear views of exhibition areas above and below the main floor. Save the "Tools and Toys"™ science specialty store to the right for last; when you do stop in, have lots of cash or a charge card because the selection of excellent products is mind-boggling.

It's also wise to reserve a seat in the Kodak Omni Theater as soon as you enter because tickets sell out quickly. The screen, reputed to be the world's largest, measures 88 feet in diameter and is 8 stories high. Be prepared for some thrilling moments; at times the movie—changed every six months—is so lifelike you may even feel a bit queasy.

Inside the atrium and hanging high above the Invention Floor is a huge aluminum sphere designed by Chuck Hoberman. In seconds, the 700-pound expandable geodesic globe unfolds robotically from a diameter of 4.5 feet to 18 feet. A colorful laser light display with varying animated images, including fish, faces, bugs, birds, and abstract geometric designs, projects up through the entire space at the rear of the atrium and can be viewed from many different angles and floors.

The three exhibit floors are divided into three categories: Environment, Health, and Invention. Children usually have their noses pressed against the three 20-foot-long meandering living salt marsh displays featured on the third floor in the Environment exhibit. They're filled with tall grasses, starfish, crabs, and numerous species of fish. The Bug Zoo is also on this floor and, while many visitors feel the live colonies of ants and bees, pink-toed tarantulas, and four-inch-long hissing Madagascar cockroaches are nauseating, they're fascinating if you have the stomach to stick around and observe. Nearby, in the Interactive Theater, watch environmentally related films while making choices that control the final outcome of the action.

If you've ever wondered about the physical properties of the earth's atmosphere and oceans, head over to the 20-foot, floor-to-ceiling "lighthouse" where, through a solar telescope, you can view sunspots and solar flares. There's also a weather station rain gauge, wind vane, and barometer on the outer deck to forecast the weather. Local scientists will be happy to assist you in The Green House for a closer look at rare insects.

The Health floor on the second level focuses on the human body. Everyone is invited to navigate a pitch-black, 100-foot-long Touch Tunnel with only the sense of touch as a guide, while the perplexing, 1,000-square-foot Illusion Labyrinth, complete with mirrors and optical illusions, is designed to challenge visual acumen. You might want to learn about your height, reflexes, balance, and flexibility in the "self-assessment" area or about your heart through EKG monitors and a capillary racer computer game.

Do stop by the hologram display, where two dimensions suddenly become three as you peer into holographic images of microscopes to see slides. Most youngsters find The Living Room intriguing. Here they can explore a laboratory, a fully equipped ambulance, and the "Empathy Belly," or pregnancy simulator. And, if you've ever wondered what effects alcohol would have on your timing and coordination, try the computer-controlled impaired-driving simulator.

The lower level, Invention, houses exhibits incorporating modern technology. Build structures with the help of a 10-foot-tall electromagnetic crane or experiment with aerodynamics, gears, and brakes. The choice is yours. Another Workshop discovery room brings ingenuity to life in self-directed or guided activities creating "tools" using a mix of ordinary objects such as popsicle sticks, scissors, and hammers as well as technical items such as computers and lasers.

Liberty Science Center's purpose is to "expose young people from all backgrounds to the sciences, encouraging them to explore careers in the field." The primary aim is to reach and engage those students whose exposure to and interest in the sciences has traditionally been low, including women, minorities, and inner-city residents.

The fun and educational exhibits are certain to make the goal a reality. Save this place for a rainy day or, if you want to take advantage of Liberty State Park, plan an entire day both indoors and outside in the sunshine.

NOTES: Don't forget a camera; the views are phenomenal. Laser Lights Café offers a wide selection of food at reasonable prices plus a great view. PATH train service with connecting buses to the park is available, as is ARCORP ferry service from Manhattan. Call (800) 53-FERRY for schedule and fares.

60. Trash Museum

LOCATION	Bergen County
	Two Dekorte Park Plaza, Lyndhurst 07071
	(201) 460-8300
SEASON	Year round
HIGHLIGHTS	Fascinating trash displays and interactive exhibits, dioramas of urban salt marsh, 1,000–gallon brackish creek housing live animals, excellent view of the Hackensack River estuary and Manhattan's skyline, nature trails, Barrier-free trail, bird-watching
ADMISSION	Fee for museum; children under 12 free. Trails free.
HOURS	Museum: 9 A.M.–5 P.M. weekdays; 10 A.M.–3 P.M. Saturday
	Trails: weather permitting, daylight hours
FACILITIES	Rest room, water, coffeehouse, meeting rooms available for rent, lecture and conference rooms
EVENTS	Trash Bash, Wildlife Carving and Art Show, weekend workshops, canoe and boat trips; call for a schedule

FOR A FUN, EDUCATIONAL, AND UNIQUE OUTING, THE "TRASH MUSEUM" IS IDEAL. Although its official name is the Hackensack Meadowlands Development Commission's (HMDC's) Environment Center Museum, locals refer to it as the Trash Museum.

There's no need to hold your nose when you enter what is believed to be the only museum of its kind in the nation. Not only isn't there any garbage aroma, but because the interior and exterior of the building are so beautiful, you may suspect you're in the wrong place.

The visitor center offers a spectacular view of the surrounding Meadowlands area and Manhattan's skyline while the lobby houses a huge diorama depicting an urban salt marsh and its inhabitants. Close by, in a 1,000-gallon brackish creek exhibit, you'll find dozens of live animals common to the area.

Along the walkway to the museum there's an interesting mosaic portraying, by way of individual aerial photographs that have been joined together, what rural New Jersey looked like in the 1930s before the landfills. Panels along the walls explain how the Meadlowlands were formed and how the Indians waded out into the river to catch clams and oysters. Later,

Discarded radiators, tire irons, and fans are only a few of the items on display in the museum's garbage rooms, where visitors can find out what it feels like to be inside a landfill—without the terrible aroma!

settlers harvested the marsh salt hay to preserve their ice during warm weather.

This once fruitful piece of land had unfortunately become a dumping ground with tons of garbage heaped all around until the Hackensack Meadowlands Development Commission was formed in 1969. Its mission wasn't simple; it was to formulate a plan to manage garbage disposal for the 32-square-mile Meadowlands region and strike a balance between orderly development and environmental concerns.

One of the commission's successes since the opening of the Trash Museum in 1989 has been in awakening visitors to the fact that over 160 million tons of garbage are thrown out annually and in teaching how each one of us can help reduce this amount. You're certain to enjoy the museum's focal point, the garbage sculpture room, where you'll be surrounded by a heap of tire irons, soap-pad boxes, bicycle tires, chicken wire, and a various assortment of tossed-out items. Being inside this room will give you a good idea of what it's like inside a landfill—thankfully, without the horrible aroma!

The garbage sculpture wasn't thrown in here but was carefully collected by Robert Richardson, a Newark artist. When Richardson went on his late-night forays through the streets of northern New Jersey, officials allowed him to include anything for the display he wished to, except for gunky, gooey stuff. Rather than toss out his own junk while renovating his home in Newark's Ironbound section, Richardson included his old radiators and windows in the display. Everything is placed with a purpose, and the drama of the glass bottles, jars, and ornaments we continuously toss into the trash shows through.

Admittedly, the message gets across—especially when there are small signs posted calling our attention to various facts, including, "Every day, we toss out enough aluminum cans to make about 30 jet planes," or "Americans throw away 38,000 tons of glass each day." Overhead, a young girl announces additional facts through loudspeakers about our waste and what's happening to our planet.

After facing these sobering images, visitors can peer through peepholes that disclose domestic scenes of a family with wasteful 20th-century habits. These include using aluminum foil and plastic cups only once, while a biodegradable display shows piles of products headed for the dump. By lifting a flap, you can see what will remain after 100 years. The story of packaging is also told, from grandma's kitchen to the bakery where you get goods in a paper bag and maybe three different layers of wrappers.

After digesting the facts presented in this wonderful museum, head outdoors and enjoy the view. Bring binoculars and relax, observing the animals and birds that frequent the Meadowlands. There are lovely, easy nature walks in the experimental park outside the visitor center. Wildflowers grow profusely in the meadows each spring and attract lots of butterflies, while the young crabapple trees are perfect for attracting many species of birds.

It's hard to imagine that this pretty park sitting atop landfill and covered with an experimental synthetic liner and recycled soda bottles could turn into something so beautiful. It's also hard to imagine that each of us can generate so much trash. Hopefully, a visit to this museum will get the message across to everyone who visits and not only give us new ideas but hope for the future.

NOTES: Medieval Times (800-828-2945), up the road from the Trash Museum, is well worth a visit. You can watch expert horsemanship, swordplay, and pageantry, plus an authentic jousting tournament, and cheer a knight of your choice to victory while you enjoy a delicious dinner. It's fun for all ages.

Additional Special Places Not to Be Missed

Gateway Region (Northeast)

American Labor Museum/Botto House National Landmark
83 Norwood Street, Haledon (973-595-7953, donation requested); hundreds of striking workers gathered here in 1913 to listen to Upton Sinclair; tours and educational programs regularly held, plus changing exhibitions in small but informative labor museum.

Aviation Hall of Fame
Teterboro Airport, Teterboro, off Routes 17 and 46 (201-288-6344, fee); dedicated to the history of flight; historic photographs and aeronautical memorabilia.

Ballantine House/Newark Museum
43–49 Washington Street, Newark, off Exit 145 of the Garden State Parkway (973-596-6550, fee); excellent art, science, and industry exhibits; planetarium; fire museum; sculpture; gardens; restored Victorian mansion.

Bergen Museum of Arts and Science
Ridgewood and Farview Avenues, Paramus (201-265-1248, fee); changing exhibits, mastodon skeleton found in Hackensack, children's discovery room, nature room, and Lenape Indian exhibit.

Branch Brook Park
Franklin and Mill streets, Newark (973-482-4198, free); during April the site of more cherry blossoms than anywhere else in the country, concerts, and annual 10K race.

East Jersey Olde Towne
Johnson Park, Highland Park (732-463-9077, fee); reconstructed colonial village along the Raritan River.

Edison National Historic Site
Main Street and Lakeside Avenue, off Exit 145 of the Garden State Parkway, West Orange (973-736-5050, fee); Edison's impressive laboratory, library, machinery, chemicals, the first light bulb, and motion picture equipment.

Great Falls Historic District
Route 80, exit 80 off Squirrel Wood Road, McBride Avenue, Paterson (973-279-9587, free); restored factories and buildings in the first planned industrial city in the nation, and the 77-foot Paterson Falls.

Lambert Castle
Valley Road, Garret Mountain Reservation, Exit 57 off Route 80, Paterson
(973-881-2761, fee); a stone castle built in 1893 housing a 5,400-piece spoon
collection, period furniture, and library.

Lorrimer Bird Sanctuary
790 Ewing Avenue, Franklin Lakes (201-891-2185, free); Audubon nature
center with trails, small museum, and regularly scheduled activities.

Medieval Times Dinner & Tournament
149 Polito Avenue, Lyndhurst (800-828-2945, fee); dinner and jousting
tournament show with knights of the realm, equestrian display, pageantry,
swordsmanship, and four-course "eat-with-your-fingers" meal served during
show. It's lots of fun.

Montclair Art Museum
3 South Mountain Avenue, Montclair (973-746-5555, fee); changing art
exhibits, concerts, lectures, art classes, and films.

New Jersey Children's Museum
599 Industrial Avenue, Paramus (201-262-5151, fee); this is a real winner for
children from one to eight and their parents. It's chock-full of child-friendly
interactive displays with 15,000 square feet of carpeted exhibit space divided
into 30 different rooms, each with its own unique and exciting theme.
Emphasis is on fun and learning. Highlights include a real helicopter for kids
to fly, a real fire engine to climb on while wearing fire gear, a 10-foot-high
fantasy castle where children can dress up in armor and gowns, and
hundreds of more interesting things to do. Open every day, the museum
also offers skits, crafts, story time, and videos, plus a protected place for
babies to enjoy, too.

New Jersey Museum of Agriculture
College Farm Road at Route 1 (732-249-2077, fee); historical farming tools,
household items, art gallery, gift shop.

New Jersey State Botanical Gardens
Skylands Manor, Morris Road (973-962-7031, free except for parking);
beautiful rock gardens and magnificent botanical garden displays during
spring, summer, and fall.

Palisades Interstate Park
Hudson Terrace near the George Washington Bridge, Fort Lee (201-461-
3956, fee for parking Memorial Day to Labor Day); reconstructed gun
batteries and a revolutionary war museum with sweeping views of the
Hudson River and New York City skyline.

Ringwood Manor
Ringwood State Park, Sloatsburg Road, Ringwood (973-962-7031, free);
period furniture in 51-room mansion once home to ironmasters.

Steuben House
Main Street off Exit 161 of the Garden State Parkway to Route 4 east to Hackensack Avenue North (201-487-1739, fee); a pre-revolutionary-war–era house filled with Indian artifacts and colonial toys.

Turtle Back Zoo
Northfield Road between Cherry Lane and Prospect Avenue, West Orange (973-731-5800, fee); over 650 animals and birds, petting zoo, train ride.

Skylands Region (Northwest)

Delaware and Raritan Canal State Park
Start at Stockton and turn north on Route 29, left on Quarry Road (609-292-2101, free); covers 60 miles, follows the 1832 canal, and continues through Mercer, Somerset, and Middlesex; great for canoeing and hiking.

Fosterfields
Route 24 on Kahdena Road, Morris Township (973-326-7645, fee); a working farm estate.

Frelinghuysen Arboretum
Morristown (973-326-7600, free); self-guiding trails through 125 acres, a historic mansion, and concerts during summer.

Lambertville
Route 29 and 179 (609-397-0055, free); quaint shops and antiques with scenic views of the Delaware River.

Morristown Museum
6 Normandy Heights Road, Morris Township (973-538-0454, fee); changing exhibits, permanent dinosaur, model train, rock, sculpture, mineral, doll, and toy exhibits, and early-American and Indian artifacts.

Speedwell Village
Speedwell Avenue, off Route 202 North, Morristown (973-540-0211, fee); site of the Vail Homestead Farm, where Morse developed the first telegraph.

Wallace House and Old Dutch Parsonage
Washington Place off Route 206, Somerville (908-725-1015, fee); Washington's headquarters during the Middlebrook encampment.

Delaware River Region (Central Southwest)

Cowtown
Route 40 off Exit 1 of the New Jersey Turnpike, Sharptown (856-769-3200, fee); the oldest rodeo on the East Coast includes a flea market; open Memorial Day to Labor Day.

Drumthwacket

354 Stockton Street, Princeton (609-683-0057, free); Governor's Mansion. Limited hours; call before going.

Parvin State Park

701 Almond Road, Pittsgrove (856-358-8616, entrance fee Memorial Day to Labor Day); camping, swimming, hiking, boating within 1,000 acres of forest and lakes.

Rancocas Nature Center

1120 Rancocas Road, Mount Holly (609-261-2495, free); Audubon nature center with exhibits and easy hiking trails through woods.

Salem

Routes 45 and 49 from the southern end of the Turnpike and Route I-295 (856-935-5004 or -7510, free except for historic buildings); sixty 18th-century buildings plus museums; 500-year-old oak near the courthouse.

The Shore Region (Central Southeast)

Cattus Island Park and Nature Center

Fischer Boulevard off Exit 82 of the Garden State Parkway to Hooper Avenue North (732-270-6960, fee); bird watching, nature trails, bay views, lovely nature museum.

Englishtown Auction

90 Wilson Avenue off Routes 9 and 527, Englishtown (732-446-9644, free); over 700 vendors selling clothing, new and used merchandise, at this 50-acre flea market.

Fort Hancock

Gateway National Recreation Area, Highlands (732-872-0115, fee for beach parking); oldest continuously operating lighthouse in the country, trails, beautiful views, beaches, and soldier's barracks plus museum.

Monmouth Battlefield State Park

Route 33, Freehold (732-462-9616, free); walk along nature trails and stop in at the visitor center at the site where Molly Pitcher made history during a revolutionary war battle.

Navesink Light Station

Twin Lights Historic Site off Route 36 on Lighthouse Road (732-872-1814, fee); two-beacon lighthouse marking western entrance into New York Harbor with museum of marine history artifacts.

Spy House Museum

119 Port Monmouth Road, Port Monmouth (732-787-1807, fee); history of the bayshore farmers of the sea and the land with special events, including annual Labor Day reenactment of the Battle of Shoal Harbor.

The Greater Atlantic City Region (Southeast)

Smithville
Route 9, Smithville (609-652-7777, free); specialty shops in an authentic 1800s village.

Lucy the Margate Elephant
Atlantic Avenue, Margate (609-823-6473, fee); a six-story-tall National Historic Landmark built in 1881 containing a museum and gift shop.

Wharton State Forest
Route 542, seven miles east of Hammonton (609-561-3262, free except for camping); easy nature trails beneath fragrant pines.

The Southern Shore Region (South)

Cape May
(609-884-5508, fee to the beaches and historic buildings); over 250 Victorian buildings and 600 summer houses, hotels, and frame buildings.

Cape May Courthouse Historical Museum
Route 9, Cape May Courthouse (609-465-3535, fee); a county historical museum with a genealogy library.

Cape May Point Lighthouse
Cape May Point State Park, Lighthouse Avenue, Cape May Point (609-884-8656, free); 1859 landmark with a 199-step climb leading to the Watch Room Gallery.

Cold Spring Historic Village
735 Seashore Road, Cold Spring (609-898-2300, fee); re-created historic village with quaint shops, crafts, and popular Old Grange Restaurant.

Overnight Accommodations

Motels

Many hotels, motels, inns, and bed-and-breakfast accommodations offer special weekend package deals. Listed below are toll-free reservation numbers for chains located within the state.

Best Western International, Inc. 1-800-528-1234
Comfort Inns 1-800-228-5150
Country Inn Hotel 1-800-456-4600
Courtyards by Marriott 1-800-321-2211
Days Inn 1-800-325-2525
Doubletree, Inc. 1-800-528-0444
Econo Lodges of America...1-800-446-6900
Embassy Suites...1-800-362-2779
Friendship Inns of America International..1-800-453-4511
Hampton Inn...1-800-426-7866
Hilton Hotels Corp. 1-800-445-8667
Holiday Inns, Inc. 1-800-465-4329
Howard Johnson...1-800-654-2000
Hyatt Corp. 1-800-228-9000
Loews Hotels...1-800-223-0888
Marriott Hotels 1-800-228-9290
Quality Inns...1-800-228-5151
Radisson Hotel Corp. 1-800-333-3333
Ramada Inns 1-800-726-6232
Red Carpet/Scottish Inns...1-800-251-1962
Red Roof Inns 1-800-843-7663
Residence Inns by Marriott...1-800-331-3131
Sheraton Hotels and Inns 1-800-325-3535
Super 8 Motels 1-800-843-1991
Travelodge International Inc./Viscount 1-800-255-3050
Treadway Inns Corp...1-800-752-3297
Trusthouse Forte Hotels...1-800-225-5843

Many budget motel accommodations are listed in the *National Directory of Budget Motels,* Carlson (New York: Pilot Books).

Bed & Breakfasts

For bed-and-breakfast accommodations consult *Bed & Breakfast U.S.A.,* Rundback and Kramer (New York: Dutton), and *Bed & Breakfast in the Mid-Atlantic States,* Chesler (Chester, CT: Globe Pequot), or try one of the following accommodations recommended by the Bed & Breakfast Innkeepers Association of New Jersey, P.O. Box 108, Spring Lake 07762.

Skylands Region

Leigh Way, Clinton	(908) 735-4311
Jerica Hill Inn, Flemington	(908) 782-0834
Cabbage Rose Inn, Flemington	(908) 788-0247
Hunterdon House, Frenchtown	(908) 996-3632
Apple Valley Inn, Glenwood	(973) 764-3735
Chestnut Hill on the Delaware, Milford	(908) 995-9761
Seven Springs Farm, Pittstown	(908) 735-7675
Whistling Swan Inn, Stanhope	(973) 347-6369
Stewart Inn, Stewartsville	(908) 479-6060

Gateway Region

Jeremiah J. Yereance House, Lyndhurst	(201) 438-9457

Delaware Region

Josiah Reeve House, Alloway	(856) 935-5640

Shore Region

Atlantic View Inn, Avon-by-the-Sea	(732) 774-8505
The Avon Manor, Avon-by-the-Sea	(732) 988-6326
Cashelmara Inn, Oceanside	(732) 776-8727
The Sands B&B Inn, Avon-by-the-Sea	(732) 776-8386
Bay Head Gables, Bay Head	(732) 892-9844
Bay Head Harbor Inn, Bay Head	(856) 899-0767
Conovers Bay Head Inn, Bay Head	(732) 892-4664
Amber Street Inn, Beach Haven	(609) 492-1611
Victoria Guest House, Beach Haven	(609) 492-4154
The Inn at the Shore, Belmar	(732) 681-3762
The Seaflower, Belmar	(732) 681-6006
Goose N. Berry Inn, Manahawkin	(609) 597-6350
Pine Tree Inn, Ocean Grove	(732) 775-3264
Beacon House, Sea Girt	(732) 449-5835
Ashling Cottage, Spring Lake	(732) 449-3553
Carriage House, Spring Lake	(732) 449-1332
Hollycroft Inn, South Belmar	(732) 681-2254
Normandy Inn, Spring Lake	(732) 449-7172
Seacrest by the Sea, Spring Lake	(732) 449-9031

Southern Shore

The Abbey, Cape May	(609) 884-4506
Abigail Adams, Cape May	(609) 884-1371
Barnard-Good House, Cape May	(609) 884-5381
Bedford Inn, Cape May	(609) 884-4158
Brass Bed, Cape May	(609) 884-8075
The King's Cottage, Cape May	(609) 884-0415
Cape Mey's Inn, Cape May	(609) 884-7793
Cliveden Inn, Cape May	(609) 884-4516

Columns by the Sea, Cape May .... (609) 884-2228
Fairthorne B&B, Cape May .... (609) 884-8791
Gingerbread House, Cape May .... (609) 884-0211
Humphrey Hughes House, Cape May .... (800) 582-3634
Inn at 22 Jackson, Cape May .... (609) 884-2226
Leith Hall, Cape May ....(609) 884-1934
Mainstay Inn, Cape May ....(609) 884-8690
Manor House, Cape May ....(609) 884-4710
The Mason Cottage, Cape May ....(609) 884-3358
Mission Inn, Cape May.. (609) 884-8380
Sea Holly Inn, Cape May ....(609) 884-6294
The Stetson Inn, Cape May.. (609) 884-1724
Twin Gables, Cape May ....(609) 884-7332
The Queen Victoria, Cape May .... (609) 884-8702
John Wesley Inn, Cape May ....(609) 884-1012
White Dove Cottage, Cape May .... (800) 321-3683
Windward House, Cape May .... (609) 884-3368
Woodleigh House, Cape May .... (609) 884-7123
Henry Ludlam Inn, Dennisville ....(609) 861-5847
Candlelight Inn, North Wildwood ....(609) 522-6200
BarnaGate B&B, Ocean City... (609) 391-9366
New Brighton Inn, Ocean City ....(609) 399-2829

State Campgrounds
Allaire State Park, Box 220, Farmingdale 07727, (732) 938-2371
Allamuchy Mountain State Park, Stephen's Section, 800 Willow Grove Street,
    Hackettstown 07840, (908) 852-3790
Bass River State Forest, Stage Rd., P.O. Box 118, New Gretna 08824, (609)
    296-1114
Belleplain State Forest, Box 450, Woodbine 08270, (609) 861-2404
Bull's Island Section, Delaware & Raritan Canal Park, 2185 Daniel Bray
    Highway, Stockton 08559, (609) 397-2949
Cheesequake State Park, Matawan 07747, (732) 566-2161
High Point State Park, 1480 State Route 23, Sussex 07461, (973) 875-4800
Jenny Jump State Forest, P.O. Box 150, Hope 07844, (908) 459-4366
Lebanon State Forest, P.O. Box 215, New Lisbon 08064, (609) 726-1191
Parvin State Park, 701 Almond Road, Pittsgrove 08318, (856) 358-8616
Round Valley Recreation Area, Box 45D, Lebanon-Stanton Road, Lebanon
    08833, (908) 236-6355
Spruce Run State Park, 289 Van Syckels Road, Clinton 08809, (908) 638-8572
Stephen's State Park, 800 Willow Grove Street, Hackettstown 07840, (908)
    852-3790
Stokes State Forest, 1 Coursen Road, Branchville 07826, (973) 948-3820
Swartswood State Park, P.O. Box 123, Swartzwood 07877, (973) 383-5230

Voorhees State Park, RD 2, Box 80, Route 513, Glen Gardner 08826, (908)
    638-6969
Wawayanda State Park, Box 198, Highland Lakes 07422, (973) 853-4462
Wharton State Forest, Batsto, RD 9, Hammonton 08037, (609) 561-0024
Worthington State Forest, HC62, Box 2, Columbia 07832, (908) 841-9575

For a listing of private campgrounds, consult the *Trailer Life RV
Campground & Services Directory* (Ventura, CA: TL Enterprises) and the *KOA
Kampgrounds Directory* (Billings, MT: Kampgrounds of America).

Appendix: Books, Maps, and Further Information

Nature Books

Annuals, Bales (Burpee American Gardening Series) (New York: Prentice Hall, 1991). Beautiful color photos and descriptions of more than 70 outstanding annuals, complete with cultural information written by Burpee's staff of horticulturists and plant breeders.

The Birds Around Us, Mace (San Francisco: Ortho Books, 1986). An enjoyable, informative, full-color guide to attracting, observing, identifying, and photographing birds.

Birds of North America, Robbins (New York: Golden Press, 1983). Great tips on identifying birds.

Complete Field Guide to North American Wildlife (Eastern edition) (New York: Harper & Row, 1981). A complete reference book with excellent illustrations.

A Field Guide to the Birds, Peterson (Boston: Houghton Mifflin, 1980). For bird lovers who want to identify almost any bird.

A Field Guide to Edible Wild Plants, Peterson (Boston: Houghton Mifflin, 1977). Fully illustrated and cross-referenced guide to more than 370 edible wild plants.

A Field Guide to Trees and Shrubs, Petrides (Boston: Houghton Mifflin, 1973). It's easy to become an expert at identifying the trees with this well-illustrated book on hand.

A Field Guide to Wildflowers (Northeastern edition), Peterson and McKenny (Boston: Houghton Mifflin, 1968). Over 1,293 species in 84 families listed, including information on how to identify all the principal wildflowers of the Northeast.

Flowering Shrubs, Druse (Burpee American Gardening Series) (New York: Prentice Hall, 1992). Beautiful color photos and descriptions of over 130 outstanding flowering shrubs.

Landforms, Adams and Wyckoff (New York: Golden Press, 1971). A guide to the rock scenery of the world, formations, and major features of the earth.

Master Tree Finder, Watts (Berkeley: Nature Study Guild, 1963). A pocket-size manual for the identification of trees by their leaves.

Ornamental Trees, Cresson (Burpee American Gardening Series) (New York: Prentice Hall, 1993). Detailed descriptions of more than 65 outstanding ornamental trees, including tips on design, planting requirements, and seasonal features.

A Practical Guide for the Amateur Naturalist, Durrell (New York: Knopf,

1982). Beautifully written reference book answering questions about the birds, bees, flora, and fauna.

Reptiles and Amphibians, Zim (New York: Golden Press, 1956). Separating fact from fable, this handy guide differentiates between reptiles and amphibians, and aids in the identification of 212 species.

Rocks and How They Were Formed, Zim (New York: Golden Press, 1961). A simple guide on mineral identification.

Seashells of North America, Abbott (New York: Golden Press, 1961). Identifying seashells is a snap with this reference book.

Stalking the Wild Asparagus, Gibbons (Putney, VT: Alan C. Hood, Inc., 1962). Hundreds of recipes for turning wild fruits and vegetables into tasty dishes, plus interesting comments on each.

Trees of North America, Brockman (New York: Golden Press, 1968). Illustrated guide with complete details, making tree identification a joy.

Wildflower Folklore, Martin (Chester, CT: Globe Pequot Press, 1984). Information on 105 wildflowers, how each was named, medicinal value and culinary uses, with myths, legends, and stories of each.

Winter Tree Finder, Watts (Berkeley: Nature Study Guild, 1970). Handy pocket-size manual for identifying deciduous trees in winter.

Books about New Jersey

Audubon Society Field Guide to the Natural Places of the Mid-Atlantic States (Inland), Lawrence and Gross (New York: Random House, 1984). Maps, tours, and descriptions of places of interest to the nature lover.

Best Hikes With Children in New Jersey, Zatz (Seattle, WA: The Mountaineers Books, 1993). Describes in detail 75 easy to difficult hikes throughout the state ranging from one to eight miles. Excellent driving directions, descriptions of history of each area, plus flora and fauna, what to take, and more.

The Bicentennial Guide to the American Revolution, Stember (New York: Dutton, 1974). Volume II presents the history of the Middle Colonies and revolutionary war sites.

30 Bicycle Tours in New Jersey, Zatz (Woodstock VT: Backcountry Publications, 1997). Tours ranging from a couple of hours to overnight, containing precise directions, detailed maps, and informative descriptions of the outstanding natural, cultural, and historic features encountered in the Garden State.

Fifty Hikes in New Jersey, Scofield, Green, and Zimmerman (Woodstock, VT: Backcountry Publications, 1988). Hikes for every level of skill and ambition, from short beach walks to a strenuous three-day backpacking trip.

Garden State Canoeing, Gertler (Silver Spring, MD: The Seneca Press, 1992). Excellent paddler's guide describing over 1,500 miles of New Jersey waterways, including tiny creeks, big rivers, and canals.

Iron in the Pines, Pierce (New Brunswick, NJ: Rutgers University Press, 1957). History of iron manufacturing in the heart of southern New Jersey.

Millstone Valley, Menzies (New Brunswick, NJ: Rutgers University Press, 1969). Describes the history of the Millstone Valley through text and photographs.

The New Jersey House, Schwartz (New Brunswick, NJ: Rutgers University Press, 1983). Photographs and details on the architecturally interesting houses found in the state.

Passage Between Rivers, Menzies (New Brunswick, NJ: Rutgers University Press, 1976). Captioned photographs detailing the history of the Delaware and Raritan Canal.

The Pine Barrens, McPhee (New York: Ballentine Books, 1991). A sentimental look at New Jersey's most mysterious region.

South Jersey Towns, McMahon (New Brunswick, NJ: Rutgers University Press, 1973). Delightful anecdotes about the people and places in southern New Jersey.

This Is New Jersey, Cunningham (New Brunswick, NJ: Rutgers University Press, 1978). All about the state's history, towns, and historic sites.

Maps

Free state road maps are available at state tourist centers or by contacting the New Jersey Department of Commerce and Economic Development, Division of Travel and Tourism, CN 826, Trenton, NJ 08625. For additional tourist information call 1-800-JERSEY-7. More detailed maps of each county are available free, or for a nominal fee, by calling the county offices listed below.

Atlantic	(609) 343-2345
Bergen	(201) 646-2553
Burlington	(609) 265-5020
Camden	(908) 757-8651
Cape May	(609) 465-1065
Cumberland	(609) 453-2175
Essex	(973) 621-5000
Gloucester	(609) 853-3271
Hudson	(201) 795-6060
Hunterdon	(908) 788-1104
Mercer	(609) 989-6475
Middlesex	(732) 745-3285
Monmouth	(732) 745-3194
Morris	(973) 285-6010
Ocean	(732) 929-2138
Passaic	(973) 881-4120
Salem	(609) 935-7510
Somerset	(973) 231-7006

Sussex...(973) 579-0900
Union..(908) 527-4966
Warren...(908) 475-5361

For Further Information on Regional Activities

Skylands
Hunterdon, Hunterdon County Chamber of Commerce, 2200 Route 31,
    Box 15, Lebanon 08833, (908) 735-5955
Morris, Morris County Chamber of Commerce, 10 Park Ave., Morristown
    07960, (973) 539-3882
Somerset, Somerset County Chamber of Commerce, 64 West End Avenue,
    Somerville 08876, (908) 725-1552
Sussex, Sussex County Chamber of Commerce, 112 Hampton House Road,
    Newton 07860, (973) 579-1811
Warren Department of Economic Development and Tourism, Wayne
    Dumont, Jr. Administration Bldg., Rt. 519, Belvidere 07823, (908) 475-8000

Gateway
Bergen, Bergen County Department of Parks, 21 Main St., Hackensack
    07602, (201) 646-2000
Essex, Essex County Parks Department, 160 Fairview Ave., Cedar Grove
    07009, (973) 857-8530
Hudson, Hudson County Public Information Office, 583 Newark Ave., Jersey
    City 07306, (201) 795-6060
Middlesex, Middlesex County Cultural and Heritage Commission, 841
    Georges Rd., North Brunswick 08902, (732) 745-4489
Passaic Special Events Information, 72 McBride Ave., Paterson 07501, (973)
    523-9201
Union, Union County Cultural and Heritage Affairs, 633 Pearl St., Elizabeth
    07202, (908) 558-2550

Delaware River
Burlington, Burlington County Chamber of Commerce, 328 High Street, Mt.
    Holly 08016, (609) 386-1012
Camden, Camden County Office of Public Information, Court House, 520
    Market Street, Camden 08102, (609) 757-6713
Gloucester, Gloucester County Office of Business and Economic
    Development, CC Budd Blvd., Woodbury 08096, (609) 384-6930
Mercer, Mercer County Cultural and Heritage Office, 640 South Broad,
    Trenton 08650, (609) 989-6701
Salem, Greater Salem Chamber of Commerce, The Old Court House, 104
    Market Street 08079, (609) 935-1415

Shore
Monmouth, Monmouth County Department of Public Information and
    Tourism, 27 E. Main St., Freehold 07728, (732) 431-7310

Ocean, Ocean Township Chamber of Commerce, 1602 Lawrence, Suite 114, P.O. Box 656, Oakhurst 07755, (732) 493-8181

Greater Atlantic City

Atlantic, Greater Atlantic City Convention & Visitors Bureau, 2314 Pacific Avenue, Atlantic City 08401, (609) 348-7100

Southern Shore

Cape May, Cape May Chamber of Commerce, P.O. Box 556, Cape May 08204, (609) 884-5508

Cumberland, Bridgeton/Cumberland Tourist Association, 50 E. Broad St., Bridgeton 08302, (609) 451-4802

Index

Other books about New Jersey and environs from The Countryman Press

Written for people of all ages and experience, these popular and carefully prepared books feature detailed trail and tour directions, notes on points of interest and natural phenomena, maps, and photographs.

New Jersey
>30 Bicycle Tours in New Jersey
>25 Mountain Bike Tours in New Jersey
>50 Hikes in New Jersey
>New Jersey's Great Gardens

Eastern Pennsylvania
>25 Bicycle Tours in Eastern Pennsylvania
>50 Hikes in Eastern Pennsylvania
>Pennsylvania Trout Streams and Their Hatches

Nearby New York State
>25 Bicycle Tours in the Hudson Valley
>25 Mountain Bike Tours in the Hudson Valley
>The Hudson Valley and Catskill Mountains: An Explorer's Guide
>Walks and Rambles in Dutchess and Putnam Counties
>Walks and Rambles on Long Island
>Walks and Rambles in Westchester and Fairfield Counties
>Walks and Rambles in the Western Hudson Valley
>The Other Islands of New York City
>Walks in Nature's Empire

Other Travel and Recreation Books
>Cape Cod and the Islands: An Explorer's Guide
>Connecticut: An Explorer's Guide
>Maine: An Explorer's Guide
>Massachusetts: An Explorer's Guide
>New Hampshire: An Explorer's Guide
>Vermont: An Explorer's Guide

Our books are available at bookstores, or they may be ordered directly from the publisher. For ordering information or for a complete catalog, please contact:

The Countryman Press
c/o W.W. Norton & Company, Inc.
800 Keystone Industrial Park
Scranton, PA 18512
1-800-245-4151